Punishment,

Communication,

and Community

STUDIES IN CRIME AND PUBLIC POLICY
Michael Tonry and Norval Morris, General Editors

Punishment, Communication, and Community

R. A. Duff

CLARKSTON CENTER

OXFORD
UNIVERSITY PRESS

OXFORD
UNIVERSITY PRESS

Oxford   New York
Auckland   Bangkok   Buenos Aires   Cape Town   Chennai
Dar es Salaam   Delhi   Hong Kong   Istanbul   Karachi   Kolkata
Kuala Lumpur   Madrid   Melbourne   Mexico City   Mumbai   Nairobi
São Paulo   Shanghai   Taipei   Tokyo   Toronto

Copyright © 2001 by Oxford University Press, Inc.

First published in 2001 by Oxford University Press, Inc.
198 Madison Avenue, New York, New York 10016

www.oup.com

First issued as an Oxford University Press paperback, 2003

Oxford is a registered trademark of Oxford University Press

Library of Congress Cataloging-in-Publication Data
Duff, Antony.
Punishment, communication, and community / R. A. Duff
p. cm. — (Studies in crime and public policy)
Includes bibliographical references and index.
ISBN 0-19-510429-3; 0-19-516666-3 (pbk.)
1. Punishment—Philosophy.   2. Criminal justice,
Administration of—Philosophy.
3. Sentences (Criminal procedure)—Philosophy.
4. Community—Philosophy.   I. Title.   II. Series
HV8693.D85 2000
364.6—dc21   99-049374

1 3 5 7 9 8 6 4 2

Printed in the United States of America
on acid-free paper

Acknowledgments

SINCE I HAVE BEEN THINKING AND WRITING ABOUT CRIMINAL PUNISHMENT for nearly twenty years, I cannot hope to acknowledge here my debts to all those who have influenced and helped my work, but I can gratefully acknowledge my debts to those who have helped me with this book (and apologize to anyone whose contribution I have failed to record).

Those debts of gratitude are owed to the University of Stirling for a grant of sabbatical leave that enabled me to write the first draft of the book; to the British Academy for a Research Leave Award that enabled me to complete the book; to my colleagues in the Philosophy Department at Stirling, who commented helpfully on various of the arguments and ideas in the book and who over the years have provided a stimulating and constructively critical philosophical environment; to audiences in Aberdeen, Birmingham, Edinburgh, Glasgow, London, Oxford, and Sheffield on whom I tried out parts of the book; to Michael Tonry for encouraging me to write it and to Stephen Morse for his helpful comments on an outline of it; to Andrew von Hirsch, who read the entire manuscript and offered a number of constructive criticisms that helped me to avoid at least some confusions; and above all to Sandra Marshall—not only for reading and commenting on the entire manuscript but for the years of discussion, support, and encouragement that we have shared.

I have made use of material from several articles, and I am grateful to the following publishers for permission to reuse it: Hart Publishing ("Punishment, Communication, and Community," in *Punishment and Political Theory*, edited by M. Matravers [1999]: 48–68); Oxford University Press ("Dangerousness and Citizenship," in *Fundamentals of Sentencing Theory*, edited by A. J Ashworth & M. Wasik [1998]: 141–64; "Law, Language, and Community: Some Preconditions of Criminal Liability," *Oxford Journal of Legal Studies* 18 [1998]: 189–206; "Inclusion and Exclusion: Citizens, Subjects, and Outlaws," *Current Legal Problems* 51 [1998]: 241–66); Sage Publications ("Penal Communities," *Punishment & Society* 1 [1999]: 23–39); and the University of Chicago Press ("Penal Communications: Recent Work in the Philosophy of Punishment," in *Crime and Justice: A Review of Research*, edited by M. Tonry, vol. 20 [1996]: 1–97).

This book is dedicated to the memory of H. L. A. Hart, who first showed me, as he showed so many others, how fruitfully philosophy could interact with the criminal law.

Stirling, Scotland   R. A. D.
December 1999

Contents

Introduction

Every year, our courts convict hundreds of thousands of people of criminal offenses.[1] These include such serious offenses against the person as murder, rape, and other violent assaults; offenses of taking or destroying property, of fraud and deception; offenses of endangerment, for instance under road traffic laws and health and safety laws; offenses involving the possession or supply of prohibited drugs; and public order offenses—to mention just some of the many offenses defined by the criminal law. Most of those convicted are sentenced to one of the various kinds of punishment provided by the law.[2] These include imprisonment for terms ranging from a few weeks to 'life', fines large and small, Community Service Orders of different types and durations, and Probation Orders to which various further conditions may be attached.

To ask, "What can justify criminal punishment?"—the central question in philosophical discussions of punishment—is to ask what can justify practices of this kind. That question is unavoidable for anyone who cares about how states should treat their citizens. And while it is often posed in impersonal terms, as if it concerned a practice in which the questioner was not personally implicated, it actually concerns every citizen. For many citizens have direct dealings with the state's penal apparatus: as suspects, defendants, or convicts who are subjected to it; as victims of crime who call upon it or find 'their' crimes taken up by it; or as officials who investigate or prosecute suspected offenders, or determine their guilt or innocence, or decide or administer the punishments imposed on convicted offenders. Many other citizens guide some of their conduct in the light of that penal apparatus, avoiding actions that might subject them to it. But all are anyway implicated in it, insofar as it purportedly operates in their names and on their behalf.

The question of justification is especially insistent at times when commentators talk, as they have talked during the past two decades, of a "penal crisis" (see, e.g., Bottoms & Preston 1980; Cavadino & Dignan 1997, ch. 1). Accounts of this crisis sometimes imply that it concerns imprisonment (our overreliance on imprisonment, the inhumane conditions in so many of our prisons) rather than punishment in general; or the material conditions and modes of punishment rather than whether it can be justified at all. But it is also a crisis of legitimacy: for when we reflect on the punishments inflicted (in our name) on so many of our fellow citizens and on the effects of those punishments on those who suffer them, we cannot but raise the question of legitimacy—of what can justify any practice of criminal punishment.

We must, however, be clear about what we are asking in raising this question: about what is to be justified and about what would count as an adequate justification.

1. What Is to Be Justified?

In considering what is to be justified, we should remind ourselves of some further aspects of contemporary penality—of the penal apparatus of which punishment is just one, albeit a central, aspect.[3]

First, few of those who have committed criminal offenses are actually convicted in the criminal courts. Because many crimes are never officially reported and the clear-up rate for reported crimes is low (see Ashworth 1995a, 7–17), only a small proportion of offenders are even detected. Of those, many are never brought to trial. Some are diverted from the criminal process—for instance, by being put under psychiatric care or required to pay penalties imposed by other agencies (such as, fixed driving penalties administered by the police or penalties imposed by customs or tax officials); some are released with an informal warning or an official caution—or perhaps with no further comment because the prosecuting authority has decided, for any of a variety of reasons, not to proceed with the case (see Galligan 1987; Ashworth 1994, 125–58; 1995a, 17–24; Sanders & Young 1994, 205–40). Of those brought to trial, some are acquitted.

Furthermore, many who have committed no offense are subjected to some part of the criminal process. They are interrogated and detained by the police as suspects or tried as defendants; some are mistakenly convicted and punished.

Although the focus of this book is on the punishment of *convicted offenders*, we must remember that no human penal system can be so designed that it will punish *all* and *only* those who commit crimes. Any system that is not to involve intolerable costs (both material and moral) will capture only a proportion, perhaps a small proportion, of actual offenders. Any human system will mistakenly punish some who have committed no crime. To justify a human system of criminal punishment must thus be to justify a system that does not even aim to punish all the guilty (see Braithwaite & Pettit 1990, chs. 6–9) and that cannot avoid punishing some innocents (see Schedler 1980; Alexander 1983; Duff 1991, 435–41).

Second, the actual impact and effects of punishment on those who are punished varies enormously—depending not only on the formal sentence but also on the conditions under which it is administered, on the offender's own character and experience (see Tonry 1994; Ashworth & Player 1998), and on how others treat the offender thereafter. For some offenders, their punishment is a mild inconvenience. For some, even if its material impact is slight, it is a source of remorse, shame, or acute embarrassment. For some, it is a serious burden but one that ends with the end of the formal sentence. For some, it involves a radical change in and reconstruction of their lives. For some, it devastates their relationships, their careers, their whole preconviction way of life (see Walker 1991, 108–10, on "incidental punishment"). People associated with the offenders may also be seriously affected—notably the offenders' families or other dependents (see Walker 1991, 106–8, on *"obiter punishment"*).

Furthermore, an offender's punishment is a stage in a larger process of subjection to the coercive powers of the criminal justice system. It is preceded by a trial, which itself follows from a process of police and prosecutorial investigation and decision. That whole process of investigation and trial can involve burdens much like those imposed by punishment: loss of freedom, for those detained for questioning or pending trial; loss of money, in lost earnings or legal costs; serious intrusions on one's time; the shame or embarrassment of being thus investigated, tried, and exposed to public scrutiny; and the sense of being subjected to the forceful disciplinary power of the state (see Feeley 1979). Such burdens also fall on those who are in the end not punished.

Although the focus of this book is on the *formal sentences* imposed by courts on convicted offenders, we must remember that those sentences vary enormously in their content, severity, and impact, that they have further foreseeable consequences both for the offenders and for others, and that the criminal justice system also imposes other burdens on those subjected to its coercive power.

Third, the punishments imposed by criminal courts by no means exhaust the realm of punishment and penalty, not even that of punishments or penalties imposed by organs of the state. The armed forces, for instance, have their own system of trials and punishments, and other agencies, such as the police and tax and customs officials, impose penalties without a formal conviction. In other contexts—in institutions, in professions, in the family—we also find formal and informal modes of punishment and penalty.

Although the focus of this book is on the punishments imposed by *criminal courts*, we must remember that there are other punishments or penalties imposed formally or informally by other agencies. (There are also other official measures for young offenders. The treatment of such offenders raises important issues that differ significantly from those raised by the punishment of adult offenders, but that do not figure in this book.)

But how can so narrow a focus, on the punishments formally imposed by criminal courts on convicted offenders, be justified? Surely what needs to be justified is not simply criminal punishment, as thus narrowly understood, but—as regards the criminal justice system—the whole coercive apparatus of penality; and—as regards punishment—punishments of all kinds, not just those formally imposed by criminal courts.

A focus on *state* penality, on the penal activities of the state's official institutions, can be readily justified. We need not claim (implausibly) that 'punishment' strictly or paradigmatically *means* 'criminal punishment by the state'—that nonstate modes of punishment can be understood as 'punishment' only by analogy to state punishment. We need only note that state punishment is distinct from other modes of punishment and that, involving as it does the state's exercise of its dominant coercive power over its citizens, it raises sharply the question of what penal powers (if any) the state should have and how they should be exercised.

However, this does not yet justify a focus on state *punishment* rather than on the broader realm of state penality. A justification of state punishment must of course ultimately expand into a larger account of the whole apparatus of criminal justice—though this is not to say that we should aspire to some unitary grand theory that will rationalize all aspects of that complex apparatus in terms of a single value or integrated set of values.[4] A justifying account of criminal punishment must also draw directly on an account of the proper aims of the criminal law and on a larger account of the proper powers of the state (see chs. 2–3). To at least that extent, normative penal theory cannot be self-standing. There is nonetheless room for a less far-reaching inquiry into the justification of state punishment in particular, rather than into all of state penality, which can then feed into further inquiries into other aspects of penality and criminal justice (*pace* Garland 1990, 9–10).

Such an inquiry would be misguided were there nothing sufficiently distinctive about criminal punishment to mark it out from other aspects of the apparatus of criminal justice—for instance, if punishment should be understood simply as one amongst other similar techniques for preventing crime or for controlling a potentially disruptive population. But there is something thus distinctive about punishment. I do not engage here in the kind of discussion of the definition of punishment that has so exercised some philosophers[5]—a discussion that is doomed to futility if it is intended to produce a definition capturing all and only those practices that properly count as 'punishment', and that must rapidly become a normative discussion of how punishment can be justified if it is to produce a useful account of what we *should* mean by 'punishment'. We need simply note the familiar points that punishment is, typically, something intended to be burdensome or painful,[6] imposed on a (supposed) offender for a (supposed) offense by someone with (supposedly) the authority to do so;[7] and that punishment, as distinct from other kinds of penalty, is typically intended to express or communicate censure (see Feinberg 1970). These points, whose significance I discuss in detail later, do not settle any normative question about what kind of state penal practice, if any, can be justified.[8] They serve only to identify a distinctive kind of practice, of imposing censure-expressing burdens on supposed offenders for their supposed offenses, which raises a distinctive justificatory question: how can such a practice be justified?

2. Theory and Practice

A further issue about what is to be justified concerns the relationship between normative theory and existing practice.

On one hand, a normative theory of criminal punishment must be recognizably a theory of this distinctive kind of human practice. Philosophy must always begin from actual human practice, with the concepts and values embodied in and given meaning only by such practice. (It must also return to practice, in that a normative theory of punishment that is to speak to us must offer some guidance about how our existing practices should be conducted, reformed, or replaced.)

On the other hand, a normative theory of punishment must be a *critical* theory. It must offer us not simply a comforting rationalization or justification of the status quo (see Murphy 1979c) but a critical standard: an ideal conception of what punishment ought to be, in whose light we can evaluate (and no doubt find seriously wanting) our existing practices. Ideals, however, are often distant from actualities. We cannot assume in advance that our existing penal practices will turn out to be more or less adequate as they are, requiring only modest reforms or refinements. We must be open to the possibility that what punishment ought to be—what it must be if it is to be adequately justified—will be radically different from what it actually now is.

Even this way of putting the point is misleading and open to the charge of "begging the institution" (Mackenzie 1981, 41), since it implicitly assumes, as philosophers of punishment are too prone to assume, that *some* practice of punishment *can* be justified—that the task is to find that justification and work out what kind of practice it justifies. But we should not assume this. We must take seriously the abolitionist challenge that state punishment *cannot* be justified and should be abolished. I argue that that challenge can be met. It must, however, be faced, not ignored.

We can make this point in another way. To say that normative theory must begin from actual practice is to say that it must begin as immanent or internal, rather than transcendent or external, critique. We cannot construct a wholly a priori account of punishment (or of any human practice) that we then bring to bear, from the outside, on our actual practice: for in what could such an account be grounded and why should it be relevant to existing practice? We must instead begin from within our existing practice, articulating the goals and values by which it is (purportedly) structured and assessing it in terms of those goals and values. Such an immanent critique can be powerful. Even if it does not reveal, as 'critical' theorists think it will (see, e.g., Norrie 1991, 1993), fundamental 'contradictions' within our practices, it can show how radically those practices fail to live up to their own purported goals and values. What begins, however, as immanent critique cannot remain purely immanent, appealing only to goals and values internal to the practice in question, because, first, the practice of punishment does not even purport to be wholly self-contained. Its internal justifications appeal to wider political, social, and moral values. Second, since to ask how punishment can be justified is to ask what role, if any, punishment should play in our political life, any adequate justification of it must ultimately appeal to such larger values. Thus what begins as an immanent critique of the practice of punishment must become a critique that, while still grounded in some account of political life, transcends that particular practice. Once the practice is thus transcended, we must raise the question whether it can be justified at all.

These points about the way in which what must begin as an immanent critique must then become a (relatively) transcendent critique also bear on the issue of what would count as an adequate answer to the question "What can justify criminal punishment?" They remind us that we cannot rule out in advance the answer "It cannot be justified"; but they also indicate something about the form that a justification should take.

3. What Kind of Justification?

An immanent critique begins with some existing, historically contingent practice. Ours must begin with the practice(s) of punishment within which we live—with criminal punishment as practiced in contemporary western societies, such as Britain and the United States, and with the normative understandings of punishment found within those practices.[9] We then seek to transcend these particular practices, towards a set of wider political or moral values in terms of which we can ask whether and how such a practice could be justified.

Philosophers have sometimes aspired to a radically transcendent theory, one that will establish some set of universal, ahistorical principles whose truth can be demonstrated to any rational being and from which we can derive an a priori account of how political society should be structured—including an account of what kind of penal practices, if any, it should maintain. I have no such aspirations, however, since I believe they are doomed to futility. I seek to articulate a set of moral and political values in the light of which a practice of punishment (but one in many ways quite different from our own) can be justified. But those values will be grounded in a particular, historically contingent, normative understanding of political society. I hope to explain that understanding in a way that makes it both intelligible and plausible to readers of this book, but I do not claim that it is one that must commend itself, a priori, to any rational thinker.

There is, however, a further question about what would count as a adequate justification of criminal punishment. If we take ourselves to be searching for '*the* justification of criminal punishment', we might suppose that what we need is some unitary (though perhaps complex) justificatory theory—a theory that will posit, if not a single goal or value, at least a coherent set of goals and values by which a practice of punishment could be unequivocally justified. But even if criminal punishment can be justified, why should we suppose that its justification will take such a unitary and coherent form? Should we not rather suspect that any such grand unitary theory will be inadequate to the complexities of a practicable system of criminal punishment (see Harrison 1988; Garland 1990, 9–10; J. Gardner 1998b, 31–33)?

There are at least two grounds for such suspicion. One has to do with the sheer variety of crimes and of punishments. Why should we expect to find a single justification that will rationalize every kind of punishment for every kind of offense: a long prison sentence for a murderer or a rapist, a Probation Order or Community Service Order for a petty thief, a heavy fine for a VAT-evading corporation, a fine and disqualification for an uninsured driver, and so on? Perhaps a justified penal system would be very different from our own, both in the range of offenses penalized and in the kinds (and levels) of punishment imposed on them. But both crimes and punishments would still be variegated enough to raise the question whether we should look for a single, unitary justification.

The second ground for suspicion concerns the familiar phenomenon of value-conflict. It is by now something of a commonplace that what moral awareness reveals to us, in public as in private realms, is not a tidily coherent set of values by which we can guide our lives and find *the* unequivocally right course to follow on every occasion, but an untidy collection of indissolubly conflicting values between which we can (because we must) reach a series of uncomfortable compromises but which we cannot securely reconcile.[10] We should not then be surprised to find such conflicts in the realm of criminal law (see Ashworth 1995b) and punishment (see Hart 1968, 1–27); and we should be suspicious of any account that claims to dissolve all such conflicts in the cleansing acid of a grand unitary 'theory of punishment'.

Nonetheless, a unitary theory is what I offer. Criminal punishment, I argue, should communicate to offenders the censure they deserve for their crimes and should aim through that communicative process to persuade them to repent those crimes, to try to reform themselves, and thus to reconcile themselves with those whom they wronged.

Now I do not suppose that any actual system of criminal justice will ever be structured by this unitary aim—or by any other unitary theory. It is implausible to suppose (and perhaps frightening to imagine) that the political and legal institutions of a liberal democracy will ever be organized by a single vision. I do argue, however, that this account provides an ideal conception of what criminal punishment ought to be that deserves a central place, even if not the only place, in our normative understanding of punishment.

4. A Brief Overview

The following brief overview of the contents of the book highlights what are, I believe, crucial aspects of any adequate normative account of criminal punishment.

Chapter 1 offers a selective survey of the main trends in normative penal theorizing of the past three decades. It does not aim for completeness or offer a detailed critique of the views it discusses (though elements of such a critique figure in later chapters). Its aim is, rather, to sketch the theoretical context from which the account I defend emerges. It covers developments in the two most familiar normative perspectives on punishment, consequentialist and retributivist (including 'mixed' theories that combine consequentialist and retributivist elements); the emergence of the idea that punishment should be understood as essentially communicative; and the abolitionist challenge to the legitimacy of criminal punishment.

Chapter 2 outlines the normative conception of political community on which my account of punishment depends. Any normative theory of punishment depends on some more or less articulated conception of the state—of the nature of political association and obligation, of the proper role and powers of the state:[11] I offer a liberal-communitarian idea(l) of political society and say something about the role of the criminal law in such a polity.

Chapter 3 begins with the question whether punishment can be consistent with community: can a system of criminal punishment still treat those punished as full members of the political community? By distinguishing 'exclusionary' from 'inclusionary' penal theories, we can see the force of some common criticisms of familiar consequentialist and retributivist theories. A communicative conception of punishment, I argue, offers the best hope for a properly inclusionary account, as well as holding out the prospect of a genuinely 'third way' in penal theory. Such a properly inclusionary account makes sense of the retributivist demand that punishment must be deserved, while also giving punishment a future-directed aim that meets the concern that punishment should be intended to "do some good"—but in a way that avoids familiar objections to consequentialist penal theories. Any such account must face the question why the communication that punishment supposedly involves should take place through the medium of penal 'hard treatment' (see Feinberg 1970). I criticize some alternative answers to that question before developing the particular (and ambitious) communicative theory that I defend, according to which punishment should be understood as a species of secular penance that aims not just to communicate censure but thereby to persuade offenders to repentance, self-reform, and reconciliation. I explain that account by showing the sense it can make of various familiar kinds of punishment, and of various kinds of program (including 'mediation' programs) that are often—but mistakenly—portrayed as *non-punitive*. This reveals how we can reconcile the often contrasted ideas of retributive and 'restorative' justice, how this account of punishment meets some of the abolitionists' concerns—which they wrongly think require the *abolition* of punishment—and how punishment can be inclusionary rather than exclusionary. I then defend this account against various criticisms, in particular the objection that it allows the state an intrusively coercive interest in its citizens' moral character that is inconsistent with the proper limits of any liberal state.

Chapter 4 takes up some central issues about sentencing (this starts to show how an ideal theory of the kind I offer can apply to practice). One much-discussed issue concerns the meaning and proper role of the principle of proportionality—the principle that the severity of punishment should be proportionate to the seriousness of the crime punished. I discuss the role that such a principle plays within a communicative, penitential system of punishment. Another issue, to which theorists have paid too little attention, concerns the material *modes* of punishment: what kinds of punishment should be available, what kinds are appropriate or inappropriate for particular kinds of offense? A communicative account of punishment as penance can, I show, throw useful light on this issue. A third issue is that of who should decide sentences. Discussions of this issue usually focus on how sentencing responsibility should be allocated among legislatures, sentencing commissions, appellate courts, and individual judges (or juries). I do not say much about this question, but do say something about the role that *offenders* (and victims) should play in determining sentences.

Chapter 5 takes up the task of connecting ideal theory to actual practice. It discusses the possibility of transforming our existing penal practices into properly communicative systems of penitential punishment, but also raises a harder set of questions about the preconditions of criminal punishment—the conditions that must be satisfied before such a system could be legitimately applied. These concern the existence of a genuine political community, within which all citizens are obligated under the law, against which offenders offend, and with which punishment can reconcile them. They also concern the moral standing of the courts (and of those in whose name they act) to judge and condemn the offenders who appear before them, and the availability of a shared language in which the communication on which punishment depends can take place. In this context we can address some critical concerns about the legitimacy of criminal punishment in societies like our own, in particular the question whether we can do penal justice in an unjust society, since I argue that such concerns are best understood as focused on the preconditions of criminal punishment. A communicative theory like mine brings these preconditions into sharp focus and raises a crucially difficult question: what should follow from a recognition that they are not satisfied? But *any* plausible normative theory of punishment must, I argue, posit some such preconditions and face the problems created by their non-satisfaction.

Punishment,
Communication,
and Community

1

Consequentialists, Retributivists, and Abolitionists

THE PHILOSOPHY OF PUNISHMENT HAS LONG BEEN A BATTLEGROUND FOR various versions of consequentialism (whose central slogan is that punishment can be justified only if it brings some consequential good) and retributivism (whose central slogan is that punishment can be justified only as being deserved). In this chapter, I sketch some recent trends in that debate and some attempts to undercut or dissolve it.

1. Pure Consequentialism and Punishment

1.1. The Structure of a Consequentialist Account

'Consequentialism', as I use the term, insists that the justification of any human practice depends on its actual or expected consequences:[1] on its *contingent* or *instrumental* contribution to an *independently identifiable* good (cf. Michael 1992). Pure consequentialism holds that the justification of a practice depends *only* on its consequences. We first identify the good(s) we should pursue (or the evils we should avert), in a way that makes no essential reference to the practice in question. We then justify the practice by showing that it is, as a matter of contingent fact, an efficient means to those ends. This involves showing not just that the practice does *some* good but also, first, that it does more good than harm—that its benefits outweigh its costs; and, second, that no available alternative means would bring as much (or more) benefit at lower (or no higher) cost. Consequentialism is thus also *aggregative*. If we are to strive for the greatest benefit at the least cost, we must sum the benefits and the costs of a practice and weigh them against each other.

A consequentialist justification of punishment must thus first identify the goods that punishment can bring and the evils that it can also bring. A complete consequentialist theory would begin with an account of the final good(s) at which all human action must aim—for instance, happiness, accord-

3

ing to classical utilitarian consequentialists. Before exploring how some penal consequentialists ground their theories in sophisticated accounts of the goods that punishment should serve, however, we can look at more familiar kinds of consequentialist account that, without discussing the final good(s), appeal to commonsense ideas of the nonfinal goods that punishment could serve.

The most obvious such good is crime prevention,[2] since if the law defines as criminal (as for any consequentialist it should) only conduct that causes or threatens harm, reducing the incidence of such conduct will do good by reducing both the incidence and the fear of such harm. Crime prevention is not a *final* good, requiring no justification beyond itself, but it is clearly an intermediate good. Other goods may also be relevant—the satisfaction of the grievances of those affected by crime (see Honderich 1984a, 28–32), for instance, or the displacement of extralegal, and dangerous, retaliatory urges (see J. Gardner 1998b). But crime prevention is the obvious candidate.

Consequentialists must also weigh the costs of punishment. The most obvious costs of punishment are the burdens it inflicts on those punished and the resources required to operate the penal system (though these costs are partly offset by the fact that they fund employment for many officials). But we must also weigh any further harmful effects of punishment and of the criminal process on those subjected to it (see pp. xii–xiii, above), as well as on other citizens (for instance, the anxious fear of being subjected to the coercive attentions of the criminal justice system). A thorough consequentialist justification of a penal system thus requires some large and complex empirical predictions and calculations (whose very possibility is far from obvious).

To identify crime prevention as an aim is not yet to specify punishment as the, or even a, means by which we should pursue it: since the end is identified independently of the practice, it is so far an open question, to be answered by empirical investigation, whether this practice is an efficient means to that end. There are indeed many *non*punitive ways of preventing crime— persuasion, education, 'situational crime prevention', for instance, and other measures aimed at removing the causes or occasions of crime. Consequentialists can advocate all these kinds of measure, but to justify a system of punishment, they need to show how it can make a distinct and efficient contribution to crime prevention. Discussion has traditionally focused on three ways in which punishment might do this.

First, the threat of punishment can deter potential offenders, while its actual infliction shows others that the threat is serious ('general' deterrence) and brings it home with special force to the person punished ('special' deterrence). Deterrence as thus portrayed is a matter of rational, prudential dissuasion. It is rational in that it aims to give potential offenders reason to refrain from crime (not just to induce an unreasoned aversion to crime) and prudential in that the reason it gives appeals not to the potential offenders' consciences but to their self-interest in avoiding the pains of punishment.

It is notoriously hard to work out how effective (let alone how efficient) any deterrent system actually is (see Beyleveld 1979; von Hirsch, Bottoms, Burney & Wikström 1999)—especially since its efficacy depends on the perceived likelihood of being detected and convicted, as well as on the severity of the threatened sanction. But it is hard to deny the commonsense supposition that a system of deterrent punishments will deter at least some potential offenders from at least some offenses (see, e.g., Walker 1991, 13–20; M. Davis 1996, 9–21)—that punishment can in this way serve the aim of crime-prevention.

Second, punishment can incapacitate potential offenders. To incapacitate someone is to do something to that person that makes it impossible for him to act in certain ways. Punishment can incapacitate potential offenders by doing things to them (locking them up, for instance, or killing them) that make it impossible for them to commit crimes. Penal incapacitation is likely to be *partial* rather than *complete*, and *temporary* rather than *permanent*. While capital punishment permanently incapacitates the executed person from *all* future crimes, other incapacitative measures make only some kinds of offense against some kinds of victim impossible. Those in prison, for instance, can still commit offenses against fellow prisoners and warders; and unless they are imprisoned for life, their incapacitation is only temporary.

Incapacitation is implausible as a general aim for our existing penal systems, since few of their punishments are incapacitative, but it offers an obvious consequentialist rationale for capital punishment and imprisonment.[3] We must remember, however, that what matters is securing an *overall* reduction in crime. We do not prevent crime efficiently by locking up a number of drug dealers or burglars if they are just replaced on the streets by other drug dealers or burglars (see Zimring & Hawkins 1995, 53–58).

Third, punishment could reform or rehabilitate potential offenders. At its simplest, a consequentialist process of reform looks for techniques that will so modify people's dispositions and motives that they will in future refrain from crime willingly—rather than, as with deterrence, doing so reluctantly from fear of punishment. More ambitiously, it might aim to induce a positive respect for the law or a motivationally efficacious recognition that crime is wrong—rather than, for instance, persuading people that it is in their long-term self-interest to be law-abiding. More ambitiously yet, it might seek a more general improvement in offenders, reaching beyond a mere refraining from crime: perhaps "the improvement of [their] personalit[ies] and the achievement of a more nearly perfect adjustment" (Diana 1970, 48).[4]

Rehabilitation, by contrast, involves seeking to improve people's skills, capacities, and opportunities, rather than to reform their dispositions or motives—by providing training that will equip them for employment, for instance, or programs to deal with their drug addiction or other problems. Here again, the aim could be simply to help people refrain from crime; or, more ambitiously, to secure some larger improvement in their lives.

There are of course other ways than these by which punishment can prevent crime. For instance, punishment could so shame offenders that they refrain from crime in future (see Braithwaite & Pettit 1990); or it might help to maintain a general respect for and trust in the law—the German notion of 'positive general prevention' (see Schünemann, von Hirsch & Jareborg 1998). But we can clarify the logical structure of a purely consequentialist account of punishment, and the basis for some familiar objections to any such account, by looking at these three familiar ways by which punishment might prevent crime.

It is a contingent question whether a system of punishment is an efficient method of preventing crime by any of these means. It is a contingent question too whether the efficient use of such means will be consistent with ordinary notions of *just* punishment, as requiring the culpable commission of a crime.

Thus in the case of deterrence it is a contingent question whether it will be cost-effective to direct the threat of punishment only against offenders—and not also against their families, for instance—or only against offenders who are by normal criteria responsible—and not also against some whose punishment might deter others even if they are not themselves responsible or deterrable (see Hart 1968, 40–44). It is a contingent question whether it will be cost-effective to inflict punishment *only* on offenders (since efficient deterrence depends on the *belief* that offenders are punished, it could in principle sometimes be secured by framing an innocent person) or on *all* convicted offenders (a system that, for instance, randomly exempted some convicted offenders from punishment could in principle be cost-effective).

In the case of incapacitation, it is a contingent question whether incapacitative measures should be imposed only on actual offenders—and not also on some who, though they have not yet offended, can be identified as dangerous by sufficiently accurate predictive techniques—or only on responsible offenders (for nonresponsible offenders can also be dangerous).

In the case of reform or rehabilitation, it is likewise a contingent question whether such measures should be applied only to actual offenders—and not also to some who have not yet offended but are predictably likely to do so—or to all actual offenders (since some might need no such treatment) or only to responsible offenders.

In all three cases, finally, there is no necessary relationship between the seriousness of the offenses that occasion the imposition of penal measures and the severity of those measures. For what kinds of measure will be cost-effective depends not on the past offenses that occasion them but on the future offenses that they prevent. Thus a harsh sanction threatened for a minor offense could in principle be a cost-effective deterrent, even if it was sometimes actually imposed, if it deterred a sufficient number of such offenses. A lengthy term of incapacitative detention or of reformative treatment imposed on someone guilty of a series of minor offenses could in principle be cost-effective if it prevented a sufficient number of future offenses of that kind.

These contingencies ground some of the familiar objections to purely consequentialist justifications of criminal punishment.

1.2. Objections to Pure Consequentialism: The Rights of the Innocent

For some time in the mid-century, consequentialism, especially in its reformative or rehabilitative form, appeared to have become the victorious orthodoxy. But the 1970s saw a striking revival of retributivist, anticonsequentialist thought.[5]

This change was stimulated in part by the perceived failure of ambitiously consequentialist strategies to achieve their declared goal of efficient crime prevention. The optimistic belief that we could rely on the human sciences (on an increasing understanding of the causes of crime, increasingly sophisticated techniques for modifying conduct and attitudes, and increasingly accurate predictions of criminal dangerousness) to build cost-effective systems of deterrent, rehabilitative, or incapacitative punishment gave way to the pessimistic belief that "nothing works": punishment is not, and cannot be, an efficient method of crime prevention (see Cohen 1985, 33–35).[6]

In other words, the contingent connection between punishment and its justifying aim of crime-prevention was thought not to be strong enough to justify it. Indeed, it is not clear that if we began from consequentialist first principles, we would construct a system of *punishment*—of imposing burdens on supposed offenders for their supposed offenses—as an appropriate method of crime-prevention (see Duff 1986, 102–4, 164–70). Deterrence admittedly requires something like a system of punishment: a system that threatens and imposes sanctions against (perceived) offenses. But, as we have seen, neither incapacitative nor reformative or rehabilitative measures need in principle be directed against actual, as distinct from potential, offenders; and while such measures are typically burdensome (as involving deprivations of freedom or simply as being imposed whether or not the person wants them), they need not be *deliberately* burdensome. It is often unclear whether those who advocate such measures, especially those who emphasize reform or rehabilitation, are seeking to rationalize *punishment*, or instead to justify modes of treatment for which punishment (given that we have a penal system) merely provides the opportunity.[7] If that is so, they should perhaps be advocating—at least as an ideal aspiration—a wholly *non*-punitive form of (if necessary coercive) treatment.

That indeed was what some critics urged: we should abandon punishment in favor of more efficient systems of 'treatment' that make more rational use of the resources of the human sciences (see, e.g., Wootton 1963; Menninger 1968). Other critics, however, had *moral* objections to purely consequentialist theories of punishment, and argued that we must justify punishment in different terms, as something other than a technique of crime-prevention.

Those moral objections reflected a rejection of the belief in social engineering that often characterized consequentialist (especially utilitarian) perspectives on social policy. Liberal theorists began to reassert the claims of justice over utility and of individual rights against the state (see, notably, Rawls 1972; R. Dworkin 1978). The picture of the state as a benevolently competent authority that could be trusted (if guided by experts) to find efficient ways of promoting social goods was replaced by a conception of the state as a dangerously oppressive set of institutions whose powers over the citizens must be strictly limited to protect individual freedom and rights. The ambitious aim of "doing more good" was replaced by one of "doing less harm" or of "doing justice" (see von Hirsch 1976; Cohen 1985, 30–35, 245–54).

The moral objections to consequentialist theories of punishment in particular focused on the rights of the innocent—on the contingency of the connection between the commission of an offense and subjection to coercive penal measures. For, as we have seen, the aim of efficient crime-prevention could in principle sanction the deliberate 'punishment' of those known to have committed no offense (as well as the infliction of sentences that are disproportionately harsh in relation to the offenses that occasion their imposition), for the sake of efficient deterrence, incapacitation, or reform.

Such objections reflect the more general charge that aggregative consequentialism fails to take seriously the moral status of individuals (see Rawls 1972, 22–33, 187–90; Nozick 1974, 33–35; but cf. Parfit 1984, 329–42) or to recognize the importance of individual rights as 'trumps' that should protect individuals from being sacrificed to social utility (see R. Dworkin 1978, ch. 4). They accuse consequentialists of being prepared to sacrifice innocent individuals to achieve the social good of crime-prevention. They also appear to embody a strongly retributivist intuition: that punishment must be *deserved* for a past crime—that it must be imposed only on offenders and be proportionate to the offense for which it is imposed.

1.3. Consequentialist Responses

Those who want to justify criminal punishment in purely consequentialist terms can make various responses to these objections.

To the objection that consequentialist strategies fail to achieve their aims, they can reply that the cry "Nothing works!" was itself an overreaction to some overambitious claims: that punishment *can*, if properly focused and based on adequate empirical research, make a cost-effective contribution to such goals as deterrence (see Wilson 1983, ch. 7; Walker 1991, 13–20), incapacitation (Greenwood & Abrahamse 1982), and rehabilitation (Palmer 1994).[8] What of the moral objections, however?

One response is to argue that if the measures to which critics object would reduce crime cost-effectively, we should accept them. This might take the

form of 'outsmarting' the critic by arguing that we *should* be ready, if necessary, to sanction the deliberate punishment of an innocent.[9] More plausibly,
it might involve arguing that some of these measures are clearly justifiable, so
long as they are not misdescribed as 'punishment'. Thus consequentialists
might avoid the charges of deliberately punishing the innocent and of imposing disproportionately harsh punishments on the guilty, while still subjecting
potential offenders to cost-effective measures of incapacitation, reform, or rehabilitation, by making such measures a matter of civil commitment rather
than of criminal punishment—and pointing out that we accept such measures in other contexts, such as quarantine and detention for psychiatric protection or treatment (see, e.g., Schoeman 1979; Walker 1980, ch. 5; Wood
1988). Such responses have the merit of challenging critics to explain both
why the deliberate punishment of the innocent is objectionable (to rebut the
countercharge that they are simply appealing to a rationally unfounded intuition) and why such measures as compulsory quarantine and psychiatric detention are nonetheless acceptable (on which see Duff 1986, 172–77; 1998a,
147–51). They are, however, unlikely to satisfy the critic, who will still argue
that consequentialists cannot find a place for the necessary connection that
should obtain between *punishment* and guilt.

Another response is to argue that even if a purely consequentialist perspective could *in principle* justify the intuitively immoral (because unjust)
kinds of punishment imagined by the critic, *in practice* it would never do so.
Given the (admittedly contingent) features of our world, it would almost
never in fact be for the best to punish a known innocent, and even more
rarely reasonable (given how fallible actual human agents are) for a penal official to decide to do so (see n.1, above). Given the great dangers involved,
we will in the long run do best if we train ourselves and our penal officials to
think and act *as if* it was intrinsically and always wrong to punish an innocent
person.[10] One problem with this argument is that it depends on some large
empirical claims about the likely effects of different practices and policies—
claims for which it is hard to find a secure empirical foundation. Another
problem is that it still makes the protection of the innocent contingent upon
those effects (particularly, in typical versions of the argument, on the effects
if it becomes publicly known that innocents might be deliberately punished). But, the critic will reply, this misrepresents the *intrinsic* wrong involved in punishing an innocent. It is an injustice whose wrongful character
does not depend on its being publicly found out.

Another strategy for the pure consequentialist is to offer a richer and subtler account of the ends that punishment and the criminal justice system as a
whole should serve: to argue both that 'crime-prevention' is not the only
such end (for it is a good only insofar as it serves other and further ends) and
that the final ends that the system is to serve should not be understood in, for
instance, such simple utilitarian terms as 'happiness'. Thus Braithwaite and
Pettit posit a 'republican' idea of 'dominion', the assured and equal freedom

of citizens living under the law, as the good that a strictly consequentialist system of justice should serve; and they argue that this end will generate a secure ground for rights, such as the right of the innocent not to be punished, that are problematic for other forms of consequentialism.[11]

The general problem with this strategy is that so long as we take (as strict consequentialists must take) the specified end to be a good that is to be maximized, so long as we say, for instance, that what the value of dominion requires of the state's institutions and officials is that they seek to maximize the overall extent to which citizens in general have and maintain dominion, we cannot rule out the possibility that dominion will be efficiently maximized by policies or actions that seriously infringe the dominion of some in order to increase that of others. This is especially true when we recognize that, while the deliberate punishment of an innocent harms both the victim's dominion and (if known or suspected) that of others whose fear of being thus victimized damages the assurance of freedom that is part of dominion, crime also harms both aspects of dominion—since it infringes on the freedom of those whom it directly victimizes and undermines the assurance of others that they will not be victimized. It is surely then possible that penal measures that efficiently reduced crime by infringing the dominion of some innocents would lead to a maximization of dominion overall.

Critics will therefore still argue that a purely consequentialist theory of punishment cannot do justice to the rights of the innocent. Innocence—the fact that a person has committed no offense—gives that person a right not to be punished. That right makes a demand of the state and its officials, that they not subject her to punishment: that is, that they not punish her if she is known to be innocent, and also that they make reasonable efforts to establish that she is guilty before punishing her, to avoid mistakenly punishing an innocent. Within a purely consequentialist theory, such a right cannot be fundamental. Any status it can have must be derivative from, contingent on, the fact that recognizing such a right will serve the consequentialist ends of the criminal justice system. But, critics argue, this is inadequate. The punishment of an innocent is still a serious wrong even if it serves (as in principle it could serve) the system's further ends. It is an *intrinsic* wrong. A purely consequentialist theory, however, simply by virtue of being consequentialist, cannot recognize it as such.

Suppose that this kind of criticism is fatal to any purely consequentialist theory. It does not follow from this that we must abandon any attempt to justify criminal punishment in consequentialist terms, but only that we must abandon any attempt to justify it in *purely* consequentialist terms. We might still justify it in partly, even primarily, consequentialist terms, insisting that a penal system can be justified only if and because it does some consequential good, while also allowing some place for nonconsequentialist values. That is what several recent theorists have sought to do: it is to these attempts that we must now turn.

2. Side-Constrained Consequentialism

Whereas consequentialists ground the rightness or wrongness of actions and practices purely in their consequences, nonconsequentialists insist that some actions or practices are right or wrong independently of their consequences, by virtue of their intrinsic character. Nonconsequentialists would say, for instance, that the deliberate punishment of an innocent is wrong not because it is on balance likely or certain to do more harm than good (indeed, even if it would on balance do more good than harm) but because it is intrinsically wrong as an act of injustice. How can we find a place for such nonconsequentialist values in a theory that still makes the consequential benefits of punishment basic to its justification?

2.1. Side-Constraints and 'Negative' Retributivism

The simplest way to do this is to portray such values as 'side-constraints' on our pursuit of those benefits.[12] Thus, on Hart's account (1968, 1–27), the "general justifying aim" of punishment lies in its beneficial consequences (such as the prevention of crime). But our pursuit of that aim is constrained by the demands that we punish only those who have voluntarily broken the law, and that the severity of the punishment be proportionate to the seriousness of the crime for which it is imposed.[13]

These are the obvious two side-constraints to posit. The resulting theory preserves the central consequentialist thought that punishment is justified only if it is a cost-effective way of achieving certain beneficial consequences. But it avoids the familiar objections to *purely* consequentialist accounts by building in side-constraints that preclude the objectionable implications of such accounts—that forbid us to punish the innocent or to punish the guilty more harshly than they deserve.[14]

To say that these side-constraints 'forbid' such actions is not to say that they rule them out *absolutely* or come what may. We can recognize a kind of action as intrinsically wrong while also believing that it can sometimes be justified by some more important value—that although lying is intrinsically wrong, for instance, we can justifiably lie to save a life—or while recognizing that we could face a tragic situation in which we 'must' do such a wrong to avert some enormous evil—in which, for instance, we are forced to kill an innocent person in order to save many other innocents.[15] It is rather to say that such actions cannot be justified merely by the fact that they would produce better consequences than any available alternative and that even if we find that we 'must' do such an action, we must recognize the moral cost involved, which pure consequentialists cannot recognize (see Hart 1968, 12).

It is, however, clearly not enough simply to assert such side-constraints. They need to be justified. *Why* is it intrinsically wrong to punish an innocent person, or to punish an offender with 'disproportionate' severity?

One obvious way to answer this question is to appeal to a retributivist notion of desert: it is wrong to punish the innocent because, having committed no crime, they do not deserve to be punished; it is wrong to punish offenders more harshly than they deserve. This is to appeal to a 'negative' version of retributivism. 'Positive' retributivism (see sec. 4, below) offers a positive justification of punishment: we *ought* to punish the guilty because they deserve it. 'Negative' retributivism, by contrast, does not tell us that or why we *ought* to punish. Rather, it tells us that whatever the positive justification for punishment is, we must *not* punish the innocent (or punish the guilty more harshly than they deserve). It tells us that it is not unjust to punish the guilty, but it does not tell us why we *should* punish them. That question is to be answered by specifying a consequentialist 'justifying aim' for punishment (see Mackie 1985, 207–8; Dolinko 1991, 539–43).

Negative retributivists, however, face the same fundamental problem as do positive retributivists: how can they explain the supposed moral connection between crime and punishment that the notion of desert is meant to capture? Given the problematic nature of this idea of penal desert (see sec. 4.1, below), side-constrained consequentialists might look for some other way of justifying their side-constraints.

Hart offers a nonretributivist rationale for the side-constraint forbidding the punishment of the innocent (Hart 1968, 1–53): that it protects individual freedom by "maximising within the framework of coercive criminal law the efficacy of the individual's informed and considered choice in determining the future and also his power to predict that future" (1968, 46). If only those who voluntarily break the law are liable to be punished, individual citizens can predict and control whether they will become liable to punishment in a way that they cannot if punishment might also be inflicted on those who have not voluntarily broken the law.[16]

(We should note that the way in which this side-constraint is justified will determine the meaning of 'innocent' and 'guilty' in this context. The simplest reading of those notions is a legal one: the 'guilty' are those who satisfy the criminal law's definition of an offense, the 'innocent' are those who do not. But this simple reading is too simple. Any morally plausible version of this side-constraint will not only forbid the punishment of those whom the law defines as 'innocent' but also set constraints on how the law should define 'guilt' and 'innocence' [see Duff 1986, 153–55]. What those constraints are, and thus how the notion of innocence should be understood, will depend on how the side-constraint is justified. If it is justified in retributivist terms, as forbidding the punishment of those who do not deserve it, the 'innocent' are those who do not deserve punishment, whatever that turns out to mean, and the law should so define 'guilt' that only those who deserve punishment count in law as guilty. If it is justified in Hartian terms, as protecting individual freedom and choice, the 'innocent' are those who have not chosen to break the law, and the law should so define 'guilt' that only those who choose to break the law count as guilty.)

I do not discuss here the adequacy of Hart's rationale, or the question whether we can find a nonretributivist rationale for the constraint forbidding the disproportionately harsh punishment of the guilty (see Feinberg 1988, 144–55). Whatever grounding these side-constraints are given, such quali-fiedly consequentialist theories face new objections, which concern not the rights of the innocent, but the rights or moral standing of the *guilty*—of those whose punishment such side-constraints permit.

2.2. Objections: Doing Justice to the Guilty

Objections to a side-constrained consequentialist system of punishment are sometimes expressed in Kantian terms. Since such a system punishes the guilty in order to achieve some further, socially beneficial end (the preven-tion of crime, through deterrence, incapacitation, or reform), it uses them "merely as means" to that further end. But this is to fail to treat them, as re-sponsible agents should be treated, "as ends" (see Kant [1785] 1948, 90–93, [1797] 1965, 99–100; Murphy 1979c, 94).

The meaning of this Kantian slogan, however, is notoriously opaque (see Murphy 1979b; Walker 1991, ch. 6; Honderich 1984a, 60–61). It certainly pre-cludes deliberately punishing an innocent to preserve the law's deterrent ef-ficacy, or subjecting to incapacitative detention a responsible agent who has not yet committed a crime, since such measures treat their victims "merely as means"—as objects whose interests can be sacrificed if it is useful to do so, rather than as moral subjects whose treatment by the state should depend on their own responsible choices. But it is less clear that the Kantian injunction precludes punishing the *guilty* for consequentialist ends. For if, as a side-constrained consequentialism requires, they are "found to be deserving of punishment before any consideration is given to the utility of [their] punish-ment" (Kant [1797] 1965, 100), they are used "as means"—but not "*merely* as means." Their choices as responsible agents are respected, since they are punished (and used) only if they choose to break the law (see Benn 1958, 325; Walker 1980, 80–85).

Nonetheless, there is force to the objection that any system of punish-ment with such consequentialist justifying aims as deterrence, incapacita-tion, or reform denies the guilty the respect due to them as responsible agents (Duff 1996a, 10–14). If it aims to incapacitate them from future of-fenses, it preempts their future choices rather than leaving them free (as re-sponsible agents should be left free) to decide for themselves whether to re-offend (see Duff 1986, 170–78). If it aims to reform them by so modifying their dispositions and motives that they will in future willingly refrain from crime, it treats them not as responsible agents who should be left free to determine their own values and attitudes but as objects to be remolded or manipulated into conformity (see Lewis 1953; H. Morris 1968). If it aims to deter them, and other potential offenders, it seeks to coerce obedience by threats rather than by the kind of moral appeal to what justifies the law's demands by which a state should seek its citizens' obedience: it treats those who are punished, and anyone whose obedience it secures by such threats, "like a dog instead of with the freedom and respect due to him as a man" (Hegel [1821] 1942, 246; see Duff 1986, 178–86).

Such a rejection of side-constrained consequentialism might seem rather too quick; and so it is. The objections mentioned in the preceding paragraph must be explained, and possible responses to them considered. We must ask whether there are side-constrained or qualified consequentialist accounts that might avoid them. The first of these tasks I take up in chapter 3, where I reformulate the objections in terms of a communitarian rather than a Kantian perspective (see ch. 3.1.2). The second task, however, I undertake now, by considering two other qualifiedly consequentialist accounts of punishment.

3. Forfeiture of Rights and Societal Defense

Can we show that the infliction of punishment on the guilty—those who have voluntarily or culpably broken the law—is consistent with the respect due to them as moral agents, even if they are punished for the sake of some further good (such as crime-prevention) that their punishment will bring? In this section I comment briefly on two arguments that aim to show that we can.[17]

3.1. *Forfeiting Rights or Moral Standing*

The objections to side-constrained consequentialism discussed in the preceding section presuppose that offenders retain the rights or moral standing of citizenship—that the state still owes them the respect, the duties of justice, that it owes to all its citizens. According to these objections, side-constrained consequentialists fail to respect those rights or moral standing. But why should we accept that presupposition? Why should we not say instead that those who (culpably) break the law thereby *forfeit* at least some of those rights, some aspects of that moral standing? They have flouted their responsibilities as citizens and violated the rights of others: how can they claim that the state should accord them the respect that they refused to accord to others?

Thus Goldman argues that if someone breaks the law, thus flouting his duties as a citizen, his "package [of citizenship rights] reverts temporarily to trusteeship by the community" (1982, 67–68). In exercising that trusteeship, the community must seek to restore him as soon as possible to full enjoyment of his rights by restoring him to membership of the law-abiding community, and must preserve as many of those rights as possible, while preventing his commission of further crimes. Incapacitation and rehabilitation are therefore the proper goals of punishment; and by emphasizing offenders' restoration to community, we avoid the charge that they are simply being sacrificed to the community's good.

C. W. Morris (1991) argues that criminals forfeit at least some of their moral rights. Their breach of the contractualist requirements of justice entails at least a temporary 'suspension' of those rights; and this allows us to punish them in order to maintain the efficacy of the law. However, although their punishment is not forbidden or constrained by the rights that they have forfeited, it is normally still constrained by considerations of benevolence, since they do not, except in extreme cases ("contract killers, war criminals, tyrants, and certain terrorists" [72]), lose *all* moral standing. Although we owe them no duties of justice, they are still "direct moral object[s]" of benevolence (61); and this constrains what we can properly do to them by way of punishment.

This line of thought is indeed tempting. First, if we are to justify criminal punishment, we must justify actions that normally violate rights. We must show how imprisonment does not wrongfully violate the right to liberty, for instance, or fines the right to dispose of one's own income. Furthermore, while we can sometimes talk of rights as being justifiably overridden or infringed, this approach does not seem appropriate here: for someone whose rights are justifiably overridden or infringed is due an apology, or even compensation, whereas those who are justly punished surely have no such claim (see C. W. Morris 1991, 64).

Second, this argument speaks to the common conception of justice and rights as being contractual or reciprocal. Even if we do not see the rights of citizenship as grounded in a social contract, and as lost by those who flout the contract, it is tempting to see them as depending on a kind of reciprocity. We can claim rights, as a matter of justice, against one another or against the state only insofar as we are willing to respect those rights in others. Someone who violates the rights of others treats them, by implication, as if they had no such rights; but he cannot then demand that they accord those rights to him—that they treat him with the respect that he denies to them.

Such 'forfeiture' accounts, however, provoke two serious worries (and see Montague 1995, 2–4).

First, just which rights are forfeited? It is implausible to say, as Goldman implies, that *any* crime entails the reversion of *all* rights of citizenship into community trusteeship until we are confident that the offender will not offend again. But it is unclear how we are to determine which rights are forfeited or suspended, or for how long (see C. W. Morris 1991, 67–68, 65). Nor is it clear whether we should be talking of certain specific rights, such as the right not to be locked up or deprived of one's money; or of some more basic and general—but so far underspecified—set of "rights of citizenship."

Second, this kind of account leaves offenders with rather weak protection against what might be done to them by way of punishment. On Goldman's account, we must do whatever is necessary to restore offenders to full membership of the community and to prevent them committing further crimes. But it is quite unclear how we can then set the kinds of retributivist limit on the severity of punishment that he wants to set (see Goldman 1982, 74–75) or how we can deny that we are now treating offenders simply as objects to be remolded or reformed into law-abiding conformity rather than as responsible moral subjects. On Morris's account, our treatment of most criminals is still constrained by the demands of benevolence, but it is not clear how strong those constraints are. They do not limit our treatment of those whose crimes are so serious that they lose *all* moral standing, for whom "torture would be no more morally objectionable than execution"; and Morris is not even sure that benevolence forbids torturing those who are still "(direct) objects of (some) considerations of benevolence" (1991, 74–75).

The main question raised by such accounts, however, is whether we should see offenders as excluding themselves from full membership in the political community—from the rights or moral standing of citizenship. It might be tempting to do so, especially from a contractualist perspective; and the ways in which they are portrayed in contemporary debates and treated by our systems of criminal justice often imply such a view of offenders, as a 'them' against whom 'we', the law-abiding citizens, must protect ourselves. (The fact that in Britain those serving prison terms lose the right to vote is a vivid expression of this loss of the standing of citizenship.) But, as I argue later, we should look for an 'inclusionary' account of criminal punishment that shows how punishment can still treat those punished as full members of the political community, rather than one that portrays them as outside the community—as having lost the rights or moral standing of membership (see ch. 3.1).

3.2. Punishment as Societal Defense

I suggested above (p. 14) that a system of deterrent punishments, even if it punishes only those who voluntarily break the law, fails to treat both those whom it punishes and those whom it threatens "with the freedom and respect due to" them as moral agents (Hegel [1821] 1942, 246). Some have argued, however, that by comparing the threat and imposition of punishment as a deterrent with the threat and use of force in defense of oneself or others, we can show that a side-constrained system of deterrent punishments does treat those it threatens or punishes with the respect that is due to them.[18]

We are justified, the argument runs, not only in *using* violence to ward off attacks upon ourselves or others, but also in *threatening* harm against potential attackers in order to deter them—and in inflicting that harm if they are not deterred. What justifies this is a principle of justice: not *retributive* justice, sanctioning the infliction on the guilty of the harm they supposedly deserve, but *distributive* justice, concerning the just distribution of harms and risks. Someone who attacks another culpably brings about a situation in which harm will occur—either the harm he will do to his victim or the harm a defender will do to him. If it is within my power as a potential defender to determine where that harm will fall (by either using defensive violence against the attacker or not preventing the attack), it is distributively just that I should make the harm fall on him rather than on the victim who did not bring this situation about. This principle is then extended to cover the threat of violence to deter an intending attacker, and the actual use of violence against an undeterred attacker to deter him or others from future attacks. This final step clearly brings us towards a deterrent system of punishment. It is distributively just that we should impose the burden of penal harm, or of the risk of such harm, on actual or intending criminals rather than leaving the burden of the fact or risk of criminal harm to fall on their actual or potential victims: for it is the (actual or intending) criminals who culpably create the situation in which one or other of these kinds of harm will ensue.

A detailed discussion of the various versions of this argument would need to ask how punishment is to be limited to the culpably guilty, since defensive force may be used even against 'innocent' attackers; what room it allows for any principle of 'proportionality'; and how far it can really justify not merely threatening or using force to deter an intending attacker, but also using force against *him* in order to deter *others*. I do not pursue these issues here, but I am not sure that the argument meets the Hegelian objection (see Duff 1996a, 14–16). We can properly use violence to ward off an attack on which someone has culpably embarked, and warn an intending attacker that we will do so. Such violence is a legitimate response to the attack that is meant simply to prevent him from carrying it through. But this account aims to justify us in threatening a degree of force that might well exceed what would be necessary to ward off the attack, and to use that force after the attack is over (since punishment is imposed after the crime) to deter future attacks. That is surely to treat potential offenders not as moral agents whom we should try to dissuade from crime by appealing to the relevant moral reasons for doing so, but as 'dogs' to be coerced by threats.

Why, however, should we observe such moral restraints when dealing with those who would attack us? If moral appeals will predictably fail to dissuade them (and deterrent threats are directed only against those who will not be dissuaded by moral appeals), why should we not then create for them prudential reasons to refrain from attacking us—which is still to address them as rational agents with reasons that will weigh with them (see Baker 1992b)?

I say more in chapter 3 (secs. 3 and 8) about the claim that a suitably side-constrained system of deterrent punishments treats actual and potential criminals with such respect as is due to them, since it can best be discussed (and criticized) in relation to my account of punishment as penance. We should note, however, that theories of punishment as 'societal defense' also raise, as did 'forfeiture' theories, a fundamental question about how we should conceive our relationships with our fellow-citizens (including those who are actual or potential criminals).

The use of deterrent threats that such theories seek to justify is morally most plausible between strangers (as potential enemies) or against outlaws: in situations in which there are no laws or ties of community to bind us or the person we threaten is deaf to the appeal of any such laws or ties (consider the contexts in which nuclear deterrence is advocated). But is this how we should see our fellow-citizens? Such justifications of punishment as deterrence are often cast in the language of 'us' and 'them': 'we' must use such threats to defend 'us', the law-abiding, against 'them', the potential criminals whom we fear (see Baker 1992b, 153–54; cf. von Hirsch 1993, 12–14, 41–44). I argue below, however, that the proper question is not how we should prevent 'them' from breaking the law but how we, as fallible moral beings, should persuade *ourselves* to refrain from crime. We should treat those who commit, or who might be tempted to commit, even serious crimes as fellow-members of the moral community; we should not abandon the moral language in which the law should speak to its citizens in favor of the brutally coercive language of deterrent threats.

It might be said that this is naive idealism. Of course, *if* we lived in societies in which people could generally be persuaded to refrain from crime by moral reminders of the concern and respect that they owe one another as fellow-citizens, by moral appeals to the values that the criminal law aims to protect, we might not need the coercive apparatus of criminal law at all—and certainly would not need a system of deterrent punishments. But we do not live in such societies. There are too many people who are, partly if not wholly, sometimes if not always, deaf to such moral persuasion, but susceptible to deterrent persuasion. We surely have the right to defend ourselves against their criminal depredations, and so to preserve the essential social conditions of peace and security, by a side-constrained system of deterrent punishments—a system that addresses them realistically as rational but immoral agents.

I say more in chapter 5 about the relationship between ideals and actualities, and in chapter 3.3 about the possibility of a *partly* deterrent justification for criminal punishment. I do not claim to have shown yet either that no such justification is possible or, more generally, that neither pure nor side-constrained consequentialist rationales for a system of punishment can be adequate; and I take up several consequentialist themes, including incapacitation and reform as well as deterrence, in other chapters. I have so far simply tried to display the structure of consequentialist theories in both their pure and their qualified or side-constrained forms, to sketch some of the ways in which those structures have been fleshed out, and to note the main objections that such theories face.

I turn now to consequentialism's familiar opponent, retributivism, and in particular to 'positive' retributivism.

4. Retributivist Themes and Variations

'Negative' retributivism sets side-constraints of desert on our pursuit of the consequentialist justifying aim of punishment (see sec. 2.1, above). The 'retributivist revival' that began in the 1970s, however, was a revival of 'positive' retributivism, which portrays 'retribution' as the positive justifying aim of punishment. We can express the difference between these two species of retributivism by saying that while a negative retributivist tells us only that we *may* punish the guilty, or that it would not be unjust to punish them, a positive retributivist holds that we *ought* to punish the guilty, or that justice *demands* their punishment.

This need not be to say that the punishment of the guilty is an *absolute* duty—that we *must* punish them, come what may (as Kant seemed sometimes to believe; see Kant [1797] 1965, 102). Such a claim would be quite implausible, because it would require us to devote all the resources we could muster to detecting and punishing those who commit offenses—which is not a realistic demand to place on a legal system (see p. xii, above). Even the more modest claim that we ought to punish all those who are duly *proved* guilty by some appropriate criminal process does not specify a plausible *absolute* duty; nor does it tell us, as a theory of punishment should tell us, why we ought to try to detect and convict (at least some of) the guilty. Retributivism is more plausibly read as holding that we have, or the state has, *a* duty to detect, convict, and punish the guilty—a duty that must compete with other duties and demands that might sometimes defeat it.

On this reading of retributivism, the state has a defeasible duty to punish the guilty (or those who are proved to be guilty). Guilt constitutes what is normally, that is, unless defeated, a *sufficient* reason for punishment—whereas negative retributivists hold that guilt is merely a *necessary* condition for punishment. Weaker versions of retributivism are also possible. It could be said, for instance, that guilt provides *a* positive reason for punishment but not one that can be sufficient by itself—that if punishment is to be justified it must *also* bring some consequential good, such as crime prevention (see von Hirsch 1976; Husak 1992b). For the moment, however, we can focus on the more familiar form of retributivism that holds that the state has a *duty* to punish the guilty, and on the central question of how such a claim is to be justified: why should the state be thought to have any such duty?

A retributivist answer to this question cannot appeal to the beneficial *consequences* of punishment, since retributivism, as normally understood, is *non-*consequentialist.[19] It justifies punishment in terms not of its contingently beneficial effects but of its *intrinsic* justice as a response to crime; the justificatory relationship holds between present punishment and past crime, not between present punishment and future effects. But how can a retributivist explain that supposed justificatory relationship?

4.1. "The Guilty Deserve to Suffer"

It might be tempting to begin with the basic intuition that "the guilty deserve to suffer" (see L. H. Davis 1972) as a basis for the claim that the state therefore has a duty to ensure that they suffer as they deserve. But this is at best a beginning. Such an intuition cries out for explanation and justification. We might feel its pull. It might seem unjust or unfair if the wicked flourish (especially when their victims do not) or "no more than they deserve" if they suffer. But we must ask what this feeling means—and whether it amounts to anything more than a morally disreputable kind of envy (that they get away with what we do not dare to do ourselves) or a vengeful hatred whose moral credentials are far from obvious (see, generally, Ardal 1984; Honderich 1984a, ch. 2, 1984b).

That explanation must tell us, first, *who* the 'guilty' are and *what* they deserve to suffer. Are the 'guilty' those who are guilty of *moral* wrongdoing (but why should it be the job of the state, or of anyone other than God, to ensure that they suffer) or those who are guilty of *legal* wrongdoing (but what should count as legal wrongdoing, and why does it make suffering deserved)? Should *any* kind of suffering that befalls the guilty count as what they deserve; or any suffering that is *caused* by their crime? Neither of these answers seems plausible. It would be absurd for sentencers to try to calculate how much offenders had already suffered in their lives and how much extra suffering, if any, must be inflicted by punishment to give them what they deserve; and not much less absurd to reduce a burglar's sentence because he caught pneumonia while carrying out the crime. This is not to say that there is no place for the idea of 'natural' punishment (see Winch 1972c, 197–200; Teichman 1973; Walker 1980, 130–31), nor that sentencers cannot sometimes properly show leniency to an offender who has "already suffered enough" (see Walker & Padfield 1996, 54–56; also Husak 1990 on "already punished enough"). But it is to say that the notion of 'suffering', as well as that of 'guilt', needs explanation if we are to agree that "the guilty deserve to suffer."

Second, it also needs to be explained why it should be the job of the state to inflict on the guilty the suffering they deserve. For the claim that the guilty deserve to suffer does not by itself entail that anyone has a right or duty to inflict that suffering on them. It could mean only that their suffering is a good. In thus portraying the penal suffering of the guilty as a good, that claim does contradict the familiar consequentialist idea that punishment itself is always an evil, precisely because it involves inflicting harm or suffering (see Bentham [1789] 1970, ch. 13, sec. 2). But it is a further step to claim that that good is one that it is the state's duty to secure. It must be shown both that it is a good that is the state's business, and that it is a sufficiently important good to justify creating a system of criminal punishment to secure it—given the significant costs that any such system involves (see Murphy 1985; Husak 1992b; Shafer-Landau 1996).[20] Retributivists thus need to show either that what the guilty deserve to suffer is precisely punishment at the hands of the state, or that it should be the state's responsibility to inflict the suffering they deserve.

Retributivists assert a justificatory relationship between past crime and present punishment. That relationship is expressed by the idea of 'desert': crime makes punishment appropriate or required because criminals deserve to be punished; punishment gives criminals their 'just deserts'. In trying to explain this idea of penal desert, they might appeal to the intuition that "the guilty deserve to suffer." But they still need to explain the notions of 'guilt' and of 'suffering' as used in this context; the justificatory relationship of 'desert' that supposedly connects guilt to suffering; and the state's duty to inflict such deserved suffering. They need, that is, to explain what it is about crime and about punishment that makes punishment appropriate or required as a response to crime; and why that is something that should concern the state.

The different versions of retributivism can be seen as so many attempts to answer these questions. I do not comment on all those versions here (see Cottingham 1979) but do comment briefly on three lines of retributivist thought that have figured in recent debates. Two are instructive failures. The third points the way towards a more fruitful but no longer purely retributivist account of punishment as deserved for crime.

4.2. The Removal of Unfair Advantage

Suppose we see a system of law as bringing benefits (security, protected freedom) to all its citizens by imposing on them all the burden of self-restraint involved in obeying the law. We can then say that a criminal, in breaking the law, takes an unfair advantage for herself over all those who obey the law. She accepts the benefits that flow from the law-abiding self-restraint of others but refuses to accept the burden of obeying the law herself; she takes the goods that the law brings but refuses to accept her fair share of the burdens on which those goods depend. She now deserves, as a matter of justice, to lose that unfair advantage, and punishment serves precisely to deprive her of it. By imposing an extra burden on her, it restores that fair balance of benefits and burdens that her crime disturbed.[21]

This account certainly addresses the tasks that a retributivist theory must discharge. It is a nonconsequentialist account. Just as the advantage that the criminal gains in breaking the law consists not in any material consequences of the crime but in that freedom from self-restraint that is intrinsic to the crime, so the removal of that advantage is not a contingent effect of punishment but intrinsic to punishment itself as the imposition of a burden. It gives an account of crime (as the taking of an unfair advantage over the law-abiding) and of punishment (as the imposition of a matching burden) that shows why crime makes punishment appropriate—as removing that unfair advantage. It also shows why this should be a proper task for the state. Since it is the state that, through the criminal law, imposes the burden of law-abiding self-restraint on its citizens, it is also a proper task for the state to try to ensure that those who accept that burden are not unfairly disadvantaged in doing so (though there remains the question whether this is an important *enough* task to justify, by itself, the creation and maintenance of a system of criminal punishment).

I do not discuss the various objections to this account that critics, including some of its own earlier adherents, have offered.[22] Those objections are, I think, conclusive—in particular the charge that it offers a distorted picture of the punishment-deserving character of crime. The criminal wrongfulness of rape, for instance, in virtue of which it merits punishment, does not consist in taking an unfair advantage over all those who obey the law. This account is, however, still worth noting, since it offers a clear illustration of one way in which the tasks facing any retributivist might be addressed and, in particular, one way of trying to explain the punishment-deserving character of crime.

It offers an abstract, formal characterization of the general nature of crimes. Their common and defining feature is that they involve taking unfair advantage over the law-abiding. It also portrays all crimes, qua deserving of punishment, as *mala prohibita*, since the unfair advantage that criminals take over the law-abiding, in virtue of which they deserve punishment, depends on the existence of a criminal law prohibiting what they do. Were there no such law, they would commit no wrong of a kind relevant to punishment, since they would not be refusing a burden of law-abiding self-restraint that others accept. Such crimes as rape involve actions that are, no doubt, wrong independently of the criminal law: but the wrong that is punished is a wrong that depends on the criminal law. If rape were not prohibited by the criminal law, someone who committed rape would not be taking an unfair advantage over the law-abiding.

It is certainly tempting for retributivists to look for some general, and thus inevitably to a degree abstract or formal, account of the character of criminal wrongs: for such an account might portray crimes in a way that also shows why they deserve punishment, thus bridging the gap between "A did wrong" and "A deserves punishment" and showing punishment to be an intrinsically appropriate response to crime. The 'unfair advantage' theory does this: the character of crime (as taking an unfair advantage) points towards punishment (a burden that removes that advantage) as an appropriate response.

Fingarette (1977) offers a structurally similar account. Retributive punishment, he argues, is required by any system of law that claims, as the law must claim, power over the citizens' wills, since a law that purported to impose binding requirements on citizens but did not in general punish breaches of those requirements would be no law at all. Here again, the character of crime (as disobedience to a power-claiming law) points towards punishment (as the reassertion of that flouted power) as the appropriate response to it. This account is not persuasive. Even if, as I argue in chapter 2 (sec. 6), the law cannot simply ignore criminal conduct, it is not clear why its response must involve *punishment*—why it must claim a kind of power that makes punishment necessary. But it illustrates the kind of account of crime that the 'unfair advantage' theory also exemplifies.

We should note a crucial limitation on both these accounts. They argue that punishment is necessary, as retribution, *given* that we have a system of criminal law of the relevant kind (a system that secures benefits for all by imposing burdens on all, or that claims power over the citizens' wills), but they do not tell us why we should have such a system of law (see Fingarette 1977, 513–15), or what its content should be. They offer, not a complete justification of criminal punishment, but a justification that depends on a prior justification of the criminal law and a prior account of what content it should have.

Dimock's account (1997), while also involving a general and abstract characterization of the punishable nature of crime, does address these issues. The primary function of law, she argues, is to create and maintain the "objective" conditions of trust—the conditions that make it reasonable for citizens to trust one another even when they are strangers who lack the kinds of personal relationship that can ground trust outside the law. The law fulfills this function partly by creating and maintaining "meta-trust, trust in trust" (51). But intrinsic to the maintenance of such trust is the punishment of crimes, since trust is undermined if society acquiesces in trust-undermining crimes. This, she argues, grounds a version of positive retributivism (although her account is not *purely* retributivist, since punishment also functions as a deterrent against conduct that undermines trust). Again, I am not concerned with the adequacy of this account here. To assess this, we would need to ask whether the function of maintaining trust and meta-trust generates a plausible account of the entire content of the criminal law (the content it *ought* to have); whether *punishment* (rather than some formal but nonpunitive condemnation and disavowal) is really necessary to reaffirm society's commitment to trust, or whether punishment itself is not being justified in primarily deterrent terms (see sec. 4.4); and whether we should accept the deterrent function that Dimock also allots to punishment (see sec. 3.2 above; ch. 3.3.1). But her account does again illustrate one way in which retributivists can try to explain the idea of penal desert, by giving a general, abstract account of the character of crime that shows how crime requires punishment.[23] There are, however, other ways, to one of which I now turn.

4.3. Punitive Emotions

Retributive punishment is often seen as expressing, or giving vent to, certain emotions—anger or indignation, "the feeling of hatred and the desire of vengeance" (Stephen [1873] 1967, 152)—that crime provokes. Many critics see this as undermining retributivism as a justification of punishment. It shows, they argue, that demands for penal retribution flow not from some rational foundation of value or principle but from nonrational, morally disreputable emotions.[24] Some retributivists, however, have sought precisely to justify punishment by relating it to the emotions that crime properly "excites in healthily constituted minds" (Stephen [1873] 1967, 152): we should, they argue, see such emotions not as nonrational passions, but as expressions of a moral *understanding* of crime and its implications—and thus should also reject the sharp distinction between 'reason' and 'emotion', and the view of emotions as wholly nonrational, that have bedeviled philosophy.

Thus Murphy, for instance, focuses on resentment and "retributive hatred." Resentment, which expresses my own self-respect, and retributive hatred, which involves a desire "to restore the proper moral balance" by inflicting on the wrongdoer suffering that deprives her of her "undeserved or ill-gotten" level of well-being, are in principle "natural, fitting and proper response[s] to certain instances of wrong-doing."[25] Such emotions could then *in principle* motivate a system of criminal punishment that aims precisely to satisfy them by depriving criminals of their undeserved well-being.

Murphy himself doubts whether this can *in practice* justify a state system of criminal punishment, given the dangers involved in allowing ourselves to be motivated by such emotions (Murphy & Hampton 1988, 98–108; Murphy 1999). But we should also wonder whether it can provide even an 'in principle' justification. It does offer an account of what it is about (at least some) crime that makes it deserving of punishment: crime arouses rational, morally justified emotions that involve a desire to make the wrongdoer suffer, and punishment inflicts that suffering. But, apart from the question whether *every* kind of conduct that should be criminal arouses such emotions, it is not clear why it should be *the state's* task to satisfy these emotions by instituting and maintaining a system of criminal punishment. Nor is it clear that to justify such emotions is also to justify a desire to make the wrongdoer suffer. We could agree that resentment and indignation are morally appropriate responses to some kinds of crime, while also arguing that we should try to free ourselves from the desire to make the wrongdoer suffer that these responses admittedly often involve—that we should find other, less destructive ways of expressing them (cf. Horder 1992, 194–97).

Part of the problem here is that it is not yet clear just *what* the wrongdoer should suffer. If she is now enjoying some profit from her crime, she should no doubt be deprived of that. But confiscation of the proceeds of crime is not itself punishment (the thief who has only to give back what she stole has not thereby been punished), and the desire to see a murderer or a rapist suffer is surely not the desire to deprive him of his "ill-gotten" level of well-being.[26]

Moore (1987) offers a different argument, focused not on the resentment or anger we feel at the wrongdoing of others but on the guilt we may feel at our own wrongdoing. If I were to commit a horrific crime I would, I hope, "feel guilty unto death." Given that feeling, I would judge that I ought to be punished. Since that emotion of guilt is virtuous (it is what a virtuous person would feel), and since virtuous emotions are good heuristic guides to the truth of the moral judgments that they generate, I can thus justify the judgment that I ought to be punished if I committed such a crime. If I am to respect actual criminals as human beings like myself, I must then make the same judgment about their penal desert as I would about my own—that they should be punished.[27] In the end, however, despite its detail and complexity, Moore's argument appears to amount to little more than an appeal to the intuition (expressed in first-person cases through the emotion of guilt) that "the guilty deserve to suffer": it does not tell us *why* they should suffer, or why guilt should generate the judgment that I ought to suffer, or *what* they ought to suffer, or why it should be a proper task for the *state* to inflict that suffering.

Although both these accounts fail, their failure is instructive. It reminds us of the need to explain what it is that the guilty supposedly deserve to suffer, what it is about crime that makes such suffering appropriate or required, and why it should be the state's task to inflict such suffering. More positively, however, these accounts suggest that we should portray state punishment as related to, or continuous with, our moral responses to wrongdoing, which are themselves structured by such rational emotions as guilt (at one's own wrongdoing) and anger or indignation. These accounts also suggest that such emotions might point us towards, if not a direct justification of criminal punishment, at least a clearer idea of what the thought that the guilty deserve to suffer might mean.

For there is surely *something* to the idea that one who has committed a serious wrong should not be able to live a life of "freedom and contentment" (Murphy & Hampton 1988, 91). He should not be able to carry on his life as if he had done no wrong. He should, we may think, suffer. But what should he suffer? One obvious answer is that he should suffer guilt: for guilt or remorse is a proper response to one's wrongdoing and is (when sincere) painful. Guilt, however, is a kind of suffering that is essentially *self*-induced, flowing from one's own recognition that one did wrong. How can it ground a justification for punishment—the infliction of suffering by others? Another obvious answer is that he deserves to suffer the angry or indignant condemnation of others. But why should that involve *punishing* him?

Before I discuss some possible answers to these questions, we should note the difference between the kind of characterization of crime as punishable wrongdoing that these emotion-based accounts offer and that offered by the accounts discussed in the preceding subsection.

Those accounts offer a general, abstract characterization of criminal wrongdoing—for instance as taking an unfair advantage over the law-abiding or as disobeying a power-claiming law. This involves portraying crimes, qua deserving of punishment, as *mala prohibita*—as punishably wrongful only because they flout the criminal law. By contrast, the emotion-based accounts discussed in this subsection suggest a less abstract conception of criminal wrongdoing, as consisting in particular, concrete kinds of moral wrong that arouse the relevant emotions; and those wrongs will typically be *mala in se*—wrongs whose emotion-arousing wrongfulness is prior to and independent of the criminal law.[28] Rape arouses our anger and indignation, not because the rapist has disobeyed the criminal law and thus taken an unfair advantage over us, or flouted the law's power, or undermined the conditions of trust, but because of the particular, concrete wrong he has done to his victim.

On accounts of this kind, unlike those discussed in the previous subsection, the moral character of crime as deserving of punishment is also likely to figure in the explanation of why such conduct should be criminal. The 'unfair advantage' theory tells us why, *given* that her conduct is criminal, an offender deserves punishment, but not why her conduct should be criminalized in the first place. An emotion-based theory, by contrast, can hold that the law ought to criminalize wrongdoing that deserves punishment *because* it is wrongful and deserving of punishment independently of the law. The former kind of theory separates *criminal* wrongs, as punishable, from prelegal *moral* wrongs. The latter kind of theory portrays them as intimately connected.

It is not at all clear, however, that this is a *merit* in such theories. Stephen argues that the criminal law "is in the nature of a persecution of the grosser forms of vice"—we should criminalize such vicious conduct precisely in order to ensure that it is punished and that the "feeling of hatred" that it "excites in healthily constituted minds" is gratified ([1873] 1967, 152). In more contemporary tones, Moore argues that the function of the criminal law is to achieve retributive justice, by "punish[ing] all and only those who are morally culpable in the doing of some morally wrongful action" (1997, 35). But such claims will provoke the liberal response that it is not the state's proper job to use the criminal law to "persecute" moral vice. "Prohibitions should not be included in the criminal law for the sole purpose of ensuring that breaches of them are visited with retributive punishment" (Walker 1980, 5).

Once again we face the question whether, even if the guilty do in some sense deserve to suffer, it should be a proper task for the state to inflict such suffering through a system of criminal law and punishment. If we can tie that desert, as the 'unfair advantage' theory does, to the commission of a *crime*, we have the beginnings of an answer to that question—but at the cost of losing the connection between criminal and prelegal wrongfulness that seems crucial in such (as normally understood) *mala in se* crimes as rape. If we instead tie that desert, as the emotion-based theories discussed in this subsection do, to the commission of moral wrongs whose wrongfulness is independent of the criminal law, we preserve that connection—but still have no clear account of why this is the state's business.

I return in chapter 2 to this question, which is one aspect of a larger question about the proper aims and role of the criminal law (see ch. 2.4). I now turn, however, to another species of retributivism, according to which punishment serves to express or communicate the condemnation or censure that criminals deserve.

4.4. Punishment as Communication

The idea that punishment serves an expressive purpose is neither new nor necessarily retributivist.[29] I argue in chapter 3 that we should talk of *communication* (as a rational process that seeks a response mediated by the other person's understanding) rather than simply of *expression* (see ch. 3.2.1). But here we need not distinguish these two ideas.

To see how a communicative or expressive conception of punishment can figure in a retributivist theory, we can consider the answers that retributivists and consequentialists might give to three questions: *what* is being expressed or communicated, *to whom*, and *why* (see Skillen 1980)?

For a consequentialist, the 'why' is straightforward: we should use punishment in this way if this will efficiently serve the consequentialist aims of the penal system, in particular the prevention of crime. The 'what' and 'to whom' are also straightforward: punishment may be used to express any content that will serve those aims, to anyone who can be usefully affected by it. A deterrent system of punishment fits this bill. The threat and the imposition of punishment communicate to potential offenders the message that they will suffer something unpleasant if they break the law, thus (we hope) persuading them not to do so.

Retributivists, by contrast, must answer these questions in terms of the offender's desert. That approach suggests that whatever punishment communicates must be communicated primarily to the offender. As for the 'what', the obvious answer is that punishment communicates the condemnation or censure that offenders deserve.[30] Punishment "is a conventional device for the expression of attitudes of resentment and indignation, and of judgments of disapproval and reprobation, on the part either of the punishing authority himself or of those 'in whose name' the punishment is inflicted" (Feinberg 1970, 98).[31]

These answers seem well suited to retributivism for two reasons. First, censure is backward-looking: it focuses, as retributivist punishment must focus, on the past offense; the offender is censured, as for retributivists offenders must be punished, *for* that offense. Second, it is not puzzling—in the way that critics of retributivism find the idea of penal desert puzzling—that offenders deserve censure for their criminal wrongdoings.

Consequentialists can also regard the expression of censure as a useful function of punishment. Censure can be an efficient means of modifying conduct: the person censured may avoid such conduct in future (realizing that it is wrong, or fearing the pain of censure); others may be dissuaded from such conduct by the prospect of censure.[32] They might indeed insist that any plausible answer to the 'why' question must be consequentialist. What is the rational point of expressing censure if not to influence future conduct (see, e.g., Walker 1991, 21–33, 78–82)? Retributivists will argue, however, that a purely consequentialist rationale for censure is morally unacceptable. To use censure simply as a useful technique for modifying conduct is to treat the person censured not as a responsible and autonomous subject, but as an object to be manipulated by whatever techniques we can find (see Charvet 1966; Duff 1986, 42–53; ch. 2.2, above).

How then can retributivists answer the 'why' question, if not in terms of the beneficial effects of punishment as communicating censure? A complete answer to this question requires a fuller account of how the state, through the criminal law, should treat and address its citizens (see chs. 2.4, 3.2). But part of the answer can be given here, by noting what is involved in meaning what we say.

If I declare firmly that a certain kind of conduct—discriminating on racial grounds in making job appointments, for instance—is seriously wrong, this has implications for my own conduct. To mean what I say commits me to avoiding such conduct myself. If I regularly engage in such conduct, with no effort to avoid it and no remorse at engaging in it, I cannot mean what I say. It also commits me to certain judgments on the conduct of others—to the judgment that those who engage in such discrimination act wrongly. But it also commits me to *expressing* those judgments in certain situations. If I find that my own institution has engaged in such discrimination, I must express my view that it acted wrongly by criticizing or censuring its action. To remain silent, to let the action pass without criticism, necessarily casts doubt on the sincerity of my declaration that such conduct is seriously wrong.[33] As with individuals, so with groups. A group (an academic department, for instance) that collectively declares racial discrimination in making appointments to be seriously wrong is thereby committed to avoiding such discrimination itself, and to condemning such discrimination by others.

So too with the law. The criminal law declares certain kinds of conduct to be wrong—to be criminal. But if the law, or the society in whose name it speaks, is to mean what it thus says, it is committed to censuring those who nonetheless engage in such conduct. To remain silent in the face of their crimes would be to undermine—by implication to go back on—its declaration that such conduct is wrong.

We can add further moral weight to this conceptual point by saying that such censure of conduct declared to be wrong is owed to its victims, as manifesting that concern for them and for their wronged condition that the declaration itself expressed. It is owed to the society whose values the law claims to embody, as showing that those values are taken seriously. And it is owed to the offenders themselves, since an honest response to another's wrongdoing, a response that respects him as a responsible moral agent, is criticism or censure of that wrongdoing. To take crimes seriously (as the law purports to take them seriously in declaring them to be wrong) as the wrongdoings of responsible agents is to be committed to censuring those who commit them (see von Hirsch 1993, ch. 2).

Suppose we agree that, for the reasons sketched above, those who commit crimes should be censured by the criminal law. Such censure is expressed by the formal convictions that follow on proof of guilt at a criminal trial. It could also be communicated through a system of purely symbolic punishments, which are burdensome or painful solely in virtue of the censure they communicate (see Duff 1986, 148–49, 240–42). Now the punishments imposed by our legal systems are not *purely* symbolic: imprisonment, fines, and compulsory community service are burdensome independently of any condemnatory meaning they might have. Such penal 'hard treatment' (see Feinberg 1970), however, *can* communicate censure. Given an appropriate set of conventions and a shared understanding of those conventions, a term of imprisonment or compulsory community service, or a fine, can communicate to those on whom it is imposed (and to others) an authoritative censure or condemnation of the crime for which it is imposed. Such punishments are then no longer *merely* hard treatment, but also symbolic acts of censure.

This is indeed true—though some questions need to be raised about the content of what is communicated and about the conditions that must be satisfied if such communication is to be possible and legitimate. But it also raises the crucial question that faces any communicative or expressive account of punishment.

That question concerns the gap between 'can' and 'should'. Granted that we *can* express or communicate the censure that criminals deserve through hard treatment punishments, why *should* we do so? Since that censure could also be expressed by formal convictions or declarations, or by purely symbolic punishments, what can justify the choice of penal hard treatment as the mode of expression—given the pains and burdens that such hard treatment imposes on those subjected to it? If a communicative theory is to justify hard treatment punishments, it must show that penal hard treatment is not just a *possible*, but a *necessary*, method of communicating the censure that offenders deserve.

We can easily find consequentialist answers to this question: that, most obviously, penal hard treatment adds a deterrent incentive to the law's moral appeal. We know that too many offenders would not be dissuaded from crime by a system of merely formal censures or of purely symbolic punishments. Thus by using penal hard treatment as our mode of communication, we give such people an additional, prudential reason to refrain from crime (see Feinberg 1970; von Hirsch 1985, ch. 5). Such an answer, however, faces the objections noted earlier to a system of deterrent punishments (see secs. 2.2, 3.2, above).[34] But can retributivists find an adequate answer to this question?

Some argue that the censure that serious wrongdoing warrants can be adequately expressed, or effectively communicated to the criminal (who might be disinclined to listen to purely symbolic punishment) only by hard treatment (see Lucas 1980, 132–36; Falls 1987; Primoratz 1989b; Kleinig 1991). But it is not clear that this suffices to justify penal hard treatment—unless the efficacy of the communication is just a matter of its *deterrent* efficacy (see Duff 1986, 240–45; Gur-Arye 1991). If the claim is that hard treatment "translates the disesteem of society into the value system of the recalcitrant individual," so that even if he does not come to see his crime as a wrong we can at least make him "see that [it] was from his point of view a mistake" (Lucas 1980, 133–34, 147), we must wonder whether such a translation can preserve the meaning of what it claims to translate. We must also ask why, if not for the sake of effective deterrence, it is so vital to drive this message home that the state should create a system of punishment to do so.[35]

I offer an alternative account of why we should use penal hard treatment to communicate the censure that offenders deserve by portraying punishment as a species of secular *penance*. That account is retributivist: it justifies punishment as the communication of deserved censure. Unlike other forms of retributivism, however, it also gives punishment the *forward-looking* purpose of persuading offenders to repent their crimes (communicative actions in general typically have a forward-looking purpose). This is not to say, however, that my account is a partly consequentialist one—that it seeks to marry a retributivist concern for desert with a consequentialist concern for future benefits: for the relation between punishment and its aim is not, as it is for consequentialists, contingent and instrumental (see sec. 1.1, above) but internal. The very aim of persuading responsible agents to repent the wrongs they have done makes punishment the appropriate method of pursuing it.[36]

I explain the meaning and significance of this point in chapter 3 (secs. 2.2, 4). Here, however, we must take note of a serious challenge to any attempt to justify criminal punishment.

5. The Abolitionist Challenge

'Abolitionism' names a broad movement (rather than a single theory) whose members generally share certain values and political sympathies and agree in opposing existing forms of state punishment, but who often differ sharply from one another about both ends and means.[37] We can, however, sketch some of the salient features of the abolitionist challenge to the institution of state punishment by focusing on three questions that any abolitionist must face: what is to be abolished, why, and what should replace it?[38] In sketching abolitionist answers to these questions, I offer a selective and composite picture. My aim is to pick out what are, for my purposes, the most significant general themes in abolitionism, broadly understood, without implying that all those who are called or who call themselves 'abolitionists' would accept every view that I ascribe to 'abolitionism'.[39]

5.1. What Is to Be Abolished?

Some abolitionist arguments focus on the abolition, not of punishment as such, but of imprisonment as a mode of punishment (see Mathiesen 1974; Sim 1994). This is certainly a radical ambition, given the extent to which imprisonment is used by our existing penal systems, and the fact that it is seen even by those who argue for significant reductions in its use as the only plausible sentence for serious and dangerous offenders. I argue (ch. 4.4.2) that imprisonment *should* still have a (very limited) role in a justifiable system of criminal punishment. The most radical form of abolitionism, however, on which I concentrate, argues precisely for the abolition of state punishment as such.

Furthermore, the most radical abolitionists are what we may call 'absolute', rather than 'contingent', abolitionists. A 'contingent' abolitionist argues that while some system of state punishment (very different from our own) would in principle be justifiable in some kind of society (very different from our own), punishment as practiced in our own societies cannot be justified, since it cannot, in those societies, be what it would need to be to be justified (see, e.g., Murphy 1979c, 103–10; also Duff 1986, ch. 10.3). Analogously, a 'contingent' pacifist argues that, while some kinds of war could in principle be justified, no war fought under our present political and military conditions could in fact be justified. 'Absolute' pacifists argue, by contrast, that no kind of war can ever be justified under any conditions (see Coates 1997, 77–87). Analogously, 'absolute' abolitionists argue that no system of state punishment could ever be justified in any kind of society.

Of course, abolitionists cannot and do not talk simply of abolishing 'punishment', as if everything else could be left as it is. The abolition of punishment must also involve either the abolition or the radical transformation of all the state institutions and practices with which punishment is bound up—the criminal law, the police, the entire criminal justice system; and abolitionist arguments typically look for yet wider social and political transformations reaching far beyond the realm of penality. A few such wider transformations are noted below, but most have to be ignored for our present purposes.

To say that state punishment should be 'abolished' need not, however, be to say that we should demand its immediate and complete abolition: that every prison gate should at once be flung open and the whole apparatus of penality be at once dismantled. Abolition can be an aspiration rather than an immediate demand: a distant goal to be striven towards (through the necessary radical, but also inevitably gradual, transformations of our political, legal, and social institutions and practices) rather than something to be fully actualized today. This does of course raise serious questions. What must we do about punishment meanwhile, pending those radical transformations? How far, if at all, can we continue to rely on or be silently complicit in our penal practices? Such questions, however, also face radical penal theorists who argue that punishment can be justified, but only if both it and the societies within which it is practiced are radically transformed (see, e.g., Murphy 1979c, 110; Lacey 1988, 195–258; ch. 5, below).

5.2. Why Abolition?

If asked *why* we should abolish punishment, abolitionists might with some justice reply that the onus instead lies on their opponents to show why we should maintain it. Punishment is, after all, a practice that severely coerces those subjected to it and inflicts burdensome sufferings on them. It requires some persuasive justification; and abolitionists could simply argue that the justifications offered for it fail and that therefore we cannot justifiably maintain it. They join in retributivist criticisms of consequentialist theories. Such criticisms concern not only the efficacy of consequentialist penal practices in achieving their declared aims, but also those aims themselves and the means by which we should try to achieve them. Our aim should not, for instance, be merely to secure obedience to the law, or conformist 'integration' with the existing normative structures; nor should we seek to coerce obedience by threats or to remold 'deviants' into conformity. They also reject retributivist theories, for reasons similar to those offered by consequentialists: the mere infliction of pain for past wrongdoing is not moral, but barbarous; and even if we can rightly seek to censure wrongdoers, we should not do so by punitive "pain-delivery" (see Christie 1977, 9; 1981, 98–105).

It is also true that distinctively abolitionist arguments against punishment often consist in positive arguments for their preferred alternatives—in showing that there are better ways of dealing with 'crime' than punishment (see ch. 3.4.3). But a little more can be said here about why they find punishment so objectionable, beyond the fact that it inflicts pain for (as they see it) no good reason.

One general objection to state penality that abolitionists emphasize is that it replaces democratic, egalitarian, and constructive ways of dealing with our problems by oppressively authoritarian, destructive institutions. The law declares certain kinds of conduct to be *wrong*, and demands that all citizens accept its declarations. This might be legitimate were there genuine consensus amongst all the citizens on the values thus asserted. But it is illegitimate in the absence of such consensus, since in the absence of consensus what is needed is open and equal discussion, not the imposition of the favored values of the powerful (see, e.g., Bianchi 1994, 71–97). When a citizen commits such a legal wrong against others, the law "steals" the "conflict" that then exists between them. Instead of allowing (or helping) those involved in that conflict to resolve it themselves, the law reconceptualizes it as a 'crime', which is taken over by the professionalized institutions of the criminal justice system and transferred into a criminal process in which neither 'victim' nor 'offender' has any real part to play (see Christie 1977; Hulsman 1991). The criminal justice system thus removes the conflict from the context in which it arose and should be resolved; it abstracts offenders from the contexts in which their actions must be understood, treating them not as socially situated agents but as 'abstract individuals' (see Hudson 1987, 125–28; Hulsman 1991, 683–84; Norrie 1991); and it insists on describing and judging their actions, not in rich and context-sensitive terms that are appropriate to them, but in the abstract and context-insensitive language of the law (see, e.g., Norrie 1993; Hudson 1994). Finally, the punishment inflicted on offenders does not (either in aim or in fact) repair the harm they have done or reconcile them with those with whom they were in conflict. It simply further subjects them to the state's oppressive power, and reinforces their exclusion, as 'criminals', from the society of the law-abiding (see, e.g., Hulsman 1991).

I argue later that there is considerable force to the abolitionist critique of our existing systems of criminal justice and of prevalent conceptions of crime and punishment, but that what is required is a transformation of those systems and those conceptions rather than their abolition. We should now, however, look briefly at some abolitionist ideas about what should replace punishment.

5.3. What Should Replace Punishment?

The abolitionist critique says more than that punishment must be abolished. It is directed against the whole apparatus of criminal justice, including the concept of crime and the criminal process. But what should take its place?

We should think not of 'crimes'—actions prohibited by an authoritative law and inviting (if not entailing) a punitive response—but of 'conflicts' or 'troubles' (see Christie 1977; Hulsman 1986). Rather than just declaring, as the criminal law declares, that 'offenders' have broken the law and wronged their victims, we should see their 'crimes' as involving (perhaps as causes of, but also as symptoms of) some conflict or trouble between the 'offenders' and their 'victims' (and their wider local communities).

Such conflicts or troubles need to be resolved. But punishment cannot resolve them. We must instead look for ways of repairing such harm as was done, of restoring the relationships that have been damaged or fractured, of reconciling the parties to the conflict with each other and with their local community. We should look for justice, but for 'restorative' or 'reparative' justice (see Matthews 1988; T. F. Marshall 1994) rather than for retributive or punitive justice, and for justice not merely to offenders, as individuals abstracted from their social contexts, but between all those involved in the conflict or trouble.

Furthermore, such justice must be negotiated, in an open and equal discussion between all those involved, rather than being imposed from above by 'the law' or by a professional class of officials. We should look for informal, participatory modes of conflict-resolution based within the communities within which the conflicts arise, rather than for the formal procedures of a legal process that 'steals' conflicts from those to whom they properly belong. There will be roles for various kinds of officials in facilitating such negotiations. But their roles must be subordinate and supportive, not dominant and decisive.

There is much to admire and to accept in such abolitionist aspirations—in particular the theme of restorative or reparative justice, which has recently been coming to prominence beyond the abolitionist movement. I also argue below, however, that abolitionists are wrong to think that we must *replace* criminal justice and punishment by nonpunitive processes of reparation and reconciliation. If we accept the sharp distinction that many penal theorists—not only abolitionists—draw between 'retributive' and 'restorative' justice, and associate 'punishment' purely with 'retributive' justice as thus understood, we will think that reparation and reconciliation cannot be pursued through punishment. But this reflects an inadequate understanding of the possibilities of punishment—of what punishment can be and can mean. I argue for a different, subtler, conception of punishment, according to which punishment can precisely serve the aims of reparation and reconciliation (once those aims themselves are properly understood) and given which we should look, not for "alternatives to punishment" (Christie 1981, 11), but for *alternative punishments* that will better serve the reparative aims that punishment should have.

2

Liberal Legal Community

A NORMATIVE THEORY OF PUNISHMENT MUST INCLUDE A CONCEPTION OF crime as that which is to be punished. Such a conception of crime presupposes a conception of the criminal law—of its proper aims and content, of its claims on the citizen. Such a conception of the criminal law presupposes a conception of the state—of its proper role and functions, of its relation to its citizens. Such a conception of the state must also include a conception of society and of the relation between state and society.

In this chapter I sketch the conceptions of crime, of the criminal law, and of the state and society on which my account of punishment depends. That account appeals to a conception of political community and might thus be classed as 'communitarian'—especially by those who think that it pays insufficient regard to the limits that 'liberals' set on the power and functions of the state. But it also gives a central place to certain values, particularly those of individual autonomy and freedom, which are central to 'liberal' political theories. I must therefore say a little about the debate between 'liberalism' and 'communitarianism' in order to locate my own account more clearly.

That debate has become increasingly complex in the past decade.[1] It is now even less clear than it might once have been just what it is to be either a 'communitarian' or a 'liberal'. Many who class themselves (or are classed) as 'liberals' insist that they can find a place for values often associated with 'communitarianism', while many who class themselves (or are classed) as 'communitarians' insist that they can find a place for values usually regarded as 'liberal'. In this chapter, without embroiling myself too deeply in either the substantive or the (ultimately fruitless) classificatory debate, I explain the kind of 'liberal-communitarianism' on which my account of criminal punishment (and the criminal law) depends.

1. 'Liberalism' and 'Communitarianism'

We can identify the (for present purposes) relevant features of the 'liberal-communitarian' debate by looking briefly, first, at the liberal values that fueled the moral reaction against consequentialist conceptions of punishment in the 1970s and much of the retributivist revival flowing from that reaction, and second, at the impact that the recently prominent political rhetoric of 'community' has had on discussions of crime and punishment.

1.1. Liberalism and Punishment

Central to any version of liberalism is an insistence on the moral standing and rights of individual agents: as agents who are, or have the potential to be, autonomous—determining their own actions in the light of their own self-determined ends and conceptions of the good; as agents who should be left free to determine those ends, goods, and actions—who should be allowed and perhaps helped to develop and to exercise that capacity for autonomy; as agents who should be allowed an extensive realm of privacy, of freedom from the uninvited interference of other people or the state, in which to exercise that freedom and autonomy; and as agents who should not simply be sacrificed for some larger social good—whose individual rights "trump" the consequentialist claims of social goods (see R. Dworkin 1978).

This conception of the rights-bearing individual inspired the familiar objections to purely consequentialist theories of punishment (ch. 1.1.2), in particular the objection that such theories sanction sacrificing the rights of *innocent* individuals to the social good of crime prevention. The right of the innocent (those who have not voluntarily broken the law) not to be punished should protect them against being thus sacrificed. It also fueled objections to side-constrained consequentialist theories that focus on the rights of the *guilty* (ch. 1.2.2). Apart from the charge that a side-constrained consequentialist system would use the guilty "as means" to the social good of crime-prevention, it was argued that to subject offenders to compulsory 'reform' was to treat them, not as autonomous subjects who must be allowed to determine their own beliefs and attitudes, but as objects to be remolded into conformity; that to subject them to purely preventive modes of incapacitation was to deny them the freedom to determine their own future conduct in relation to the law; and (less often) that to seek their obedience by deterrent threats was to treat them as "dogs" rather than as responsible agents. (But some liberals do justify some such penal policies.)

Two further liberal themes are also implicit in liberal objections to using punishment as a technique of 'reform'. The first is an aspect of the liberal concern for privacy. The state has a proper interest in preventing conduct that infringes others' rights or that harms or threatens their legitimate interests; it may use the criminal law to prevent such conduct. But it has no such proper interest in its citizens' moral character—in the condition of their souls; it should not use the coercive power of the criminal law as a means of moral reform to make its citizens morally better.[2] The second, related theme is that of 'neutrality'. The state should protect and enforce *rights* (partly through a criminal law that punishes rights violations) but should not seek to enforce any particular conception of the *good*—of what constitutes a good or flourishing human life, of what ends we should pursue. It should instead leave individuals free to determine and pursue their own diverse conceptions of the good, within the framework of rights and security provided in part by the criminal law. Hence the importance for liberals of such ideas as "the priority of the right over the good" and value-pluralism.[3]

If we now ask what positive account of punishment liberals who are thus concerned with individuals and their rights could offer, we might begin, as liberal theorizing often begins, with the idea of a social contract—not a contract actually entered into by present or past citizens, but one into which they *would* enter as rational agents were they called upon to decide the terms of their political association from a suitably impartial vantage point (for instance, from behind the "veil of ignorance" that structures the Rawlsian "original position"). We should note three features of such a contractualist perspective.

First, contracts involve *choice*—or if not active choice at least the kind of acquiescence that constitutes consent—and choice or consent offers an obvious way of founding obligation. Whether or not we can ground *all* obligations in choice or consent, we might at least hope to ground the obligations that go with political association in the choice or consent of those obligated, thus providing a neat solution to the problem of political obligation. Even if we cannot posit an *actual* choice or consent (either explicit or 'tacit') on the part of every citizen to accept the social contract that defines the terms and obligations of political association, we might at least hope to show that that contract is one to which every citizen as a rational agent *would* consent—and thus that it is one by which each is now actually bound. This clearly bears directly on the problem of punishment. Even if we cannot simply argue that criminals choose or consent to their own punishment,[4] we might ground their obligation to obey the law in their hypothetical consent to a social contract and argue that that contract would include provisions for the punishment of those who break the law—thus justifying their punishment in terms of the contract to which they would consent.[5]

Second, contracts are suitable to govern the dealings of *strangers*. If people are bound together by strong bonds of mutual affection or concern, or by a shared commitment to some common activity in pursuit of a common good, there may be less need and less proper room for contractual definitions of their respective rights and obligations. But when they lack such bonds (and the trust that goes with such bonds), there is room, and need, for contracts to regulate their mutual dealings (see Waldron 1988). Now political association, in any modern state, is between strangers—people between whom there may be no prior bonds of affection or commitment (Hobbes's state of nature offers a radical example of this conception). Indeed, that is how we *should* understand political association if we are to respect individual freedom and choice. While we can *choose* to enter or to remain in intimate associations with some others, we should not be *forced* into intimacy with others just because they are our fellow citizens; we should be free to relate to them, if we wish, as strangers with whom we have only a limited, contractual relationship.

Third, contracts define the *limits* of the relationships they govern. They specify what we can demand of one another and thus also what we *cannot* demand of one another simply by virtue of our contractual relationship. If our contract obligates me to perform or to avoid certain actions, other parties to it have the right to demand such performance or avoidance from me, to call me to account if I breach my obligations, and perhaps to enforce those obligations. But they have no right to interfere in aspects of my life that fall outside the contract's terms. Liberals who are concerned to protect individual freedom and privacy against the coercive power of the state can thus argue that the social contract gives the state a legitimate interest in those aspects of its citizens' conduct that fall within the contract's terms, but forbids it to intrude into what falls outside those terms.

But what kinds of penal provision might a liberal social contract include?[6] We can expect the scope of the criminal law to be strictly limited—perhaps in accordance with the Harm Principle and the demand that it focus on (external) conduct rather than on (internal) motives or attitudes (see n.2, above). But what provision will it make for those who breach its requirements? The basic idea of the social contract generates no determinate answer to this question. What answer we can offer will depend on what values and concerns we ascribe to the imaginary contractors.

We might expect that, given their concern for individual freedom and privacy, liberals would reject purely reformative or incapacitative justifications of punishment, for the reasons noted above: punishments that aim simply to re-form offenders' moral attitudes intrude coercively on the private sphere of thought and conscience, infringing both privacy and autonomy; and punishments that aim simply to incapacitate offenders from further crimes infringe their autonomy by preempting their future choices. But even this is not certain. For if we understand *all* the rights of citizenship in contractualist terms, we might think that offenders, who refuse to respect the rights of others, *forfeit* some or all of their own rights. By flouting their contractual obligations, they put themselves outside the contract's protection (see ch. 1.3.1). In that case, however, they might lose the protection against reformative or incapacitative coercion that liberal rights provide.

I am not suggesting that liberals typically would, or in consistency should, see offenders as forfeiting their rights as citizens, or their rights to be respected as responsible agents. My point is only that a contractualist model leaves this possibility open, unless we insist that offenders retain their status as parties to the contract and retain at least some basic rights of autonomy and privacy. Even if we do insist on this, however (as many liberals do), we are left with at least two possible justifications of punishment—retributivist and deterrent.

Murphy once argued that rational contractors would choose a retributive penal system that deprives criminals of the 'unfair advantage' they gained by their crimes (Murphy 1979c; see ch. 1.4.2). And they would indeed do so *if* they saw crime in those terms, and thought that even a side-constrained consequentialist system would use those punished "merely as means" to the end of preventing crime in a way that rational (Kantian) agents would find unacceptable (see ch. 1.2.2). But it seems equally consistent with the idea of a social contract to justify punishment as a deterrent (subject to suitable side-constraints). Rational agents can see that they benefit from an effective system of criminal law that prohibits certain kinds of harmful conduct, that if no sanctions are attached to the law too many people will disobey it—thus directly causing harm and undermining the confidence of others in the law's efficacy—and that a system of deterrent sanctions will avert this danger. They would therefore agree to such a system. To the charge of using those punished "merely as means" to the social end of preventing crime they could reply that offenders are not being used *merely* as means: for only those who voluntarily break the law are liable to punishment; and they would, as rational agents, have consented to such a system (see ch. 1.2.2).

I return in chapter 3 to the question of how punishment can be rendered consistent with the central liberal values of autonomy, freedom, and privacy, and to the viability of a more sophisticated account that combines censure and deterrence. I now turn to the role that communitarian ideas have played in recent penal discourse.

1.2. The Penal Rhetoric of 'Community'

While much recent penal theory has drawn explicitly on liberal ideas and values, there has been less explicit appeal to communitarian ideas (but see H. Morris 1981; Lacey 1988; Reitan 1996). Indeed, the most prominent appeals to ideas of 'community' are found in abolitionist writings (see ch. 1.5). However, political discussions of crime and punishment have in recent years been infused with the rhetoric of 'community' (see Nelken 1985; Lacey & Zedner 1995).

The 'community' figures as the *victim* of crime: we must build safer communities and protect them against criminal depredations. It figures as an *agent* of crime prevention (Nelken 1985): it should be involved in "situational crime prevention" and help to police itself. It figures as a *locus* of punishment: more punishments should be administered "in the community" rather than in prison (Home Office 1988; see Dean-Myrda & Cullen 1998). It figures as the *beneficiary* of punishment: it is protected by punishment; and "punishments in the community," such as Community Service Orders, enable offenders to make reparation to the community (Home Office 1988, pars. 1.5, 2.3). It figures, less frequently, as the offender's proper place: even if rehabilitation is no longer a central penal purpose, one supposed benefit of "punishment in the community" is that it allows offenders to retain their place in the community—a place that imprisonment threatens to destroy (Home Office 1988). This concern to preserve the offender's place in the community is often displaced, in the dominant rhetoric of 'law and order', by an emphasis on the need to protect the (law-abiding) community against criminals: but it is important to my argument.

We must of course treat such invocations of 'community' with proper skepticism. Too often they amount to little more than rhetorical appeals to vague but currently resonant ideas or to romanticized images of a premodern golden age of small, stable communities. Too often 'community' actually signifies only a geographical location. Criminals are punished outside the walls of the prison; the mentally disordered are cared for, or neglected, outside the walls of psychiatric institutions. But such people are not in any substantial sense in or of the 'community' whose members pass them by with distaste or averted eyes; and what drives policies of decarceration is often, not a vision of the importance of community for human well-being, but a cruder economic calculation that these are cheaper ways of appearing to pursue the aims of crime reduction or psychiatric care (see Scull 1984; Cohen 1985).

Nonetheless, I want to take the idea of community seriously in the context of criminal law and punishment: not just because we can thus expose the hollowness of the rhetoric in which strategies of decarceration are often garbed, but because it can illuminate a central problem of criminal punishment—and point us towards a way of dealing with that problem.

The rhetoric of community is often accompanied by that of 'inclusion' and 'exclusion' (communities 'include' their members, but also 'exclude' those who are not members). In (re)building our political community, we must include those who are or have been excluded—hence the British government's creation of the "Social Exclusion Unit."[7] However, the rhetoric of inclusion can cut both ways in the context of crime and punishment. It can, on one hand, be used to *include* offenders—to emphasize that they are still members of the community whose laws they have broken and to encourage penal policies that seek to keep them in or restore them to the community. But, on the other hand, it can often be used to *exclude* offenders (or those who are publicly perceived as 'serious' offenders) from the community of the law-abiding. In building and protecting safer communities, we seek to create structures that will protect 'us', the law-abiding, from 'them', the criminals who would prey on us.[8] In punishing offenders, and too often shunning them thereafter, we exclude them (if they were not already excluded) from many of the rights and advantages of law-abiding community.

Whether the communitarian rhetoric of inclusion is used to include or to exclude offenders from 'the community', it will arouse familiar liberal worries, of three kinds.

First, an emphasis on 'community' seems to *subordinate* individuals to the communities to which they belong, and thus to open the way to sacrificing individual rights or interests to the interests of 'the community'. This might be done directly, by claims that the good of 'the community' is so much more important than the good of any individual that individuals can be sacrificed for the sake of that communal good (especially if they have attacked that good by committing crimes). Or it might be done more subtly, by claims that individuals can find their own goods and their own identities only within the community—which makes it easier to sacrifice their interests to those of the community (cf. Lacey 1988, 164, 171–73).

Second, if offenders are (either explicitly or implicitly) *excluded* from the community of the law-abiding, they are deprived of the protections that liberal rights provide. They are defined as the 'enemy' against whom 'we' must defend ourselves by whatever means are necessary, or as 'outsiders' whose interests need not concern us in the way that the interests of fellow members must concern us. As I noted above (p. 38), a social contract model could be applied to exclude offenders from the protections provided by the contract. But a communitarian perspective seems at least as apt to exclude offenders from 'the community'.

Third, if offenders are still *included* within the community, punishment might then be intended to preserve or restore their place in the community. Crime, as a violation of the community's law and an attack on its good (as a breach of community), threatens to destroy the criminal's relationship with the community. Punishment aims to restore that relationship, to repair that breach, by bringing the criminal back into (law-abiding) community. But that aim suggests that punishment will be used as a method of coercive rehabilitation or reform. The community will try to coerce those who reject or deviate from its values into conformity—into submissive acceptance of its conceptions of the good and the right. But this is inconsistent with the liberal values of autonomy, freedom, and privacy (see sec. 1.1, above).

More generally, invocations of 'community' in political discourse often suggest the (to liberals disturbing) image of small, close-knit communities bound together by a rich set of values and a determinate conception of human good that all are expected (even forced) to share, their members taking a close and intimate interest in every aspect of one another's lives. Liberal critics have two objections to taking such an idea of community as a model for the life of a political society.

First, it is utterly unrealistic. Such communities might exist *within* the framework of a political society, but we could not hope to transform an entire modern society such as Britain or the United States into a community of this kind.

Second, any such aspiration is inconsistent with such central liberal values as autonomy, freedom, and privacy, and with the liberal ideal of a pluralistic society. Communities of this intimate, all-embracing kind would be suffocating. They would deprive their members of the freedom to determine and pursue their own conceptions of the good, and subject them to the oppressively intrusive attentions of their fellows and of the state. Liberals can value such intimate communities, but only if they are both diverse and optional. Individuals should be free to choose to create or to live in such communities, with those with whom they wish to associate on such intimate terms. But a liberal polity should protect them against being forced to live in such communities, and should leave them free to relate to their fellow citizens as strangers bound only by the terms of the social contract rather than as intimate friends or relatives.

I share many of these liberal worries about some of the more extreme manifestations of communitarian thought. But communitarianism need not take this form. In what follows, I offer a form of communitarianism—of 'liberal communitarianism'—that gives a central place to versions of the values dear to liberal hearts. This account of political community raises the question on which I to focus, whether criminal punishment can be consistent with community. Can a system of criminal punishment still treat those who are punished as full members of the political community?

It might seem that I should first define 'communitarianism' as distinct from 'liberalism', but it is even harder with 'communitarianism' than it is with 'liberalism' to specify a defining set of values or beliefs—partly because 'communitarianism' is not a single theory or movement. It is therefore easier to explain the sense in which my account is 'communitarian' *after* I outline the account itself.

2. A Normative Idea(l) of Community

The question I want to ask, whether criminal punishment can be consistent with community, is of course vacuous without some substantial account of 'community'. We need an account of political or legal community—of a political community living under the law. But its central structural features can be clarified by beginning with a simpler example.

2.1. A Model: Academic Community

Many communitarians take the family as a paradigm of community (see Simmons 1996, 251–52). Others argue that we should take friendship rather than the family as a model on which to base an account of political community (see S. E. Marshall 1998). I, however, use the example of academic community, as that idea is used by those who insist on its importance, or bewail its passing in our contemporary university systems. Academic community might seem remote from political community, but it exhibits some of the structural features that are central to my account of political community.

Those who preach the importance of academic community are not giving 'community' a merely geographical sense. Geographical contiguity is not, as I show below, a necessary condition of community. Nor are they referring simply to a certain institutional structure. The existence of the institutional structure of a university is not enough to create an academic community: universities should aspire, but can fail, to be academic communities. What then do they mean? There are two related aspects to this idea(l) of community.

First, community requires a shared commitment by the community's members to certain defining values—here, the pursuit and transmission of knowledge and understanding within the various intellectual disciplines. Those values structure the community's activities and define its goods—the goods of pursuing and gaining such knowledge and understanding. These goods might be understood in partly instrumental terms, as serving ends external to the academy (for instance, as fostering useful skills for the wider society), but they cannot be *merely* instrumental goods. There must be *intrinsic* goods internal to the community's academic activity; it must constitute a "practice" (MacIntyre 1985, ch. 14). These goods are also *communal* goods: they are seen by members of the community as 'our' goods, in that their character as goods depends on their being shared. There are, of course, individual goods within such a community: I enhance my own understanding (and my career and reputation) by the work I do; I can claim some kind of property in 'my' ideas and 'my' publications. But such individual goods take their character as goods—as goods internal to the practice—from their place within the community's shared pursuits; and they count as goods internal to the practice only if they are understood as contributing to the shared goods of the community—to the advancement of knowledge and understanding in which all its members share.

Second, the members of the community must have a regard for one another as fellow members that is itself structured by the community's defining values. They must understand their own and one another's good, as members, in terms of the values and goods that define the community. They must have a mutual regard for one another as being committed to those values and as finding their good in those goods. This regard involves a willingness to help one another, to cooperate, in their academic activities; a refusal to exploit one another simply as means to their own ends (see Mason 1993; Reitan 1996, 58–61); and a readiness to treat one another in ways consistent with the defining values of the community.

(This raises a question about just who counts as a member of the community: how about the students, administrators, cleaners, and research assistants on short-term contracts? We should simply note here that on a plausible [democratic] conception of the community's goods, the community should be as broadly inclusive as possible, because they are goods in which many can and should be able to share; that there are different degrees of 'sharing', in that those not directly involved with such goods can still value them and see themselves as contributing to them; and that only those who are treated as members of the community can be held to be bound by its values—for instance, by the demands of intellectual rigor and honesty.)

My aim in sketching this ideal conception of an academic community is to highlight some general features of the idea of community that I use in relation to the law. To that end, we should note some further aspects of this conception.

First, community of this kind is clearly a matter of aspiration as much as of fact. To see ourselves as members of such a community is to see ourselves as subject to the demands of its defining values, which we often fail to satisfy. We may hope to avoid the grosser forms of academic wrongdoing, but we must recognize our frequent deficiencies in academic virtue and commitment— in our relations to academic values and to our fellow academics. Community as thus conceived is an ideal towards which we should aspire and in whose light we must judge ourselves and our activities.[9]

Second, even if we agree on the structural features of community (mutual regard and a commitment to shared intrinsic values), we can disagree fiercely about just what those values are, about what that regard requires, about who should count as members of the community. Some such disagreements can render community impossible: we can no longer respect one another as being committed to the same goals and values. But not all such disagreements, even if profound, destroy community.

Third, academic communities, such as universities, have formal structures of authority and rules that should express the community's defining values and assist the pursuit of its distinctive goods. Their members must be able to accept the rules as being thus justified. They must be able to see them as 'our' rules, and as rules that suitably order their academic activities. If they cannot accept the rules as embodying at least a reasonable conception of the community and its goods, they must see them as alien impositions, which they might have to obey but cannot accept as theirs.

Fourth, an academic community is not typically the only community in which its members live. Its goods are not the only goods they pursue, its relationships not their only significant relationships. They also live in other (sometimes overlapping) communities that have their own distinctive structures of values, goods, and relationships.

Fifth, academic community is partial rather than total: there are limits to the interest that its members properly take in one another's lives. These limits are determined by the values that define the community, and are of two kinds. On one hand, there are limits to the kinds of support that members can claim from one another. I can expect my colleagues to take a sympathetic interest in my academic activities, but I cannot demand that they take such an interest in other aspects of my life—in my financial or marital problems, for instance. Such interest is not (at least if invited) *forbidden*, and might often be forthcoming, but it is not *expected* simply in virtue of our fellow membership of an academic community. On the other hand, there are limits to the interest that members can properly insist on taking in one another. The nature of the community defines a distinction between the 'public' and the 'private'—between those aspects of our lives that are of proper interest and concern to our fellows and those that are not. I am answerable to my colleagues for my philosophical ideas and for my performance of my academic duties. They can insist on discussing my ideas and challenge me about my teaching; these are 'public' aspects of my academic life. But if my colleagues seek to inquire into my personal life or my moral or political views (insofar as these do not directly impinge on my academic activities), I can reply that that is not their business. I need not, as a member of this academic community, open myself to such—as it would now be—intrusive interest. (Note, however, that the distinction between the 'public' and the 'private' is relative to the community. What counts as 'public' or 'private' depends on the character of the community; and what is 'public', or 'private', in this context might not be so in the context of other communities to which I belong.)

Sixth, while most academics find their closest community in a university where they work in physical proximity to their colleagues, such geographical contiguity is not necessary for community. The geographically dispersed character of the British Open University does not preclude its constituting an academic community; and as a philosopher I can see myself as a member not just of my department but of the wider community of Scottish philosophers, or British philosophers, or philosophers. To see myself thus is to see myself as engaged, with these others, in a common practice (although we might disagree about its precise point and meaning), to see my own philosophical activity as contributing to that common pursuit, and to recognize other philosophers as fellow members of this community—a recognition manifested in how I treat them, their work, and their ideas.

Seventh, membership of academic communities is typically *voluntary*: members choose to join (though perhaps under pressure) and can choose to leave (though often at significant cost). This fact, and the fact that there is life outside the academy, make it easier to say with a clear conscience that those who are unwilling to accept the community's values should leave, or to expel those who persistently flout its demands. This might seem a crucial disanalogy between academic and political community, since membership of a political community and subjection to its normative demands are not typically seen as voluntary. The law claims to bind even those who never chose to join the polity and who cannot in practice choose to leave it, but who have no commitment to its defining values. I discuss this issue below (sec. 5), since it is crucial to the justification of criminal punishment: how can those who do not wish to see themselves as members of the political community be nonetheless bound by its laws and properly liable to punishment if they break them? For the moment, however, we need simply note that not only voluntary communities can bind their members. We have commitments as members of communities that we never chose to join and cannot choose to leave. The family is one such community: we can argue about the claims that members of my family have on me and about the conditions (if any) under which I can free myself from those claims, but we cannot plausibly say that I am bound by them only if I choose to remain in the family (see Melden 1959, 1977, ch. 3; Horton 1992, 145–51). Our moral commitments are also grounded in moral communities into which we are born and inducted without choice. Although we may rebel against them, such rebellion must appeal to shared values that we did not choose (see Beardsmore 1969; R. Dworkin 1986, 195–202).

It might seem a piece of typical academic conceit to suppose that this (as some would say, romanticized) sketch of academic community can illuminate the realm of criminal law and punishment. However, by drawing on the central structural features of this normative ideal of community, we can provide a plausible account of political and legal community—of a political community living under the law, defined by values that are embodied in its laws; and this account should quieten at least some of the anxieties aroused in liberals by talk of 'community' in this context.

2.2. Political Community

The example of academic community shows that there can be normative communities whose members are bound together by a shared commitment to certain defining values and by mutual respect and concern in the light of those values, but that do not have the intimate, all-embracing and potentially oppressive character that liberals fear. Academic community can indeed be partly structured by versions of some central liberal values: by a concern for freedom and autonomy—members must be encouraged to pursue their own intellectual explorations and to develop and exercise their capacities for independent thought; a respect for privacy—a recognition of which matters are and which are not of proper concern to other members of the community; and a respect for and encouragement of diversity—of different approaches to the various academic disciplines and to their teaching. Academic community need not involve emotional intimacy or physical proximity. It can exist between colleagues who have nothing to do with one another outside their shared academic activities and between people who have no direct contact with one another. What makes it true that I and another philosopher I have no contact with are fellow members of the philosophical community is not any direct relationship that we have with each other (for we have none) but the fact that we are both engaged in this practice and *would* recognize and treat each other as fellows *if* we came into contact.

As with academic community, so too with political community. Those who want to make a notion of 'community' central to political theory can commend and argue for a *liberal* political community, a polity defined and structured by a shared commitment to such central liberal values as freedom, autonomy, privacy, and pluralism, and by a mutual regard that reflects those values.[10] A liberal political community will recognize individual freedom and autonomy as crucial values: as human goods to be fostered and encouraged and as rights that must be respected by other citizens and by the state. It will accord to individuals, and to the various other communities that they form and within which they find their particular goods, extensive spheres of freedom within which they can pursue a variety of such goods. It will thus also accord them extensive spheres of privacy: spheres of thought and action into which other citizens and the state must not intrude. Although it will insist upon autonomy, freedom, and privacy as central goods, it will not insist on or seek to enforce any single all-embracing or comprehensive conception of human good. It will seek instead to encourage a diversity of substantive and particular conceptions of human good—which is done in part precisely by fostering and respecting individual autonomy, freedom, and privacy.

(Although the values of autonomy, freedom, privacy, and pluralism are the most relevant to such a community's [self-]definition as a liberal community,[11] its members will share other values that also help to constitute them as a community. These include, for instance, the political and procedural values of liberal democracy; welfare values concerning the physical, psychological, and material goods that matter to us simply as human beings or as preconditions of the pursuit of any substantive conceptions of the good [see Lacey 1988, chs. 5, 8; Brudner 1993]; and 'other-regarding' values concerning the community's relations to nonmembers, both human and nonhuman. Those tempted by value-monism might want to portray these as derivative from some more basic value [for instance, autonomy], but such a reduction is neither plausible nor necessary [see Brudner 1993; J. Gardner 1998a]. We should, in this as in other contexts, recognize an irreducible diversity of values.)

Now members of such a community will be related to most of their fellow citizens as (relative) strangers; community does not entail intimacy. Their membership of this political community and their relationships as fellow citizens might not loom large in their lives. The political community will be only one of the communities to which they belong, and might well not be one in which they find their most important goods or to which they devote much of their time or attention. Indeed, they will have no direct or individual contact with most other members. Their relationships as fellow citizens will be a matter not so much of how they do interact as individuals but of their places within the various practices and institutions by which the community's life is ordered, and of how they *would* respond to one another *if* they came into direct contact.[12]

They constitute a community insofar as they aspire, and know that they aspire, to share the community-defining values of autonomy, freedom, and privacy (values that underpin a plurality of specific, substantive conceptions of the good, which not all will share) and insofar as they aspire, and know that they aspire, to an appropriate mutual concern for one another in the light of those values. That mutual concern will involve a readiness to assist one another in pursuing and preserving the community's distinctive goods—though such assistance will often be organized and directly provided by the state—and, more crucially for present purposes, a respect for one another as fellow members of the community that precludes simply exploiting others for one's own ends or treating them in ways that are inconsistent with the community's defining values. That is to say, in such dealings as they have as fellow citizens, they must address one another as citizens whose status as members of the community is no different from (no lower or more doubtful than) their own. They must not treat one another in ways that infringe their autonomy or legitimate freedoms. They must respect one another's privacy, not seeking to intrude into matters that are not of proper concern to them simply as fellow citizens. They must not merely tolerate but respect the diverse ways of life, the diverse conceptions of human good, that the political community embraces.

Such concern and such respect must also, of course, inform the state's institutions and activities. For the state must be so structured and organized that it fosters and respects the community's defining values, and must treat and address the citizens in ways that embody those values. In section 4, below, I show what this involves as far as the criminal law is concerned.

This sketch of a political community might sound little different from at least one kind of liberal ideal. So why should I call it 'communitarian' (or 'liberal-communitarian'), rather than simply 'liberal'? What substantive work is the notion of 'community' doing here?

3. 'Communitarianism' and 'Liberalism' (Again)

A recent feature of the 'liberal-communitarian' debate has been a blurring of the boundaries between these supposedly opposed schools—a realization of the ways in which we can be 'communitarian-liberals' or 'liberal-communitarians' (see, e.g., Kymlicka 1989; Taylor 1989; Mulhall & Swift 1992, pts. 2–3). There are, however, significant differences between the liberal-communitarian conception of political community sketched in the previous section and some familiar forms of liberalism.

3.1. Metaphysical and Normative Issues

Communitarian critics of liberalism have often focused on metaphysical issues about the nature of social and human reality. Thus it was argued against Rawls that in grounding his theory in an account of what rational agents would decide in the "Original Position," he relied on a metaphysical conception of the person as identifiable independently of her or his ends and social situation. This conception, critics argued, is untenable, since individual persons are at least in part constituted by their ends and their place in a human community.[13] Similarly, liberals who seek to ground political obligation in the idea of a social contract, arguing that obligation must always be based on consent or choice (if not on actual consent or choice, then on what a rational agent would consent to or choose), are accused of ignoring the fact that contracts presuppose a normative community within which they can be made or even understood, and that choice likewise presupposes some socially constituted framework of (unchosen) values and norms. We cannot find the ultimate ground of political obligation in the idea of a social contract made between or chosen or consented to by presocial individuals, since such individuals could have no basis on which to deliberate or to choose.

Such metaphysical debates are important. Our political theories should be informed by some tenable metaphysics of human and social reality. However, although I think that metaphysical communitarians are largely right as against metaphysical liberals, these debates are not crucial here. For one liberal response to such metaphysical communitarian objections is that liberalism should be understood as a normative rather than as a metaphysical theory. It concerns the ways in which we should structure and justify our political institutions, and neither implies nor depends upon the metaphysical conceptions that communitarians attack.[14]

There are difficult questions to be asked about what kinds of normative political theory are consistent with what metaphysical conceptions of human beings and society, and indeed about how far we can separate the metaphysical from the normative (see Taylor 1989; also Gaita 1991; Marshall & Duff 1982). But it seems at least plausible that one could allow to metaphysical communitarians most if not all of what they claim about the necessary social embeddedness of individuals and about the impossibility of deliberating from an asocial "view from nowhere" (the dependence of rational deliberation and choice on a social context of given, unchosen values) and still construct a normative political theory of a recognizably liberal, contractualist, and individualist kind that differs in important ways from the liberal-communitarian account sketched in the previous section.

The consistency of such a normative individualism with a communitarian metaphysics is due in part to the related facts, emphasized above, that political community is partial, not total, and that members of a political community will also belong to a variety of other communities. It is also due to the facts, which metaphysical communitarians cannot deny, that 'socially constituted' selves can be individualist selves who have clear conceptions of their own interests and give those interests paramount importance in their lives; and that even if we cannot detach ourselves from *every* community to which we belong, we can detach ourselves from any *particular* community in which we now live, including any political community to which we belong or are said to belong.

When I begin to reflect on my commitments and my values, I find myself as an individual already embedded in a particular social context—a context that includes various particular associations, practices, and values. I belong to this family, to this church, to this country, . . . Each of these associations gives me an aspect of my identity. I am a member (a son, brother, cousin, . . .) of this family, a fellow believer with these others in this religion, a fellow citizen with these others of this country. At the same time, they give me a substantial normative framework of values, goods, and obligations. To be a son, in the normative sense appropriate to this context, is to be committed to certain familial values, to find important aspects of my good in the life and flourishing of this family, to recognize certain obligations to other members of the family.

Suppose we accept this kind of communitarian argument.[15] We must also, however, recognize certain further truths. First, I have acquired a conception of 'my' interests as distinct from those of others, and it is both conceptually and (usually) psychologically possible for me to attach paramount importance to 'my' interests.[16] Second, I belong to a range of associations or communities, and yet others are accessible to me. There is a range of normative frameworks within which I can think, a range of normative discourses that I can speak; and it is both conceptually and (often) psychologically possible to detach myself (in thought if not in fact) from any particular association or community to which I currently belong, and ask myself whether and why and on what terms I should belong to it.

There are of course (controversial) limits on how much I can detach myself from while still being able both to think rationally and to understand that from which I have detached myself. It is, for instance, a controversial question in moral philosophy whether I can detach myself not merely from some set of moral beliefs but from 'morality' as such, and rationally ask myself (while still understanding that about which I am asking) whether I have good reason to commit myself to any moral values at all.[17] But it surely is, in contemporary western societies if not at all times and in all places, both conceptually and psychologically possible to detach oneself, in thought, from any *political* society or associations to which one currently belongs; and to ask whether, why, and on what terms one should commit oneself to this, or to any other kind of, political association. And this, the contractarian individualist might argue, is just what each of us *should* do (see Matravers 2000, ch. 7).

We must be able to justify the demands that political association makes on us—the obligation claims that belong with such association. We must be able to justify those demands to those who do not (yet) accept them—those who are detached from political association. We must also, if our own commitments are to be rational, justify them to ourselves. To do so involves detaching ourselves, at least in thought, from political association and asking whether we have good reason to commit ourselves to it. More precisely, this is not something that 'we' must do collectively (if we have detached ourselves, there is no such 'we') but something each of us must do individually for herself or himself: I must detach myself and then choose whether to (re)commit myself. But if I now ask myself, as on this view I must, "To what kind of political association, if any, should I commit myself, and on what terms?" an individualist contractarian answer seems plausible. I should commit myself to (a particular form of) political association if and because I realize that it will be in my best interests to do so. Since that association will be with others each of whom can and rationally should ask herself or himself the same question, it must be one to which each can agree on the same grounds; and an obvious way to portray that association will then be as something like a contract between all these individuals, to which each will agree as being beneficial to herself or himself.

This is the crudest sketch of a contractarian individualism that aims to avoid positing a dubious metaphysical picture of presocial rational individuals who could decide, from outside any social framework of thought and value, what political structures to accept. I do not try here to put more flesh on these bones nor to ask how successfully such an account can meet the metaphysical communitarian's objections. I want simply to use this sketch to draw out, by contrast with it, the respects in which the account of political community offered in the previous section can be usefully called 'communitarian'.

3.2. 'I' and 'We'

For the liberal individualist we must each begin, in normative deliberation if not in metaphysical reality, in isolation and then find reasons to enter into association or solidarity with others. Even if we cannot begin metaphysically with isolated, asocial 'I's, each of us must begin our practical deliberation about political association as an 'I' detached from his or her existing political commitments; we must each ask whether and on what terms this 'I' should associate himself or herself with these other people. For communitarians, by contrast, we begin our normative deliberations not in isolation as detached individuals but as a 'we'—as individuals already in association or solidarity with historically contingent groups of others, who should (and can) detach themselves from such associations only if given reason to do so. The question is not how *I* should live or what associations *I* should form, but how *we* should live—how we should live together. I must ask that question for myself and find an answer to it that *I* can accept. But the content of the question is set in the first-person plural, not the first-person singular.

Who constitutes this 'we'? Initially, the communities and associations in which we find ourselves: these form the given from which we begin. This is not to say that we must simply accept, as unchangeable givens, whatever such communities we are born or brought up into. We can, and sometimes must, question not only the particular values and practices of communities of which we are and remain members but also our very membership of a community. Should I remain a member of this church or of this polity or of this union? But this is not a question that I *must always* raise, if my continued membership of a community is to be rationally justified. Nor, if it is raised, must it always be answered in terms of *my* interests. Suppose I live in a family, or in a group of friends who came together not through any deliberate choice but through the various unchosen contingencies of our lives. Why is it rationally incumbent on me to detach myself in thought from my family or my friends so as to ask, from the outside, whether I should remain in this community (as distinct from asking, from the inside, how we should lead our lives together)? Or, if I do ask (or am asked) such a question, why should my reflective answer not simply be, "But these people are my family/friends"? Such an answer expresses my recognition of a particular kind of fellowship with these other people: I might not have *chosen* them, but we are now bound together. That fellowship need not be unconditional.[18] It could happen that, for a variety of possible reasons, I come to realize that I should cut myself off from my family or my friends. But in the absence of such reasons, I see myself as bound in fellowship with them.

So too with citizenship of a polity. I am born into a particular polity and grow up to see myself as a member of it—as a fellow citizen of this polity with these other people. I did not choose to be English or British or American. I might not have chosen such fellow citizens had I been given the choice. But we are here together. Of course, we should look critically at the structures and practices of our polity. They are not given, as the unchangeable framework of our political and social lives. Of course, I may be led, and sometimes should be led, to question my membership of this polity: perhaps it is so corrupt that I should leave it—either geographically or morally (or perhaps I should stay and fight to change it). Of course, the boundaries of the polity are not set in stone. I may come to see myself not as British but as Scottish, and join an ultimately successful campaign for independence. Or I may come to see myself as a member of an oppressed minority in an oppressive state and think that we (and here again I will think of what 'we' should do) should strive to maintain as best we can our own distinct way of life. But nonetheless I can, unless I am very unlucky in my situation, recognize myself as a fellow member of a political community.

This is not to say that for communitarians we must begin (metaphysically or morally) with communities *rather than* with individuals, as if individuals were subordinate to the communities to which they belong—which might imply that their interests may be readily sacrificed to the interests of the community. It is to say that we must begin with *individuals in community*, with individuals who already recognize themselves as living in community with others.

Two further aspects of the contrast between the communitarian and the individualist perspectives should make these comments clearer.

3.3. Choice and Recognition

I talk of the 'recognition' of fellowship—in a family, in a group of friends, in a political community. By contrast, liberal individualists typically talk of choice or decision: I must *choose* whether and on what terms to commit myself to an association, and find reasons for choosing one way or the other.

This contrast runs deep in moral philosophy. One kind of moral theorist insists that we must choose what to believe, what principles to accept, what respect or concern to accord to other beings (human or nonhuman). This way of talking is most obviously characteristic of various species of subjectivism. By contrast, others insist that attention, perception, and recognition, rather than choice or decision, are basic to moral life and thought (see, e.g., Murdoch 1970; Diamond 1978; Gaita 1991; Blum 1994). We must attend to the world and to other people as sources of moral demands on us; we must strive to see what is right or good and what we must do, and (most crucially for present purposes) we must recognize others as our fellows—as fellow human beings (see Gaita 1991, ch. 3),[19] or as fellow members of the various more particular communities in which we find ourselves with them.

A kind of recognition is of course involved in the liberal individualist's deliberation: I must recognize other people as rational beings like myself with interests, commitments, and conceptions of the good (and as beings whose interests, commitments, and conceptions of the good differ from mine). What the individualist cannot recognize, however, is fellowship with those from whom she has in thought detached herself—a fellowship with other members of a historically contingent community, which involves having a concern for them (and a claim on them) as my fellows: for that is the kind of connection from which, if she ever had it, she has detached herself. It is precisely such a recognition on which communitarians insist. This is the sense in which the normative bonds of community are, for normative communitarians, *given* rather than chosen.

To say that such bonds are given is not to say that they that they can never be rationally questioned. The detachment that liberal individualists demand is conceptually and (usually) psychologically possible, and we might sometimes have to question or reject our existing attachments. It is rather to say that they are given in moral experience. They are part of what we recognize when we think about our relations to those around us. In the absence of some particular reason to question them, they are not open to serious question, and although I might find them burdensome, when they demand that I constrain or sacrifice some of my own interests, I cannot honestly deny them.[20] I might not, given the choice, have *chosen* to be bound to these others or to be a member of this community; I might not be *required* by either psychology or logic to accept these bonds and the demands that flow from them: but I am, morally, stuck with them—these are my fellows, whether I like it or not.

3.4. Individual Goods and Shared Goods

A common communitarian complaint against 'liberals' is that they cannot do justice to the good. In their insistence on the priority of 'the right' over 'the good', and on the 'neutrality' of the state as between different conceptions of the good, they ignore the way in which any substantial notion of 'the right' depends upon a prior conception of the good, and wrongly suppose that a state could remain neutral as between *all* possible conceptions of the good. In their insistence that individuals must be left free to choose their own goods, they ignore the way in which all goods are 'socially constituted' and cannot do justice to the nature and importance of 'communal' or 'common' goods (see Mulhall & Swift 1992, pt. 1, passim; Kymlicka 1989, chs. 3, 5). To which some liberals reply that even if they are committed to autonomy and freedom as fundamental goods to which the state should *not* be neutral, these are formal or meta-goods whose value consists partly in the fact that they involve the capacity and opportunity to choose between a wide range of substantive goods as between which the state should indeed remain neutral (see Kymlicka 1989, ch. 5; Sher 1997, 14). These liberals also reply that while we can recognize a variety of ways in which goods are 'socially constituted', the goods thus constituted could still be the goods of individuals and be good only because they are chosen and valued by those individuals (see Sher 1997, ch. 7), and that we can recognize certain social or communal goods precisely as being important *to individuals* (see, e.g., Kymlicka 1989).[21]

Rather than pursue these general debates here, I focus on the way in which a liberal-communitarian will understand the defining goods of a liberal polity—autonomy, freedom, and privacy—as being not only socially constituted but also communal, in that they count as goods only insofar as they are shared.

To say that such goods are 'socially constituted' is to say that they can be understood, as goods, only within a social context that makes them possible and gives them their meaning and significance. Thus *autonomy*,[22] understood as a set of capacities for rational thought and action (including thought about ends or goods, as well as instrumental thought about the means to such ends or goods), is not something that could be identified or valued in isolated, asocial, 'rational agents': for those capacities are capacities to participate in forms of social life and thought, within the structures of reason and of norms embedded in such forms of life; they can be identified, developed, and valued only within such social contexts.[23] Similarly, we must understand *freedom* not in merely negative terms as the absence of certain kinds of external constraint on the actions of individual agents, but in richer, positive terms of the opportunities that social agents have to act in their social space— opportunities that are determined and are given their content and significance by their social context.[24] We must understand *privacy* not as concerning a realm of the 'private' that is given a priori in advance of any particular social context but as concerning a sphere that is socially defined by a particular community (see p. 45, above; also Sypnowich, forthcoming).

As I note above, however, liberal individualists need not deny that goods are in this sense socially constituted, since goods that are thus constituted can still be *individual* goods. The significant communitarian claim is that these goods should be understood as shared or communal goods. This is not to say that they must be seen as collective goods *rather than* as individual goods. It is individual people who achieve (or are denied) these goods, and whose lives go well or badly depending on whether they achieve them. Similarly, in an academic community it is individual academics who achieve or fail to achieve the goods of knowledge and understanding. Nor is it to say that they *cannot* be seen in purely individualist terms. As an academic, I can see my intellectual advances or achievements purely as *my* goods, contributing to *my* academic career; as a citizen, I could care for my autonomy, freedom, and privacy as being of value to me independently of the extent to which others achieve such goods. But it is to say that to see these goods in such purely individualist terms is to fail to understand them as the community's defining goods, to fail to relate myself to them as a member of the community. As an academic, I *should* care about the extent to which *we* achieve the goods of knowledge and understanding, and see my advances not just as *mine* but as contributions to our common pursuit. That is what it is to be a member of an academic community. As a citizen, I *should* care about the extent to which *all* citizens achieve the goods of autonomy, freedom, and privacy, and value my own autonomy, freedom, and privacy only insofar as others too can achieve those goods. That is what it is to be a citizen of a liberal political community.

This is not to say that I should *subordinate* my autonomy, freedom, or privacy to some mysterious collective good, or that I can be properly called on to *sacrifice* my autonomy, freedom, or privacy for the sake of the autonomy, freedom, or privacy of others. It is rather to say that within a liberal polity my autonomy has value as that of an autonomous citizen among other autonomous citizens; and so too with freedom and privacy. If I have the freedom to pursue my own projects, while many of my fellow citizens do not, the very character of my freedom differs from that of the freedom of a free citizen amongst other free citizens; nor does it have the value that freedom has when it is shared in by all—the value that defines it as the good of citizens in a liberal polity.[25]

I have tried in this section to explain the sense in which my account of a liberal polity is a 'communitarian', albeit a 'liberal-communitarian', account by contrasting it with familiar forms of liberal individualism. I have not tried to *prove* that we should favor this liberal-communitarian perspective over the various forms of liberal individualism, since I do not think that anything that could properly count as a 'proof' is available in normative political theorizing. I have tried to show, however, that we are not rationally *required* to take the individualist's standpoint—to detach ourselves as individuals from our exist-

ing associations and commitments and to ask whether we have reason to
choose to recommit ourselves to them; and I have tried to say enough to render the liberal-communitarian alternative both intelligible and attractive. In
the end, in political as in moral argument, we can only say to those whom we
are trying to persuade, "Can't you see it like this?" painting a picture that we
hope the other will find persuasive.

There is a further issue I must tackle—that of nonvoluntary membership
of a political community. But that can best be done after we have discussed
the role of the criminal law in a liberal polity.

4. The Criminal Law of a Liberal Polity

What role will the criminal law play in a liberal political community of the
kind sketched above in sections 2.2 and 3? It defines certain kinds of conduct
as 'criminal', but what does this mean? It might be tempting to say that to define conduct as criminal is to make its agents liable to punishment, but that
would be too quick. While punishment does presuppose crime, we have yet
to see whether or why crime should entail punishment—or, if crime does entail punishment, why we should have a *criminal* law at all. We must begin
with an account of crime (an account that will meet abolitionist critiques of
the concept of crime; see ch. 1.5.2–3), before we can ask whether and why
criminals should be punished.

According to the *Model Penal Code* (sec. 1.02(a)) the "general purpose" of
the substantive criminal law is "to forbid and prevent conduct that unjustifi-
ably and inexcusably inflicts or threatens substantial harm to individual or
public interests." This account of the purpose of the criminal law implies a
normative conception of crime—of the kind of conduct that should be criminalized. But it raises several questions. In particular, does the criminal law
'forbid' and aim to 'prevent' the conduct that it defines as criminal? And why
should we have a criminal rather than a civil law to deal with conduct that
harms or threatens to harm 'individual interests'? In answering these questions, I argue that the criminal law of a liberal polity should be a 'common
law'.

4.1. Prohibitions and Declarations

It seems natural to say that the criminal law 'prohibits' conduct it defines
as criminal. We supposedly have an obligation to obey the law and may be
punished if we disobey it; and to obey the law is to refrain from doing what it
prohibits, because it is legally prohibited.[26]

To portray the criminal law thus is to portray it as giving citizens *content-
independent* reasons for action. If their reasons for refraining from conduct defined as criminal had to do solely with the nature or effects of that conduct,
independently of the fact that it was defined as criminal (for instance, with its

prelegal moral wrongfulness), their reasons would be *content-dependent*: they would depend on the particular content of the law, not on the fact that it was the law. In that case, however, they would not be *obeying* the law: for to obey *X* is to act in conformity with what *X* requires, *because X* requires it (see, e.g., Hart 1994, 19–20, 51–61), whereas these citizens would be acting as they do because of what it is that the law 'requires' rather than because the law requires it. To see the criminal law as *prohibiting* conduct, and as requiring our *obedience* to its prohibitions, is to see it as offering us reasons for action that are at least partly independent of its particular content:[27] These are reasons that we would not otherwise have for acting thus, reasons having to do with the authority or power of the law itself.

This is indeed how traditional legal positivism portrays the law—as a set of commands addressed to the citizens by a sovereign. It is also how the law *should* be portrayed if it should be understood as a set of edicts imposed by a sovereign on her subjects.[28] But it is not how we should understand the criminal law of a liberal polity.

Consider the central kinds of criminal *mala in se*—crimes, such as murder, rape, serious assault, theft, involving conduct that is wrongful independently of its being defined as criminal. To say that the criminal law 'prohibits' such conduct is to say that it offers citizens reasons for refraining from it that are independent of its prelegal wrongfulness: reasons having to do presumably, either with the law's authority (citizens should obey because they recognize an obligation to do so) or with its power (they are to obey because the threat of sanctions for disobedience obliges them to do so). Many citizens will of course refrain from such conduct independently of the law's prohibition, because they see it to be (prelegally) wrongful. On this account, however, the law must be addressed, not to those who would anyway refrain from such conduct, but to those who might otherwise engage in it; and it offers *them* new or additional reasons to refrain from it.

One point to notice about this picture concerns the motivation of those who do *obey* the law. Few, if any, will obey out of *respect* for the law's *authority*: for what kind of person would it be who, though not motivated to refrain from murder or rape by the prelegal wrongfulness of such conduct, was motivated thus to refrain by his respect for the law?[29] One can imagine cases in which this would be intelligible—in particular cases in which the law makes a determinate ruling on matters that are morally controversial or uncertain. Someone, for instance, who thinks that voluntary euthanasia is morally permissible, or that a property holder can be morally justified in using fatal force to prevent its theft, *might* be dissuaded from such conduct by respect for the law that defines it as criminal (see further sec. 4.4, below). Such instances will, however, be rare. Most of those who obey the law will do so from fear of the threatened sanctions—from fear of its power rather than from respect for its authority.

In either instance, however, whether the law exerts its power or its authority over those who obey it, the other and more important point to notice concerns the way in which it addresses the citizens. For on this account it says nothing directly to those who conform to but do not obey its requirements—those who refrain from criminal conduct because they see it to be wrong independently of its legal status as criminal. It might at most address them indirectly—assuring them that it does seek obedience from those who might not otherwise conform. As for those from whom it does seek obedience, it addresses them in the peremptory tones of authority or of power. It says to them either, "Act thus, because you have an obligation to obey the law" or, "Act thus, or else you will suffer sanctions." But these are not the tones in which the law should address the citizens of a liberal polity.

Now on this picture there is, first, a radical lack of fit between the reasons that the law offers the citizens for acting as it demands and the reasons that supposedly justify the content of those demands. The law 'prohibits' murder, rape, and the like because such conduct is *wrongful* in a way that properly concerns the law (see further sec. 4.3, below)—wrongful in terms of the shared values of the political community. The reasons it offers citizens for obeying those prohibitions, however, refer not to the wrongfulness of the conduct prohibited but to the law's own authority or power—to their supposed obligation to obey the law or to the sanctions threatened for disobedience. There is thus a lack of "transparency" in the way the law addresses the citizens (see Bickenbach 1988, 770–71). The reasons it offers them are different from the reasons that justify its demands on them.

But, second, to address them thus is to *fail* to address them as members of the normative political community whose law this is. As members of that community, they are supposed to share a commitment to its central and defining values, which determine the content of the criminal law. If the law is to address them as members of the community, it must therefore address them in terms of those values—the values that determine its content and that should guide their conduct.

We can express this point by portraying the law, not as *prohibiting* the central kinds of *mala in se*, but as *declaring* their wrongfulness. By defining them as crimes it formally declares that they are wrongs in terms of the community's own values and, further, that they are 'public' wrongs that properly concern the whole community and that must be formally recognized and condemned as such by the community.

This is also to say that we should not see the criminal law as aiming (just or primarily) to 'prevent' such conduct (*Model Penal Code* sec. 1.02(a)). In defining conduct as criminal, the law does of course declare that it should not be done; and internal to such a declaration is the intention that those to whom it is addressed will refrain from the conduct it thus condemns. But talk of 'prevention' implies an instrumentalist perspective. We identify an end, that people not engage in such conduct, and then look for cost-effective means of achieving that end—means that might, as far as cost-effectiveness is concerned, involve appeals to the law's content-independent authority or power. If, however, the law's primary role in relation to the central *mala in se* is not to prohibit them but to declare their wrongfulness, then its aim is not so much to 'prevent' them as to *remind* citizens (if they need reminding) that and why such conduct is wrong.[30]

Before I comment on the idea of a 'public' wrong, (sec. 4.3, below) and on some ways in which the criminal law can still be read as 'forbidding' conduct that it defines as criminal (sec. 4.4, below), we should note how this conception of the criminal law connects with the idea of a 'common' law.

4.2. The Criminal Law as a Common Law

The idea of the 'common' law has come to be used to distinguish statute law, as passed by a legislature, from nonstatutory law, which is declared, if not created, by the courts. But in its classical formulation, by theorists such as Coke, Hale, and Blackstone, the idea of the 'common' law transcended the distinction between statutory and nonstatutory law.[31]

The genius of the common law, according to its classical defenders, lies in its relation to the community whose law it is. It is not (as statute law can too easily be) a law *imposed on* a people by a sovereign, which they must receive and obey as subjects. Rather, it is the law of the community itself. It embodies the shared values and normative understandings of the community. It flows not from the will of a separate sovereign but from the traditions and practices of the community. The task of judges who administer and develop the common law is not to *create* law, in the light either of their own values or of a 'natural' law distinct from the life of this particular, historical community. Rather, it is to articulate the values embedded in the community's life—although that articulation will often involve providing more precise *determinationes* of those values.[32] Statute law should also, on this conception, be a common law (see Postema 1986, 14–27). The legislature's task is not to impose its own will on the population, but to give more adequate and practicable expression to the values that already structure the community's life and understanding.

This conception of the 'common' law provides an (ideal) picture of the law of a liberal polity—of a law fit for citizens rather than subjects. The law is not the law of a distinct sovereign, but the community's own law. It is *'our'* law as members of the community. The law does not address the citizens in the voice of a separate sovereign who exercises power or authority over them. It speaks in their own voice, in the language of their own values.[33]

This idea has obvious Kantian resonances, since Kant famously talked of the laws that as *homo noumenon* I can or must will to be binding on myself as *homo phainomenon*—laws that I must address to myself in the first person (see Kant [1797] 1948, 105). But it differs in at least one crucial respect from Kant's idea. The voice of the Kantian is a first-person *singular* voice, which expresses my individual recognition of the demands of the moral law. By contrast, the voice with which I am concerned is a first-person *plural* voice. The voice of the law is (or aspires to be) the voice of the community addressing itself, the voice of all the citizens addressing one another and themselves. It speaks of what 'we', the community, require or demand.

But what will this 'we' thus require or demand: what kind of content should the criminal law of a liberal polity have?

Before we can answer this question, however, we face a prior question: why should a liberal polity have a *criminal* law at all? To say that its law must be a 'common' law is not yet to say that it must include a criminal law; and the abolitionist challenge to the practice of state punishment is in part a challenge to the concept of crime on which that practice depends (see ch. 1.5.2). If we are to meet that challenge, we must show why the law of a liberal polity should include a criminal law that condemns certain kinds of conduct as 'public' wrongs, as well as a civil law that deals with 'conflicts' or 'troubles' between its citizens. We must explain and justify the concept of crime.

4.3. The Concept of Crime

It might be tempting to define crime in terms of punishment. Crimes are legal wrongs that make the agent liable to punishment (see, e.g., G. Williams 1983, 27–29; Smith & Hogan 1996, 16–23); thus to justify a system of criminal law is to justify a system of punishment. However, we are not yet in a position to tackle the issue of punishment; and we can anyway identify some central features of the concept of crime that leave open (as it should be left open) the question whether crimes should be punished.

Crimes, it is often said, are 'public' wrongs, as distinct from torts, which constitute only 'private' wrongs. But what is a 'public' wrong? If we say that it is a wrong that injures 'the public', or the community as a whole, as distinct from those that injure only individuals, we will be led to look for some such 'public' injury as the identifying feature of crimes. Now there certainly are familiar crimes that injure the community as a whole rather than identifiable individuals: crimes of public endangerment, for instance, and frauds against the public purse. However, if we then extend this perspective to crimes that directly victimize individuals, such as the central crimes against the person, the search for some injury to the public or to the community is liable to turn our attention away from the wrong done to the direct victim—and thus to distort our understanding of the criminal wrongfulness of such crimes.

We might say, for instance, that such attacks on the person should be a matter for the criminal law because they threaten the social order by causing "social volatility" (see Becker 1974) or by undermining the conditions of trust (see Dimock 1997), or because the criminal takes an unfair advantage over those who obey the law (see ch.1.4.2). But this seems to distract us from the wrong done to the direct victims of such crimes, which surely should be central to our understanding of their criminal character. Murderers and rapists should be prosecuted not because their crimes undermine trust or cause social volatility or because they take an unfair advantage over the law-abiding, but for and because of the wrongs they do to their victims—in which case that is also the central reason why such conduct should be criminalized.

We can give a better account of crimes as 'public' wrongs by beginning with the idea, not of wrongs against 'the public', but of wrongs in which 'the public', the community as a whole, is properly interested. There are two aspects to this proper interest.

First, it involves an authoritative, communal condemnation of such wrongs. They are not simply matters of private conscience or matters on which only those directly involved have the standing to pronounce, but matters on which the community as a whole can and should take a stand, through the authoritative voice of the law.

Second, such wrongs merit a public, communal response. Those who commit them should be called to account and censured by the community. This is one central feature of a criminal process that deals with crimes, as distinct from a civil process that deals with private torts—of a criminal as distinct from a civil trial. A civil process is initiated and controlled by the complainant, the person who believes she has been wronged. The community, through the civil law, declares the norms to which she appeals. It provides the institutions through which she can bring her case, have it decided, and have the verdict enforced. But the case is *hers* (it is the case of "*P v. D*"). She decides whether to bring it, whether to pursue it, and whether to enforce any verdict in her favor. By contrast, a criminal procedure is controlled by the community: the case is "*People* [or *Commonwealth*] *v. D*";[34] and while it might often in fact be brought or pursued only if the victim is willing that it should be, it can be pursued or dropped against the victim's wishes. A criminal process thus relieves the victim of the burden of bringing the case, but also deprives the victim of the authority to decide whether and how the case should proceed.[35]

These two aspects of the criminal law provoke the abolitionist charge that, in defining and prosecuting 'crimes', the law 'steals' what we should instead see as 'conflicts' or 'troubles' from those to whom they properly belong—from those directly involved in them (see Christie 1977; Hulsman 1986, 1991). For the law *imposes* a purportedly authoritative, but controversial, standard of right and wrong. Instead of allowing the issue to be discussed and worked out—as it should be—by the people directly involved, it declares as it were from on high, or from the outside, that one party is to be condemned as a wrongdoer.[36] It allows neither offender nor victim any active role in resolving their conflict.

Now there is indeed much in our existing systems of criminal justice that invites such a charge. We can object that our existing criminal law is not a genuinely common law, since it too often fails to reflect values that are shared by the whole community—and since too many of those supposedly bound by it are effectively excluded from any voice in its formulation or interpretation. We can object that it deals with matters that should not fall within its realm and exceeds the limits that the criminal law of a liberal polity should respect (see sec. 4.5, below). We can object that our criminal process too often excludes both offenders and victims from the kind of active participation in it that they should have (see ch. 3.4.2–3; ch. 3.3.2). We can also agree that there are many conflicts or disputes that involve (what the law now counts as) crimes, but that would be better resolved by a process of negotiation and compromise that does not aim to censure one party as a wrongdoer—that it is often a mistake to look to the law (either criminal or civil) as the first resort to deal with the conflicts in which we find ourselves with our neighbors. This is *not* to say, however, as some abolitionists seem to say, that we should abandon the concept of crime—of 'public' wrongs that are properly condemned and dealt with as wrongs by the community as a whole.

The case of domestic violence illustrates this point (see Dobash & Dobash 1992, ch. 5). The police often used to see cases of domestic violence, in which one partner (usually male) regularly assaulted the other (usually female), as 'domestic disturbances' or 'disputes' into which the criminal justice system should not intrude. The rights and wrongs of the situation were often hard to determine; the couple should work out their problems between themselves. The violence was thus seen as 'their conflict', to which they must negotiate a solution: as if we must ask, "How wrong was the assailant, how right was the victim?" (Christie 1977, 8; see n.36, above) and recognize that there might be no clear answer to that question. But whatever else is unclear about the rights and wrongs of a domestic dispute, whatever else needs to be negotiated if the relationship is to survive, whatever else should be seen as a matter for compromise between the legitimate claims of the people concerned, such violence should surely *not* be seen as a matter for negotiation or compromise. It should be condemned by the whole community as unqualifiedly wrong; and this is done by defining and prosecuting it as a crime.

The same is true of other central *mala in se*. To say to the victim of a rape or an unprovoked assault or a mugging that she has a 'conflict' with her assailant that we must allow and help the two of them to work out, to refuse to judge and declare that she was wronged, would add insult to the wrong she has already suffered. There is sometimes room for doubt and debate about the rights and wrongs of such cases—about whether what the 'victim' portrays as a crime was really and unqualifiedly a crime. But there is often no moral room for such debate; and one thing that the victim should not be expected to see as being up for discussion is whether assault or mugging or rape is wrong.

This is to say that the central crimes should be kinds of conduct that are categorically wrong—kinds of conduct from which all citizens should be able to expect, categorically, to be safe in the course of their normal lives. Some risks of harm we can be expected to accept, either as aspects of normal life or as risks to which we have voluntarily exposed ourselves. We may have a right to compensation if they are actualized through another's culpable conduct, but that is something for us to pursue through a civil process—and the amount of compensation may be reduced by our contributory negligence. Other kinds of harm, however, we should not be expected to accept in this way. We might have to recognize that we will in fact be vulnerable to them if we behave in certain ways or fail to take certain precautions: that house-holders who fail to secure their homes might be burgled, that strangers who visit 'dangerous' areas might be attacked, that women who dress or behave 'provocatively' might be raped. We *might* criticize as imprudent those who thus expose themselves to danger. But we must also recognize that they have been wronged; that the assailant's guilt is not mitigated by the victim's im-prudence (hence the justified criticisms of judges who suggest that a rapist's guilt is mitigated by his victim's 'contributory negligence'), and that if com-pensation is possible at all, it must be of a kind that aims to make reparation not just for whatever material harm they have suffered but for the wrong done to them.[37]

We could also say that these are wrongs in which the community shares. As members of the community, we should see them not merely as the vic-tim's wrongs but as 'our' wrongs. Just as the central goods of the community are shared goods (see sec. 3.4, above), so attacks on those goods are wrongs in which we share with the victim as fellow citizens (see Marshall & Duff 1998). This is not to say that they are wrongs against 'the community' *rather than* against their direct victims. They are wrongs against their direct victims as members of the community, and so also wrongs against the community.

These comments clearly do not provide determinate criteria for deciding which wrongs should be the concern of the criminal law. Rather, they are in-tended to clarify the concept of crime as a 'public' wrong—as a categorical wrong in which the community should share. I do not think that we could find general criteria for determining just which wrongs should be thus seen as 'public'. One could, for instance, imagine a community whose valuations of reputation and of private property were such that libel was seen as a public wrong and theft as only a private wrong. However, any political community will have some set of shared values given which some wrongs will count as public wrongs in the sense explained here; and we can assume that this cate-gory of public wrongs will at least include the kinds of serious attack on the person that form the core of our *mala in se*.[38]

I cannot embark here on a more detailed discussion of the content of the criminal law of a liberal polity—either of how it will define the central kinds of *mala in se*, or of how far and in which directions it will extend beyond that central core. But I must briefly discuss two further topics, which will throw further light on this complex question. One concerns the authority of the criminal law, in relation both to *mala in se* and to *mala prohibita*. The other concerns the kinds of limit a liberal polity will set on the scope of its criminal law.

4.4. *The Authority of the Criminal Law*

As I argued in section 4.1, above, we should not see the criminal law as *prohibiting* the conduct that it defines as *mala in se*—as offering the citizens content-independent reasons to refrain from such conduct. We should see it instead as *declaring* such conduct to constitute a public wrong properly condemned by the community, for which the agent is answerable to the community through a criminal process.

This is one aspect of the authority that the law claims to have. Though the law does not *create* these wrongs as wrongs (since they are already wrong in terms of the community's prelegal values), it identifies them as public wrongs and thus imposes on the citizens a duty to answer for their alleged commissions of such wrongs through the criminal process. This is a duty that they could not have were there no system of criminal justice. The law's definitions of central *mala in se* can thus be seen as laying down both "rules for courts" and "rules for citizens" (see Alldridge 1990; Robinson 1990). As rules for courts, they specify the kinds of conduct for which the courts should convict those who commit them. As rules for citizens, they admittedly do not (subject to the qualifications to be noted shortly) *forbid* citizens to engage in the conduct they define as criminal, but they remind citizens that such conduct flouts the community's public values, and so warn them that they will be liable to be called to public account for such conduct through the criminal process. They also indirectly, in association with the laws governing the criminal process, require citizens to answer through that process for their alleged commissions of such wrongs.

The criminal law also, however, claims the authority to prohibit conduct, to *make* wrong conduct that is not or might not be wrong independently of the law, in relation both to some aspects of *mala in se* and to *mala prohibita*; and in such cases we can properly talk, as we cannot talk in relation to the central *mala in se*, of an obligation to *obey* the law and of acting out of *respect* for the law's authority.[39]

In relation to *mala in se*, the law will sometimes have to provide precise *determinationes* of values whose precise prelegal meanings or implications are uncertain or controversial. The law defines just what counts as murder or theft or rape, as well as what counts as a justification for what would otherwise be a criminal action. In doing so, it specifies more determinate legal meanings for normative concepts whose prelegal meanings are typically less determinate, and it takes an authoritative stand on issues that may be controversial in the political community, such as the permissibility of euthanasia. A liberal polity's law, which respects its citizens' autonomy, will as far as possible respect their different and conflicting interpretations of the community's values. Where there is, as with euthanasia, reasonable disagreement about just what those values (the value of respect for life, for instance) require, it should try to avoid taking a stand that requires some citizens to act against their consciences. But this will not always be possible. Sometimes the law will have either to allow what some citizens firmly believe to be a public wrong or to declare as a public wrong what some citizens firmly believe to be permissible (or to be a private matter that should not concern the law)— when both sides to the controversy found their beliefs on a not unreasonable interpretation of the value at stake. In such instances, what the law says to those who dissent from the stand it takes is not simply and unqualifiedly that the conduct in question is wrong, but rather that this is now the community's authoritative view. Even if they dissent from its content, they have an obligation as members of the community to accept its authority—to obey the law, even if they are not persuaded by its content, unless and until they can secure a change in it through the normal political process.[40]

As for *mala prohibita*, we cannot simply say that these are wrong only qua prohibited by the law,[41] and thus that the law does now offer the citizens genuinely content-independent reasons for *obeying* its prohibitions or requirements. This is straightforwardly true in instances in which the citizens would have *no* reason to refrain from or to engage in the kind of conduct in question were it not for the law that prohibits or requires such conduct. If, for example, the law did not require me to display a tax disc or an inspection sticker on my car, I would have no reason to do so. Even in these instances, the law's requirements must be justifiable to those on whom they are imposed, in terms of their contribution to some aspect of the common good. Citizens should obey the law not *just* because it is the law, but because it marks a reasonable attempt by the legislature to serve the common good. In other instances, however, what might formally count as *mala prohibita* should be seen as more or less artificial *determinationes* of genuine *mala in se*.

It is an offense to drive at forty miles an hour on a road subject to a thirty-mile-an hour speed limit, or to drive with more than the legally permitted proportion of alcohol in one's blood. These are *mala prohibita*, in that such conduct might not be either criminal or wrongful independently of the law that prohibits it. Depending on the conditions and the driver's skill, driving at forty miles an hour in that context might not be dangerous; that amount of alcohol might not impair a particular driver's capacity or commitment to drive safely. If such laws are to be justified, however, it must also be true that *most* instances of the kinds of conduct they render criminal would be wrongful independently of the law: that driving in excess of the specified speed limit would usually be dangerous, that most drivers with that much alcohol in their blood would be less able or willing to drive safely, and thus that most of those who engaged in the prohibited conduct would be acting wrongfully in that they would be exposing others to unreasonable risks of harm.[42]

Now there are obvious practical reasons for formulating the law in this way, rather than simply declaring it to be an offense to drive at a dangerously high speed or to drive if one's capacities are impaired by alcohol (kinds of conduct that are wrongful independently of the law). Formulating the law in this way makes it easier to enforce the law by making it easier to obtain convictions and also, in effect, forbids drivers to try to decide for themselves whether they can safely drive at such a speed or after consuming that much alcohol—decisions that are notoriously fallible.[43] However, the law's message to the citizen is now more complex than it is for the central *mala in se*. Rather than simply declaring that certain kinds of conduct, which citizens should already recognize as wrongful, constitute public wrongs, it requires citizens to accept certain legal constraints on their conduct—to obey the law's own definitions of safe and permissible driving rather than deciding for themselves what is safe.

I will not try to discuss here the proper scope of *mala prohibita* in the criminal law—either of pure *mala prohibita* or of those that provide artificial *determinationes* of *mala in se*. My aim is simply to indicate some of the ways in which the criminal law does properly claim authority over the citizens' conduct, by rendering criminal kinds of conduct that might not otherwise be wrongful, and thus also to indicate the different kinds of 'wrongdoing' with which the criminal law is concerned. In the simplest instances, of actions that uncontroversially constitute central *mala in se*, a crime is wrongful independently of the criminal law, and the charge against the offender is not so much that he 'broke the law' as that he committed a wrong that properly counts as a public wrong in the sense explained above. In other instances, however, the charge is at least in part that he broke a law that, as a citizen, he had an obligation to obey: that he flouted the law's precise definition of a *malum in se*; that he committed a *malum prohibitum* in breach of a law designed to serve some aspect of the common good; or that he acted on his own judgment of whether his conduct was safe rather than accepting the law's authoritative guidance.

4.5. A Limited Criminal Law

Although I have not tried to say anything determinate about the scope of the criminal law of a liberal polity, in relation either to *mala in se* or to *mala prohibita*, we should note that such a polity will set strict limits to the reach of its criminal law.

One fear aroused in liberal minds by communitarian talk of 'community' in the political realm is that it could encourage oppressive attempts to coerce members into conformity with some all-embracing set of values—and thus sanction the use of the criminal law to enforce all aspects of the community's morality. Now it is true that, on the account I have sketched, the criminal law aims to 'enforce morality' in the sense that, at least in relation to *mala in se*, it defines conduct as criminal because it is immoral—because it is inconsistent with the central moral values of the political community. However, *any* morally plausible account of the criminal law will portray it as 'enforcing morality' in this sense (see MacCormick 1982). The question is not whether it should do so, but which aspects of what morality it should enforce; and a liberal communitarian can agree with other kinds of liberal that it should enforce only the essential aspects of a liberal political morality.

As we have seen (sec. 2.2, above), a liberal political community is a *limited* community, which does not aim to embrace all aspects of its members' lives. Such a community is structured by the central values of individual autonomy, freedom, privacy, and pluralism. It follows from this that its shared, public morality will be similarly limited in scope, and will be oriented around those values. Furthermore, those very values will give the community reason not to use the criminal law to give force to all aspects of that morality: to use it only as a weapon of last resort. The criminal law, as a set of authoritative declarations and demands, need not in principle infringe autonomy: for it offers the citizens reasons to accept its demands and leaves them to decide, as autonomous agents, whether to accept those reasons (though we have yet to ask whether punishment infringes autonomy). But a polity committed to allowing its citizens as extensive as possible a sphere of freedom and privacy in which to determine and lead their own lives will thus also be committed to limiting as far as possible the extent to which the criminal law intrudes into their lives. This commitment will be reinforced by a recognition of the potential for oppression and abuse that is intrinsic to any human system of criminal justice.

The limits a liberal polity sets on the reach of the criminal law will be of two kinds. One concerns the *scope* of the criminal law—the conduct that it will define or prohibit as criminal. It will extend beyond the central *mala in se* that typically involve serious wrongs done to individual rights and interests to cover offenses against social goods and important social institutions, such as corruption, tax evasion, and perjury. It will include minor as well as serious offenses. Many traffic offenses, for instance, are minor, but are properly criminal insofar as they constitute (relatively minor) kinds of wrongdoing that, since they do not typically harm identifiable individuals, are best dealt with by the criminal law. It will include a range of *mala prohibita*, of the two kinds indicated above, though many of these will be minor offenses.[44] It will include a range of 'nonconsummate' offenses, involving conduct that does not actually cause but is liable to cause some relevant kind of criminal harm.[45] However, it will criminalize only conduct that attacks or injures or threatens important individual rights or interests, or social goods and interests that cannot otherwise be adequately protected.[46]

The other kind of limit concerns the *depth* of the criminal law: the extent to which the law's definitions of offenses, and the courts' inquiries into guilt, should be concerned with agents' underlying motives, attitudes, and moral character. One aspect of the privacy that a liberal polity accords its members is privacy of thought and feeling: hence the familiar slogans that the criminal law should not punish 'mere thoughts' or attitudes and should not be concerned with citizens' general moral character. Such slogans are neither clear nor uncontroversial (see Husak 1998; Duff 1996b, chs. 7, 9.1, 11.4.), but they gesture towards another significant limit on a liberal criminal law. The criminal law, we can say, should be concerned only with *actions* that attack, injure, or threaten some legally protected interest; and while 'action' in this context involves more than 'external' bodily movements and their circumstances and consequences (since it includes the intentions and attitudes manifest in the agent's conduct), it involves less than the agent's entire moral character (see Duff 1996b, chs. 7, 9–11).

I have more to say about these limits below—especially the second, which is important in the context of punishment. But first there is another issue that must be considered.

However strict the limits that a liberal polity sets on the scope and depth of its criminal law, that law will claim to be binding on some who do not accept it—on some who do not share or actively reject the values that the law embodies. It will claim to bind them as members of the political community regardless of whether they wish to be, or see themselves as, members of that community: for membership of a political community is not typically voluntary (see sec. 2.1, above). But how can such a claim be justified?

5. Nonvoluntary Membership

I said (in sec. 2.2, above) that members of a liberal polity constitute a community insofar as they aspire, and know that they aspire, to share the defining values of the community and to hold an appropriate regard for one another in the light of those values. I also discussed (in sec. 3.3, above) what is involved in recognizing oneself as a member of a community, in fellowship with others. A community can exist only if *most* of its members recognize themselves as members of it and share in those values and aspirations. The law speaks to such members in what they can hear as their own voice—in terms of values to which they are already committed and of what they owe to others whom they already recognize as their fellow citizens. Sometimes, in defining *mala in se*, the law reminds them of normative demands by which they already recognize that they are bound—though given the various kinds of moral weakness to which we are prone, such formal public reminders can play a useful motivational role. Sometimes, in creating *mala prohibita*, the law imposes new duties on them. But they can recognize that those duties bind them insofar as they are designed to serve a common good that they see as theirs. For such members, the law is indeed their 'common' law (see sec. 4.2, above).

Ideally, *all* members of a liberal political community would see themselves as members in this way. All would be 'voluntary' members—not because they *choose* to be members (see sec. 3.3, above) but because they recognize or identify themselves as members. But, although what I sketch in this chapter is an *ideal* conception of political community, of what a liberal polity *ought* to be, it would be dishonest to dispose of the problem of political and legal obligation simply by saying that, ideally, all citizens would recognize and accept their political and legal obligations because they would see themselves as members of the political community. Any actual human polity will include some people who do *not* recognize or accept the normative bonds of community—the demands by which they are, supposedly, bound as members of the polity. Even an ideal account of political community must have something to say about whether and how such people are nonetheless bound by those demands. It must, that is, have something to say about political obligation, as a kind of obligation that can bind even those who reject it.[47]

There are of course different species of rejection or nonacceptance. In particular, we should distinguish those who reject the values of a political community because they are committed to some opposing set of political values from those who reject (or do not accept) them because they have no such commitment at all—that is, because they have no commitment to any values or concerns extending beyond their individual self-interest or beyond the interests of some smaller group to which they recognize themselves as belonging (a family, a sect, a self-defining collective, or whatever). In an authentically liberal polity, structured by such values as autonomy, freedom, and pluralism, there might be few dissenters of either kind—for as we have seen, the demands of political community will be relatively modest, and consistent with a plurality of specific conceptions of human good; membership of the political community will be consistent with membership of a range of other communities; and there will be room for substantial disagreement even about the community's central and defining goods, so long as there is agreement on how such disagreements are to be dealt with. But there will no doubt still be some dissenters of both kinds. We must therefore ask what, if anything, can be said to them to justify the claim that they are still bound by the normative demands of the political community, whether they like it or not.

Matters would be relatively straightforward if we could make out one of the following four familiar arguments: that they must either accept the bonds of community or leave; that they have (either explicitly or tacitly) consented to those bonds; that as rational beings they are bound, on pain of demonstrable irrationality, to accept them; or that to deny those bonds would be to deny their own identities as human beings, since their identities are inescapably bound up with their membership of the political community. But none of these arguments can succeed. I do not discuss the reasons why they fail here, since my main concern is with what can be said to dissenters if we accept that these arguments do fail. But I should indicate briefly why I think they fail.

The first argument can succeed only when departure from the community is a genuine option. But in modern societies it often is not. For some groups or individuals emigration might be possible, if they can find a place in another society more in tune with their beliefs; some groups might be able (and should be enabled) to constitute themselves as separate, more or less independent, political communities. But for many, neither emigration nor independence is a realistic possibility; nor can a liberal polity justly say to them that they must either accept the normative bonds of community or become outlaws who owe nothing to and can claim nothing from the polity.

The second argument fails for similar reasons. Dissenters are hardly likely to give their explicit consent to bonds that they claim to reject; and while 'tacit' consent can sometimes be properly inferred from or constituted by a failure to dissent or to leave, that is true only if departure is a genuine possibility. We cannot properly say to a dissenter who had no choice about entering the community (since she was born into it), and who can leave the community (if she can leave it at all) only at very significant cost, that by not leaving she tacitly consents to be bound by the community's norms.[48]

The third argument could succeed only if we could show that some moral demands are demands of reason itself, which it would be demonstrably irrational to reject, and that the normative demands of an appropriate kind of political community are included among or can be derived from those demands. Philosophers have often tried to show something like this, but the effort is doomed to failure. Someone who is quite unmoved by *any* kind of moral consideration might indeed be lacking in reason (as psychopaths are said to be). But such a person is not even subject to the demands of morality, since he cannot understand them; and while those who either reject or remain deaf to particular moral demands may be criticized as misguided or immoral, they cannot generally be convicted of a failure of reason.

The fourth argument has appealed to some communitarians.[49] It would be sound if our identities were indeed inescapably bound up with our membership of a particular political community. But they need not be. Since political community is partial rather than total, and since we all belong to a variety of other communities within which we can find our identities and our goods, it is possible to detach oneself from the political community without losing one's identity (see sec. 3.1, above).

What then could we say to the dissenters to justify the claim that they are bound by the normative bonds of a liberal political community to which, as we see it, we and they belong? We can speak to them as we can speak to anyone who fails or refuses to recognize a moral demand that we take to be binding on them as it is on us. If people are unmoved by the needs of strangers, we can appeal to them to recognize the others as fellow human beings. If they are unmoved by the sufferings of other animals, we can appeal to them to recognize the animals as their fellow creatures (see Diamond 1978). In both instances, we try to find ways of bringing them to recognize a certain kind of fellowship and to accept the moral demands that it makes. So too

with political community. We can do no more and no less than to try to persuade them to recognize their fellowship as citizens with the other members
of the polity.

This involves appealing to them to recognize these others as fellows in a
community that they did not choose to join but in which they find themselves,[50] and to accept as theirs the values of that community—as values that
are worthy of their acceptance. Such appeals may, like any moral appeal, fail.
Those to whom we appeal may remain deaf or unpersuaded, and we may not
be able to show that they are irrational in doing so. We must regret such a
failure, but it does not render illegitimate or unjustified our insistence that
they ought to be persuaded—that they ought to recognize this fellowship
and accept these values. Nor does it disallow us from criticizing their conduct
in the light of the fellowship and the values that they do not accept.

Are we then trying, illegitimately, to 'impose' our own values on them?
Not necessarily. We are certainly trying to bring them to accept values that
we think are binding on them as they are on us; and our attempt might be
forceful and persistent. But so long as we appeal to their moral understanding, imagination, and sensibility; so long as we do not use illegitimate methods of deception, manipulation, or coercion to try to persuade them; so
long as we leave it, in the end, to them either to recognize and accept what
we urge on them or to refuse to do so: we are not trying improperly to 'impose' anything on them. We are instead addressing them—as we should—as
responsible moral agents, seeking by appropriate means to persuade them of
what we take to be the truth.

The same is true, in principle, when they are addressed not just by other
individuals but by the law. The law claims to speak with authority—with the
authority of the community's values that it embodies and applies; and while
we are depressingly familiar with the many ways in which claims to authority
can be transformed into exercises of more or less naked power, such claims
need not of their nature be improperly or oppressively coercive. They can
and should still address those to whom they are made as rational and responsible agents, seeking but not coercing their assent. The law of a liberal polity
addresses its citizens in such terms (see sec. 4.1–2, above). It does not merely
assert its power to coerce their obedience, but it seeks their assent to demands that are justified to them in terms of the values that claim their allegiance as members of the political community.

These comments, while true, might seem somewhat disingenuous. The
criminal law does not simply appeal to the citizens to accept its demands. It
inflicts its coercive attentions on those who breach those demands, subjecting them to a process of trial and punishment. In doing this, the law (and the
community in whose name it speaks) is surely involved not just in a rational
moral appeal to defaulting citizens but in an attempt to *coerce* their obedience. We must therefore now turn our attention, at last, to the ways in which
a liberal polity can properly respond to breaches of its criminal law.

6. Responses to Crime

I argued above (sec. 4.3) that to understand crimes as 'public' wrongs is to understand them as wrongs to which the community should respond. I also argued (pp. 27–29) that that response should involve censure. That a community should respond thus to crimes depends not merely on the pragmatic point that the law would otherwise be ineffective in dissuading people from the conduct it condemns or prohibits. It depends on the conceptual point that to mean what we say in condemning some conduct as wrong is to be committed to censuring those who engage in it (assuming that we have the standing to do so), and on the moral point that such a response is owed both to the victims of such wrongs and to their perpetrators.

This is not yet to say that that response must be a *formal* response, administered through an institutionalized system of criminal trials and convictions. The law could in principle make no provision for any such formal response to crime, leaving it to members of the community to respond, informally, for themselves. Or it could provide for systems of 'informal justice' in which local communities can deal through a participatory, informal, nonprofessionalized process with their own wrongs.[51] I say more in the following chapters about the possible role of more participatory and informal processes in a system of punishment (chs. 3.4.2–3, 4.3.2), but for the moment we need simply note that there are good reasons for a liberal polity to provide for a formal response involving something like a system of criminal trials.

A criminal trial calls a citizen to answer a charge of wrongdoing. He is called to answer by and to the community whose law he has allegedly broken, for a 'public' wrong in which the community is properly interested. If the charge is proved against him, he is censured for it by a formal conviction (see Duff 1986, ch. 4). Such a procedure makes clear that the wrong allegedly committed is the concern of the whole political community, and makes it clear to both victims and defendants that they are seen and treated as members of that community—that the community shares in the wrong suffered by the victim (see sec. 4.3, above), and that the defendant is both bound by the community's values and protected by the various rules of the criminal process.

If such a procedure is properly used and applied (and recent experience in both Britain and the United States makes clear how large and important that 'if' is), it also protects both victims and offenders against the various kinds of unreliability that are liable to affect purely informal processes. It ensures that there will be an appropriate response when it is needed, rather than relying on the active sentiments of other members of the community. It ensures that those suspected of crimes are tried fairly, and thus guards against over-hasty findings or assumptions of guilt.

Now a criminal procedure of trial and conviction is coercive in that defendants are likely, not only to be summoned to trial, but also to be forced to attend if they try to avoid it.[52] They cannot be *forced* to answer to the charge or to play any active part in their trial. But they can be forced to be present at the trial and to hear—even if they will not listen to—the verdict. This kind of coercion is, however, consistent with a proper regard for defendants, whether innocent or guilty, as members of the political community. It limits their freedom, but only in accordance with the duty that they have, as citizens, to answer charges properly brought against them. It does not infringe their autonomy, since it is left up to them whether and how to answer the charge and how to respond to their conviction if they are convicted. It respects their privacy, both in that they are not forced to answer or to confess and in that the trial will deal only with the charge that they have committed a public wrong—something that is not a private matter.

But of course the trial and conviction do not mark the end of the criminal law's dealings with offenders. Having been convicted, they are then liable to be punished; and we must thus, finally, face the question whether a system of criminal punishment can be consistent with the values of a liberal political community—whether and how it can still treat those punished as members of the political community.

3

Punishment,
Communication,
and Community

IN CHAPTER 2 I DISCUSSED THE NATURE OF A LIBERAL POLITICAL COMMUNITY as structured by the defining values of autonomy, freedom, privacy, and pluralism; the role of the criminal law in such a polity as defining or creating a range of 'public' wrongs that concern the whole community; and the role of the criminal trial as a process through which members of the community are called to answer for their alleged commissions of such wrongs, and to be publicly censured if those allegations are proved. Such a criminal process treats those subjected to it as members of the political community. They are called to answer for their alleged wrongdoings by a law that claims to be their law—to bind them as members of the community; and the process respects their autonomy, freedom, and privacy.

But what of the punishments that normally follow upon conviction? What role, if any, could they properly play in a liberal polity? More precisely, what role could there be for 'hard treatment', as distinct from purely symbolic, punishment (see p. 29, above)?

1. Can Criminal Punishment Be Consistent with Liberal Community?

We must ask whether criminal punishment can be consistent with liberal community. Can a system of criminal punishment still treat those punished (or threatened with punishment) as full members of the political community? Can criminal punishment be inclusionary rather than exclusionary (see ch. 2.1.2)?

To give this question a sharper focus we should distinguish four interrelated dimensions of inclusion in, or exclusion from, such a community.

1.1. Modes of Inclusion and Exclusion

First, there is *political* inclusion or exclusion: the extent to which people can participate in the political process through which the community's governance is organized, its public policies decided, its laws made. There is room for argument about whether such participation should be merely *available*, or should be *required* of citizens. But a liberal polity must be democratic; and while the requirements of 'democracy' are controversial, it must at least provide all citizens with a role in political decisions and a way of making their voices heard in political deliberations—including decisions and deliberations about the laws that are to bind them. People are excluded from the political community insofar as they are, either deliberately or in fact, excluded from such political participation.

Second, there is *material* inclusion or exclusion: the extent to which people can share in the material resources and benefits available within the community—the extent to which they can acquire the resources necessary for a decent human life and for the pursuit of any of the diverse specific goods available in a pluralist society, such as health care, housing, education, employment, and money. We might disagree about what resources should be seen as essential, about how far people should have only equal *opportunities* to try to acquire such resources or equal *guarantees* of being provided with them. But whatever our views on such questions, people are excluded from full membership of the community insofar as they are, either deliberately or in fact, denied fair access to such resources and benefits.

Third, there is *normative* inclusion or exclusion: the extent to which people are treated as sharing in the community's values. To be treated as sharing in a liberal polity's values of autonomy, freedom, and privacy is to be treated in ways consistent with those values: to have one's autonomy, freedom, and privacy fostered and respected by the state and by one's fellow citizens. It is also to be treated as being subject to the demands of those values: to be expected to respect them in one's dealings with others, to be subject to censure if one flouts them. People are excluded from the normative community insofar as they are treated, either deliberately or in fact, as if these values did not apply to them—as if their autonomy, freedom, or privacy were unimportant or as if they did not share in the obligations flowing from these values.

Fourth, there is *linguistic* inclusion or exclusion: the extent to which people share—can understand and speak—the language in which the public or political life of the community is conducted. A normative political community must be a linguistic community. Its members might speak different languages in their private, nonpolitical lives, but they must share a normative language embodying their shared values in which they can discuss and conduct their activities as a political community—and in which they can articulate and develop those values themselves. This requirement underpins the possibility of both political and normative inclusion. I can participate in the political process only if it is conducted in a language I can understand and speak; and I can be bound by a community's values only if I can understand and speak the language of those values. People are included in a political community insofar as they can understand and speak its normative language and are addressed in that language. They are excluded insofar as that language is alien to them, like a foreign language that they can neither understand nor speak for themselves, or insofar as they are not addressed in that language by their fellow citizens or by the state.

Now punishment as practiced in our existing systems of criminal justice is very often exclusionary in all these ways—either as itself excluding, or fostering the exclusion of, those who are punished or as reflecting exclusions that they are already suffering. In Britain, those serving terms of imprisonment suffer formal political exclusion by being denied the right to vote. More generally, many of those who are punished feel that they have no part in the political process or in discussions of penal policy—which are typically conducted in terms of what 'we', the law-abiding, should do about 'them', the criminals.[1] Many offenders have already suffered various kinds of material exclusion, and their punishments (especially imprisonment), apart from such material deprivations as they directly involve, often lead to further exclusion—for instance, from the chance of employment. Offenders are normatively included in that they are punished for breaches of laws by which they are supposedly bound. But apart from the infringements of autonomy, freedom, and privacy often intrinsic to their punishment (especially, again, imprisonment), the administration of their punishment often displays little regard for those values. Finally, offenders are often linguistically excluded. They are excluded, for instance, insofar as their trial is an alien process that they cannot understand and in which they can play no real part (see, e.g., Baldwin & McConville 1977, ch. 5) and insofar as, given the content of their punishment and the context and manner of its imposition, the language in which they can understand it as addressing them is not that of legitimate authority but that of brute power (see, e.g., Mathiesen 1990, ch. 3).[2]

The question is, however, whether this *must* be so. Must criminal punishment be in its nature exclusionary? To many, the answer is obviously "Yes": given which, some argue that punishment is nonetheless justified, since offenders 'forfeit' the rights or moral standing of citizenship (see ch. 1.3.1); and others argue that punishment is therefore unjustifiable, since it is inconsistent with true community (see Bianchi 1994; also Christie 1981; Hulsman 1991). I believe, however, that criminal punishment could and should be inclusionary, as something that we can do, not to a 'them' who are implicitly excluded from the (law-abiding) community of citizens, but to *ourselves* as full, if imperfect, members of that community.

1.2. Exclusionary Punishments

Some kinds of punishment are indeed intrinsically exclusionary, and are objectionable for just that reason. Two simple examples can illustrate this point and also clarify the force of the question whether punishment could be inclusionary.

Suppose, first, that the sole purpose of a given kind of punishment was to incapacitate offenders, temporarily or permanently, from committing further crimes. Now if people were liable to such punishment only when they had culpably committed a crime, they would be treated as citizens until that point. The law would speak to them, as it must speak to members of a liberal polity, in terms of values binding on them as members of the community. But it would leave them free, as a liberal polity that respects autonomy must leave its citizens free, to decide for themselves whether or not to offend. Once they had committed a crime, however, they would be treated not as members of the community but as dangerous enemies against whom 'we', the law-abiding, must protect ourselves by incapacitating them. The law (and those in whose name it speaks and acts) now abandons the attempt to guide their future conduct by appealing to them to accept its normative demands—demands flowing from the values of the community to which they belong. Indeed, it abandons the attempt to *guide* their future conduct at all, seeking instead merely to constrain it by force. But this is to cease to treat them as autonomous, responsible citizens of a liberal polity. Respect for another as an autonomous agent does not preclude the attempt to persuade her to behave as we think she should behave. We can offer her what we take (and hope that she will see) to be good reasons for refraining from crime. We can insist that she ought thus to refrain, and forcefully criticize her if she does not. Nor does it preclude preventing her, if necessary by force, from carrying through a crime on which she has already embarked. Defensive force can be an appropriate response to another's attempted wrongdoing (see Duff 1986, 227). But it does preclude an attempt to *incapacitate* her from *future* wrongdoing. Apart from the fact that incapacitation will also typically incapacitate the person from quite legitimate activities, it deprives her of the ability to determine her own conduct in the light of her own grasp of reasons for action—an ability that is crucial to autonomous agency. To subject offenders to purely incapacitative punishment is thus to exclude them from the normative community—to cease to treat them as citizens whose autonomy must be respected (see Dubber 1995).[3]

Suppose, second, that the sole purpose of punishment was rational deterrence: to provide potential offenders with prudential reason to obey the law. Such a penal system could be appropriate for a society (if one could be imagined) of rational egoists, who all realize that they will benefit from a social contract that includes penalty clauses whose sole point is to give self-interested agents prudential reason to obey its terms. But it is not appropriate for a liberal political community. The law of that community, as its common law, must address its members in terms of the values it embodies—values to which they should, as members of the community, already be committed. It portrays criminal conduct as wrongful in terms of those values; and the reasons that citizens have to refrain from such conduct, the reasons to which the law refers and on which it depends, are precisely the moral reasons that make such conduct wrong. A purely deterrent law, however, addresses those whom it seeks to deter, not in terms of the communal values that it aims to protect, but simply in the brute language of self-interest. It thus addresses them, not as members of the normative community of citizens, but as threatening outsiders against whom the community must protect itself. It implicitly excludes them from membership of the citizen community by no longer addressing them in terms of that community's values.[4]

This is not yet to say that deterrence can have *no* proper role in a liberal polity. There are certainly some kinds of community in which deterrence has no proper place—in which it would be inconsistent with the normative character of the community. Consider, for instance, someone who uses deterrent threats to try to modify a friend's or a spouse's behavior or to try to bully his academic colleagues into accepting the policies he favors. But this does not yet show that a liberal political community could not have a system of punishment whose function is *partly* deterrent (see sec. 3, below). It shows only that such a community cannot consistently operate a *purely* deterrent system of punishment.

These two justifications of punishment render it inconsistent with liberal political community.[5] Is there any account of its justification and its purpose that would render it consistent with such community?

2. Punishment and Communication

The most promising starting point for an argument that punishment can be consistent with liberal political community is a communicative conception of punishment as communicating to offenders the censure that their crimes deserve (see ch. 1.4.4).

2.1. Communication and Expression

Although some theorists talk of the 'expressive' purpose of punishment (see ch. 1, n.30), we should rather talk of its communicative purpose: for communication involves, as expression need not, a *reciprocal* and *rational* engagement.

Expression requires only one who expresses. If there is (as there need not be) someone at whom it is directed, that person need figure only as its passive object or recipient; and if it aims (as it need not) to bring about any effect on its recipient, that intended effect could be entirely nonrational—it need not be mediated by the recipient's reason or understanding. By contrast, communication requires someone to or with whom we try to communicate. It aims to engage that person as an active participant in the process who will receive and respond to the communication, and it appeals to the other's reason and understanding—the response it seeks is one that is mediated by the other's rational grasp of its content. Communication thus addresses the other as a rational agent, whereas expression need not.

2.2. Communication and the Criminal Law

The criminal law of a liberal polity, and the criminal process of trial and conviction to which offenders are subjected, are communicative enterprises that address the citizens, as rational moral agents, in the normative language of the community's values.

The criminal law, as the common law of the political community, addresses the citizens in terms of the values that are or should be theirs as citizens. It declares and defines *mala in se*, and creates *mala prohibita*, as public wrongs from which citizens should refrain. In claiming authority over the citizens, it claims that there are good reasons, grounded in the community's values, for them to eschew such wrongs (see ch. 2.4). It speaks to the citizens as members of the normative community. It seeks not just (as might a sovereign) their obedience to its demands, but their understanding and acceptance of what is required of them as citizens.

A criminal trial is also a communicative enterprise in which a citizen is called to answer a charge of wrongdoing and to take part in the process by which that charge is tested (see Duff 1986, ch. 4). If he is convicted, his conviction communicates to him (and to others) the censure that he has been proved to deserve for his crime. He is expected (but not compelled) to understand and accept the censure as justified: to understand and accept that he committed a wrong for which the community now properly censures him. His trial and conviction thus address him and seek a response from him as a member of the political community who is both bound and protected by its laws.

An important aspect of communication in both these contexts is that it aims not merely to secure present understanding and assent but to affect future conduct. In defining certain kinds of conduct as public wrongs, the law seeks to persuade citizens (those who need persuading) to refrain from such conduct. That aim is internal to the law insofar as it consists in such declarations and definitions of wrongs, since to declare certain kinds of conduct to be wrong is to urge those to whom the declarations are addressed to refrain from such conduct. Analogously, convictions seek to persuade offenders to repent their past wrongs and thus to reform their future conduct. They communicate the censure that those wrongs deserve; internal to censure is the intention or hope that the person censured will accept it as justified; and to accept censure as justified is to accept that one did wrong, which entails repenting that wrong and seeing the need to avoid such wrongdoing in future.[6]

To say this is not, however, to posit a *consequentialist* aim for the criminal law or for criminal convictions—to portray them as contingently efficient means to the independently identifiable end of crime-prevention (see ch. 1.1.1). The aim is not simply that citizens refrain from crime or that offenders refrain from repeating their crimes (those aims leave quite open the question of what means we may use to achieve them). It is, rather, that citizens recognize and accept the law's requirements as being justified and refrain from crime for that reason, or that offenders recognize the wrongfulness of their past crimes and refrain from future crimes for that reason. But such an aim also specifies the kind of means by which it can properly be pursued, since it can be achieved only by a process of rational and 'transparent' persuasion (see ch. 2.4.1).

If I try to persuade another person to do what (I think) she morally ought to do, my aim is of course that she should come to do what is right. But if I am to treat her as a moral agent, as a member of the moral community to which we both belong, my aim cannot be simply to find some efficient means of bringing it about that her conduct conforms to what morality requires—that she pays her debt, for instance, or tells the truth. Such an aim could in principle be achieved by deceiving her or bullying her or manipulating her emotions or beliefs—methods that fail to respect her as a moral agent. Nor should we say that, while my aim is indeed the consequentialist aim of modifying her future conduct, there are moral side-constraints on the methods I can use to achieve that aim, which preclude deception, bullying, or manipulation. The demand that I respect her as a moral agent determines the ends I can pursue, as well as the means by which I can properly pursue them. My aim must be that she does what is right *because she sees it to be right*; and intrinsic to that aim is a specification of the means by which it can be achieved—that it can be achieved only by a process of rational moral persuasion. If I get her to pay her debt by deception or bullying or manipulation, it is not that I have achieved my aim by improper means (as a 'side-constraint' account would portray it). I have not achieved my proper aim at all.

So too with the criminal law and the criminal process of a liberal polity. If the law is to treat and address the citizens as responsible members of the political community (a community whose defining values include that of autonomy), its aim cannot be merely to bring about that they conform their conduct to the law's requirements. Nor can its aim be to bring that effect about, subject to certain side-constraints on how it is brought about. Its aim must instead be to persuade them to refrain from criminal wrongdoing because they realize that it is wrong. *That* aim can of its nature be achieved only by a communicative process that seeks to bring citizens to recognize and to accept not just that certain kinds of conduct are 'prohibited' by the law (see ch. 2.4.1) but that and why such conduct is wrong.

Furthermore, if a citizen does commit such a wrong, the law should aim to bring him to recognize and to repent that wrongdoing: not just because that is a method of persuading him not to repeat it, but because that is owed both to him and to his victim (see pp. 28–29, above). To take wrongs seriously as wrongs involves responding to them with criticism and censure; and the aim internal to censure is that of persuading the wrongdoer to recognize and repent his wrongdoing. This is not to say that we should censure a wrongdoer only when we believe that there is some chance of thus persuading him. We may think that we owe it to his victim, to the values he has flouted, and even to him, to censure his wrongdoing even if we are sure that he will be unmoved and unpersuaded by the censure. But our censure still takes the form of an attempt (albeit what we believe is a futile attempt) to persuade him.

2.3. Punishment, Communication, and Hard Treatment

What then of punishment? It *can* communicate censure (see ch. 1.4.4), and in so doing it addresses offenders as members of the normative community. It calls on them, as do criminal convictions, to recognize that they have done wrong. It addresses them as citizens who are both bound and protected by the community's values. But censure can be expressed by a formal conviction, or by a purely symbolic punishment that burdens the offender only insofar as she takes its message of censure seriously. Why then should we express it through the kinds of hard treatment punishment that our existing penal systems impose—punishments that are burdensome or painful independently of their communicative content?

There are two ways in which we could try to answer this question. One justifies penal hard treatment in communicative terms. We should use hard treatment punishments of certain kinds because they can serve the communicative aims of punishment more adequately than can mere convictions or symbolic punishments; a communicative conception of punishment thus provides its *complete* justification. The other accepts that the hard treatment dimension of punishment cannot be justified in communicative terms. It is not *necessary* to the adequate communication of deserved censure, and must thus be justified in other terms—in particular in terms of deterrence. I argue for an account of the former kind later in this chapter, but first attend to two accounts of the latter kind.

3. Communication, Deterrence, and Prudential Supplements

A *purely* deterrent system of punishment is inconsistent with the values of a liberal polity (see sec. 1.2, above). It fails to address those punished, or those threatened with punishment, as members of the normative political community. However, this leaves open the possibility of arguing that hard treatment punishment can be justified in *partly* deterrent terms.

3.1. Communication Plus Deterrence

Suppose we insist, as I have argued, that the criminal law, the criminal process, and punishment itself must be initially understood in communicative terms. The law declares certain kinds of conduct to be wrong, and to be avoided for that reason. Convictions formally censure proved offenders for their wrongdoings. Punishment also communicates that censure to them. But when we ask why that censure should be communicated through *hard treatment* punishments, the answer is that such hard treatment adds to the law's initial moral appeal a prudential, deterrent incentive for obedience (see, e.g., Feinberg 1970; von Hirsch 1985, ch. 5).

Ideally, in communities more virtuous than our own, that moral appeal would suffice by itself. Citizens would generally refrain from crime because they saw it to be wrong, and any citizens who did occasionally succumb to criminal temptation would need no more than a formal censure to remind them of the error of their ways. But in societies more like our own, whose members are not so wholeheartedly committed to its central values, such methods of purely moral persuasion would be intolerably ineffective: not because they would not prevent *all* crime—for a liberal society must accept a certain level of crime as the price of freedom—but because they would not prevent *enough* crime to preserve the very social structures within which autonomy and freedom can be protected and individuals can pursue their own goods.

Surely, then, it is consistent with—indeed required by—the values of such a community to use penal hard treatment as a deterrent for those who would not otherwise obey the law. So long as punishment still communicates the censure that the wrongdoer deserves, it still addresses those who are punished or threatened with punishment (those who would not obey the law without that deterrent threat) as members of the political community—as members whose commitment to the community's values is deficient. They share in the protection that an effective criminal law provides. If they are not willing to guide their own conduct by the values that the law protects, it is legitimate to try to persuade them to behave as they should by offering them prudential reasons that will motivate them.

This account is not, however, consistent with the ideal of a liberal political community. For the law addresses those whom it threatens with punishment, not just in the appropriate language of the communal values in which it is grounded, but in the coercive language of deterrence. But this is to cease to address them as members of the normative community (and note how easy it is now to talk of what 'we' must do to deter 'them' from breaking the law). Admittedly, it *began* by addressing them in the appropriate terms of the values it embodies and protects. But when that moral appeal fails, it turns instead to the inappropriate, coercive language of threats. It is as if, when my attempt to persuade you to do what you ought to do by offering you relevant moral reasons fails, I try instead to coerce you into conformity by threats. But that is to abandon what should be my proper aim in trying to persuade you, and to cease to treat you as a moral agent (see sec. 2.2, above).

It might be argued in response to this objection that such a qualified system of deterrent punishments does still respect those whom it punishes or threatens (see Lipkin 1988; Baker 1992b). Its threats are addressed not to those citizens who accept and respect the values it embodies (*they* do not need deterring) but to those who do not share those values, or do not care for them sufficiently to be dissuaded from crime. It addresses such people in terms of their own values, by offering them what they will see as good reason to refrain from crime. It thus addresses them as rational agents, by offering them reasons for compliance; and as autonomous agents, by appealing to their own values. Admittedly it does not address them as members of the normative community that shares the values embodied in the law. But they are not members of that community, if membership involves accepting its values. We should instead recognize that they are, as far as that normative community is concerned, outsiders to whom we must speak, as a deterrent system of punishment speaks, in a language to which they will be willing to listen. Such a system of deterrent punishments recognizes the limits of normative community, and respects the autonomy of those who do not see themselves as belonging to such a community.

There are three initial objections to this argument. First, it (re)creates a conception of 'us' and 'them'. 'We', who accept and are motivated by the values embodied in the law, must find a way of persuading 'them', who do not accept or are insufficiently motivated by those values. However, apart from the question whether it is *morally* appropriate to see potential offenders in this light, we must ask whether it is *empirically* plausible to portray them thus. No doubt some actual and potential offenders are estranged from the values that the law embodies. They have no serious regard for those values, either because they are committed to other conflicting values or because they care much more for their own self-interest than for any such other-directed values. But we must surely recognize (especially if we attend to the full range of crimes and of criminal motivations) that many actual and potential offenders do to some significant extent share in those values. What leads or tempts them to crime is not that they have no serious regard for those values but that their regard is not wholehearted, or consistent, or always sufficient to overcome the temptations of self-interest. They—or rather *we*, since these comments surely apply to many of us—are not wholly deaf to the law's moral appeal, though we do not attend to it consistently or carefully enough. So should the law really abandon that moral appeal in favor of the brute language of deterrence?

Second, those against whom punishment is threatened must still be normatively bound by the laws that the threat of punishment is to persuade them to obey. We are not dealing here with a cold war between strangers, in which such peace as exists is preserved only by deterrent threats. Nor are we dealing with the mere oppression of one group by another that seeks to enforce obedience to its will by threats. We are dealing with how a political

community should respond to crimes committed by those who are normatively bound by its laws. However, I can be bound by the law only if I am a
member of the community whose law it is (see p. 44, and sec. 1.1, above). To
cease to treat me as a member of that normative community by ceasing to address me in terms of its values thus undermines the claim that I am normatively bound by those values or obligated (as distinct from coercively
obliged) by its laws. But that then undermines the justification for punishing
me or threatening me with punishment.

Third, the argument obscures a crucial distinction: between *pointing out*
reasons that already exist and that might persuade the person to whom I
point them out; and *creating* new reasons by which I aim to coerce her. If we
could show that obedience to the law was, independently of any threat of
punishment, in the self-interest even of those insufficiently impressed by its
moral appeal, we *might* then offer them that reason for obeying the law. So
too, if I am trying to persuade you to do what you ought to do, and you are insufficiently impressed by the moral reasons I offer, I *might* then point out (if it
is true) that it would also serve your self-interest to act thus. It is not clear
that this kind of persuasion can be morally appropriate. But we need not settle that issue here, since this is not the kind of persuasion that is involved in a
system of deterrent punishment. Such a system does not remind those whom
it threatens with punishment of *preexisting* prudential reasons that they already have to obey the law. Instead, it creates a *new* reason—the threat of
punishment—to make it in their interest to obey laws that they would otherwise have no such reason to obey. But this is no longer to address them as autonomous agents, in a language to which they will listen. It is to seek to *coerce*
their obedience by threats that treat them like "dog[s] instead of with the
freedom and respect due to [them]" as moral agents (Hegel [1821] 1942, 246).

It might still be claimed that such a qualified deterrent account of punishment marks a realistic recognition of the limits of community—of the extent
to which our own societies fall short of constituting genuine normative communities whose members all share in their defining values. This is the best
we can do (and the least we must do) in societies in which the normative
bonds of community are insufficient to keep the peace upon which a tolerable social life and the very possibility of community depend—societies in
which some people do not see themselves as members of such a normative
community at all, while others are only tenuously or inconstantly committed
to its values.

I say more about this argument in section 8, below, since it gains part of its
force from objections to the account that I defend. There is, however, another way of explaining the hard treatment dimension of punishment as
offering citizens prudential reasons to obey the law, which might avoid
the objections made here to portraying hard treatment punishment as a
deterrent.

3.2. Censure and Prudential Supplements

The problem with the qualified deterrent account discussed in section 3.1, above, is that it *replaces* the law's initial moral appeal to the citizens by the brute language of threats. When moral persuasion, appealing to the values in which the law is grounded, fails, we turn instead to deterrent threats. Perhaps, however, we can still find room for a system of modest deterrents *within* a system of communicative punishments whose primary aim is to convey the censure that criminals deserve.

Most of us are to some degree sensitive to moral considerations, but also morally weak and fallible. All too often, if the only available motives for right action are moral motives, we fail to act as we should. If I am aware of my moral weakness, I might offer myself further incentives to right action. I might promise myself some modest reward for doing my duty or threaten myself with some modest penalty for failing, or I might think of the welcome praise I will receive from others for acting rightly or the unwelcome condemnation I would receive for acting wrongly. That I need these prudential incentives to right action is a sign of my own moral inadequacy. But they can surely be appropriate, if less than ideal, ways of motivating myself as an imperfect moral agent. They would be inappropriate if they simply *replaced* the moral reasons that would ideally motivate me, since my action would then be disconnected from the moral reasons that should guide it. But they *supplement*, rather than replace, those moral reasons. First, they are not meant to be sufficient to motivate me by themselves: they are meant to provide a further reason for acting in accordance with the moral reasons by which I am still, albeit insufficiently, motivated. Second, what makes them motivationally effective is not merely their character as benefits or harms from a perspective of pure self-interest, but their character as *deserved* rewards or penalties, as *deserved* praise or criticism: they thus retain an essential connection to the moral reasons by which I would ideally be motivated.

Von Hirsch and Narayan offer an analogous rationale for penal hard treatment, as giving moral but imperfect beings like ourselves an appropriate prudential supplement to the moral reasons on which the law primarily depends.[7] We express the censure that offenders deserve through hard treatment, rather than merely by formal convictions or symbolic punishments, because this provides an additional, prudential incentive to refrain from crime. But this is to supplement, not replace, the moral force of the censure. The language of deterrence in which penal hard treatment speaks is to add motivating force to, not to replace or drown, the moral language of censure in which punishment must still speak.[8]

One merit of this account is that it avoids the exclusionary conception of offenders as a 'them' against whom 'we' must protect ourselves. Punishment, as a system of prudentially supplemented censure, is something that we can plausibly threaten against and impose on *ourselves*, as moral agents who recognize our own moral weaknesses, to help us to act as we know we should. It addresses potential offenders not as outsiders, whose membership of the normative community is thus cast in doubt, but as fellow members of that community who are still within the reach of its values—who can be expected to listen to those values, even if they are also (like all of us) often prone not to attend to them. As for the Hegelian objection that such a system of punishment treats those whom it threatens "like dogs" by creating new and inappropriately coercive reasons to obey the law, we can admit that it falls short of the ideal of moral persuasion that would appeal only to the values in which the law is grounded. We could argue, however, that that objection assumes an oversimplified dichotomy—as if we must treat people either *merely* "like dogs" by using *only* threats to secure their obedience or as *purely* moral agents, offering them *only* relevant moral reasons to refrain from crime; and that we should instead treat people (including ourselves) as what they are— as moral but imperfect beings who need prudential incentives to strengthen their often weak moral wills.

Another merit of this account, for liberals who want to constrain the coercive powers of the state, is that it sets relatively modest aims for the penal system. It is not vastly ambitious about preventing crime; it recognizes that the preventive efficacy of any morally tolerable penal system will be limited (see von Hirsch 1993, 40–46). Nor does it aim to bring about ambitious moral changes, such as repentance and reform, in offenders. Punishment as censure gives offenders the *opportunity* to listen to the law's moral voice and so to repent their crimes and seek their own moral reform. But it does not find its justifying purpose in an attempt to elicit (or coerce) such moral responses (see von Hirsch 1993, ch. 8; Narayan 1993, 174–75). More ambitious theories might seek to "plant the flag of truth within the fortress of a rebel soul" (Lewis 1940, 83; see Hampton 1992a, 1), but for liberals that is not a proper task for the state. Punishment gives offenders an opportunity to examine their souls, but should not *invade* them (see sec. 8, below).

Such an account seems most plausible in relation to relatively minor offenses. The fine I would receive for speeding might not by itself, as a purely prudential disincentive, suffice to dissuade me. But as a *punishment*, conveying censure, it could provide a useful and modest supplement to the moral appeal of the law—an appeal to which I am often not sufficiently attentive. It is more problematic, however, in relation to more serious crimes, since there may then be a tension between preserving the communication of censure as the primary aim of punishment and using hard treatment as a prudential supplement that will have some preventive efficacy.

If penal hard treatment is to supplement rather than replace censure, it must not be so harsh that it effectively drowns out the law's moral voice. Von Hirsch (1993, ch. 5) therefore advocates a "decremental strategy" of gradually reducing current sentencing levels towards a system that might allow no prison sentence of more than three years (or five years for homicide). Such a system might well not deter "the most recalcitrant," but it should give "ordinary persons good reasons for compliance" and induce "most people" to refrain from crime—which is the most that a penal system should aim for (1993, 44). But we must ask whether prison sentences of up to three (or five) years can really be seen as *supplements* to the law's moral appeal; and whether punishments modest enough to be mere supplements might not be so ineffective, failing to dissuade many more than "the most recalcitrant," as to fall radically short even of von Hirsch's modest preventive aims.[9]

Although a three- (or five-) year term of imprisonment is dramatically less coercive than the maximum terms imposed under our existing systems, it still seems rather too severe to serve merely as "an aid to carrying out what [the agent] himself recognizes as the proper course of conduct" (von Hirsch 1993, 13). As a prudential "incentive" it would surely replace, rather than merely supplement, the moral voice of censure. But if we really lowered sentence levels to the point at which the hard treatment provided no more than a prudential supplement to censure, there is surely reason to fear that they would be *radically* ineffective in preventing serious crime: indeed, that they would not be significantly more effective than a system of purely symbolic punishments (but see von Hirsch 1999, 71).

To suggest that there is reason to fear this is not of course to say, let alone to show, that such punishments *would* be intolerably ineffective. I do not claim to have proved that the von Hirsch–Narayan account is untenable. Alternatively it might be argued that we cannot avoid some such tension between addressing actual and potential offenders as moral agents and securing even a minimally tolerable level of crime prevention. This kind of account, then, might be the most plausible way of dealing with that tension. But there is another possibility: to provide a more ambitiously communicative account of punishment that justifies penal hard treatment as part of the morally communicative process itself (see p. 82, above). This can best be done by portraying that process as one that aims to bring offenders to repent their crimes and to reform their future conduct.

4. Punishment as Purposive Communication

I argued in section 2.2 above that the criminal law and the criminal process should be communicative enterprises in which the law engages with the citizens—in which, if the law is genuinely a common law, the citizens engage as a political community with themselves (see ch. 2.4.2.). As communicative enterprises, they serve aims to which they are internally rather than merely instrumentally related. The law aims to dissuade citizens from crime by declaring certain kinds of conduct to constitute public wrongs. Such declarations are not merely instrumental means to the independently identifiable goal of 'preventing' crime, to be assessed in terms of their consequential cost-effectiveness. They are intrinsically appropriate to the law's proper aim of persuading citizens to refrain from crime because they realize that they should. Similarly, criminal convictions aim to bring offenders to recognize and repent their crimes by censuring them for those crimes. That is an aim internal to censure as an appropriate response to the wrongdoing of a responsible moral agent.

We can justify punishment in a similar way: as a communicative enterprise focused on the past crime, as that for which the censure that punishment communicates is deserved; but also looking to a future aim to which it is related, not merely contingently as an instrumental technique, but internally as an intrinsically appropriate means. We can thus provide a unitary justification of punishment (rather than one which, like those discussed in section 3, above, appeals both to a retributivist notion of censure and to a consequentialist concern for crime-prevention) that which will undercut the traditional opposition between retributivist or backward-looking and consequentialist or forward-looking theories. Punishment will now look both back (as retributivists insist it must) to a past crime as that which merits this response, and forward (as consequentialists insist it must) to some future good that it aims to achieve. But these two perspectives will not be separate and potentially conflicting, as they are on familiar kinds of 'mixed' theory (see ch. 1.2), since the claim will be that the punishment that is deserved for the past crime is itself the intrinsically appropriate way of pursuing the forward-looking goals that punishment should serve.

We can clarify this (perhaps still somewhat obscure) possibility by looking briefly at the suggestion that punishment should be justified as a mode of moral education.

4.1. Punishment as Moral Education?

The idea that wrongdoing manifests a species of ignorance is as old as Plato (see, e.g., the *Gorgias*). Those who do wrong, who commit what are properly defined as crimes, can do so only because they are ignorant of or mistaken about the good. Anyone who really recognized and understood the good would thereby be sufficiently motivated to refrain from wrongdoing. So perhaps we could portray punishment (at least in ideal theory) as a mode of moral (re-)education, aimed at remedying the offender's moral ignorance.[10]

Two features of such accounts are particularly important for my present purposes. First, they portray crime (in a well-ordered polity, in which crimes are indeed genuine wrongs) as manifesting some defect in the offender: not some pathological defect of which the crime is a symptom (as those who argue that criminals need therapy rather than punishment might say), but a *moral* defect that is partly *constituted* by her crime (see Duff 1993, 371–80). That defect might also be portrayed as a defect in the relationships that constitute her moral identity and thus her own good: in her relationships with her fellow citizens and with her community and its values, upon which, from one communitarian perspective, her own identity as a moral agent and her own good depend.[11] Punishment can then be seen as *benefiting* the offender. By repairing the relationships that her crime breached, it restores her to her own good.[12]

This kind of moral paternalism is anathema to traditional liberals who take their stand on Mill's famous principle that "the only purpose for which power can be rightfully exercised over any member of a civilized community against his will, is to prevent harm to others. His own good, either physical or moral, is not a sufficient warrant" (Mill 1859, ch. 1, par. 9). I now think (cf. Duff 1986, 254–66) that this is a sound objection to theories that seek the (or a) justifying *aim* of punishment in the offender's own good. The species of liberal communitarianism that I defended in chapter 2 does not allow us to claim, as such theories must claim, that members of a political community can find their good *only* in allegiance to that community and its values (see ch. 2.5). We can argue that they *ought* to do so—that they ought to recognize their moral fellowship with their fellow citizens and find their own good within the moral structures of that fellowship, and that they owe it to their fellow citizens not to commit themselves to ends that are inconsistent with the bonds of political community. But these are claims about their moral duties, not about what their own good must consist in; and whatever we might think, as moralists, about the Platonic identification of my good with allegiance to the Good, it cannot form part of the normative structure of a liberal polity. However, we should retain some aspects of this picture, particularly the idea that crime involves a breach in or damage to the offender's relationships—both with the direct victim, when there is one, and with the whole normative community—and the idea that we owe it to the offender, as well as to others, to try to repair that breach or that damage rather than excluding the offender from the community.

The second important feature of theories of punishment as moral education concerns the notion of moral reform. Moral education is clearly a species of moral reform: the offender's moral attitudes or character are reformed. But we must be clear what 'reform' means in this context. A simple consequentialist view of punishment as reformative, for instance, portrays 'reform' as an end that can be identified independently of punishment (that the offender's attitudes and dispositions are so modified that he will willingly obey the law) and must then justify punishment as a contingently cost-effective technique for achieving that end. To this view critics object that it treats offenders as objects to be remolded into law-abiding conformity rather than as autonomous, responsible agents (see ch. 1.1.2; ch. 1.2.2). Similarly, if we set out to indoctrinate people, our aim is to bring it about that they come to have the beliefs or attitudes that we want to induce, and to find some contingently cost-effective technique of achieving that end. To this view critics will object that it manipulates offenders, thus failing to respect them as autonomous agents. But moral education, as understood within this kind of account, is a quite different matter. Of course it aims to bring about a change in offenders' attitudes and dispositions—to bring them to accept and care for the values that they have so far failed adequately to grasp. But it aims more precisely to bring them to accept and care for those values *as responsible moral agents,* and *that* aim can be achieved only by methods that address them as responsible moral agents (H. Morris 1981, 265; Hampton 1984, 222). Punishment as moral education thus aims not so much to reform the offender as to persuade offenders that and why they should reform themselves.

Now one crucial question for such theories is that of how punishment, especially hard treatment punishment, could be a method of moral education. I do not pursue this question here, though I answer a similar question about my account in the rest of this chapter. But there are two further aspects of conceptions of punishment as 'moral education' that should, I think, lead us to reject them.

First, it is far from clear that what most offenders need, even if their crimes are genuine wrongs, is moral *education.* Some might indeed think that their crimes are morally justified, or at least permissible, and we might say that they require 'correction' (hence the labeling of punishment as 'correction' in some North American jurisdictions). Even here, however, to say that they need 'education' suggests a paternalist view of them as rather like children who have not yet received the education they need. Such a view might cast doubt on their responsibility for their ill-educated condition, whereas we should see them as responsible moral agents (as our equals) who have taken a wrong moral path. But in many instances it would be wrong to suggest that offenders commit their crimes from moral ignorance or error (see Narayan 1993, 173). The problem is not that they do not realize that what they are doing is wrong but that they do not care enough about it, or fail to attend to that aspect of their conduct, or give in to temptation. They do not need education to teach them what they already know.[13]

Second, it is unclear why punishment, even if it is a *possible* method of moral education, should be the preferred method. The aim of moral education is to bring people to understand that and why certain kinds of conduct are wrong in a way that will motivate them to refrain from such conduct. But there are many possible ways in which we can do this—by argument, by dramatic representations of the nature and effects of such conduct, by sermons, and so on. Why then should we, with offenders, seek to do it by *punishing* them? What justifies attempting to (re-)educate them is admittedly the fact that they have committed a crime. Only then can a liberal state properly intervene with the coercive apparatus of the law. But it does not follow from this, or from the aim of moral education itself, that that intervention must take the form of punishment rather than of some other method of moral education.

The account I offer preserves the idea that punishment should be a communicative enterprise that seeks to persuade wrongdoers of the error of their

ways and to repair the damage done by their crimes to their communal relationships. But it avoids these problems: for it portrays punishment as a matter of correction or persuasion rather than of education; and it shows why that
correction or persuasion should involve punishment—including certain
kinds of hard treatment punishment.

I can best introduce this account by an example, based on the wide variety
of victim-offender mediation programs that have been attracting growing interest from theorists and practitioners of criminal justice. It will strike many
as odd to portray such schemes, as I portray them, as involving punishment.
Not only are they very different from the kinds of punishment—notably imprisonment and fines—that are most salient in our penal practices and in our
existing conceptions of criminal punishment. They are also seen by many of
their advocates precisely as *alternatives* to punishment. However, I sketch a
model of victim-offender mediation that does provide, I argue, an appropriate paradigm of punishment as a communicative enterprise; and although I
do show that we can find a proper place in a communicative penal system for
more familiar kinds of hard treatment punishment, part of my argument is
that we should shift our orthodox paradigms of criminal punishment in this
direction.

4.2. Mediation: Civil versus Criminal

Victim-offender mediation schemes come in a wide variety of forms, related in different ways to the orthodox criminal process.[14] I do not discuss
these variations here. Instead, I set up two simple models, of 'civil' and of
'criminal' mediation. Actual schemes no doubt include elements of each
model, but the contrast between them helps me show how mediation can be
appropriate *as a mode of punishment.*

Civil mediation is a matter of negotiation and compromise, aimed at resolving a conflict between the parties (see ch. 1.5.3). I find myself in conflict
with my neighbor. She objects to my late-night parties, I complain about her
early morning do-it-yourself work. We call on a mediator to help us resolve
our conflict, since we realize that we must find a way of living together, if not
as friends, at least as neighbors. The process might include explaining to
each other why we find the other's behavior so annoying, and each coming to
admit that we have no doubt been in the wrong in various ways. But we will
probably recognize that it will be unproductive to harp on each other's alleged past wrongdoings: that we must instead look to the future and try to
negotiate some mutually acceptable modus vivendi. That will involve negotiating a compromise between our conflicting desires and habits. We might
agree that I will hold no more than one late-night party a fortnight, with advance warning to her, and that she will avoid noisy do-it-yourself work before
10:00 A.M. at weekends. It might also include agreeing to pay compensation
for any past damage (damage to her hedge by my guests, damage to my walls

by her do-it-yourself work) and perhaps an exchange of general apologies for any past wrongs. But the compensation will be focused purely on any material damage that was done, and the apologies might be both formal (we do not aim to become the sort of close friends between whom apologies are worthwhile only if sincere) and unfocused (we do not list and demand or offer apologies for every wrong).

Criminal mediation, by contrast, is precisely focused on a wrong that has been done. A woman has been regularly beaten up by her husband, or her house has been burgled and vandalized (see Hulsman 1991). The parties agree to enter a mediation process. It matters, first, that the relevant facts be established, either before the mediation or as its first stage—that this was a case of what the criminal law defines as serious assault, or of burglary and criminal damage. The process will also include discussion and mutual explanations of those facts. The victim will explain how the crime affected her; the offender will try to explain how he came to commit it. The offender's explanations might appeal to excusing or mitigating factors (which need not all be formally recognized by the law). But he will not be allowed to argue that his conduct was justified—that husbands have the right to 'chastise' their wives in this way, or that the burglary was a legitimate response to the fact that she had sacked him from his gardening job; or that the crime was partly her fault—that she 'provoked' him by not providing meals on time or 'encouraged' him by leaving her windows open (see pp. 62–63, above). For the criminal law, under whose aegis the process takes place, defines what must count as a crime and what can count as a justification. Whatever else is negotiable during the mediation process, the wrongfulness of the offender's crime is not.[15]

Part of the point of the criminal mediation process consists precisely in this exchange of explanations. The victim can explain her suffering to the offender. Her explanation will consist not in a neutral account of how the crime affected her, but in one that expresses and tries to communicate to the offender her hurt and anger, and that condemns his crime as a wrong. She will also have a chance to come to understand (which will not be to condone) the offender's action from his perspective. The offender will be vividly confronted, through his victim's voice, with his crime. But he will also have a chance to explain himself. More, however, is hoped for and intended than this.

The most ambitious hope is for a reconciliation between victim and offender (and some versions of these programs are called "Victim-Offender Reconciliation Programs"). If they are, as might be true of the burglary, related only as fellow citizens, they might have no further dealings with each other. But reconciliation is still valuable since it restores those bonds of citizenship, of mutual respect and concern, that the crime damaged. If they are related more closely than that, as in the case of domestic violence, reconciliation *might* enable them to repair and maintain their marriage. But even if that is impossible, there is still value in a reconciliation that enables them to part on morally satisfactory terms. We must, however, be clear what kind of 'reconciliation' is required and what it can or must involve.

Given that the wrongfulness of the crime is not negotiable, one thing that reconciliation cannot properly involve is some compromise between the conflicting 'desires' of victim and offender, such as a compromise that might allow the husband occasionally to beat his wife or the burglar to steal from the victim's car but not from her house. Whatever else they might negotiate, the offender's commitment to refrain from repeating the crime must be a nonnegotiable demand.

Reconciliation will also require some kind of reparation, some attempt by the offender to 'make up' to the victim for what he did to her. This might involve something materially similar to the kind of compensation that can result from civil mediation. The burglar, for instance, might repair or pay for the damage he caused, or replace the goods he stole. But compensation of this kind will not always be possible; nor, even when there is some material loss that can be repaired, will such material compensation suffice by or in itself. What needs 'repairing' or 'making up for' is not just such material harm as was caused (which might anyway be irreparable) but the *wrong* that was done to the victim, and what *that* requires is, minimally, an apology that expresses both a repentant recognition of the wrong done and a commitment to avoid its repetition.

Of course, apologies do not always presuppose wrongdoing. I may apologize to another for some harm that I inadvertently and nonculpably, or intentionally but justifiably, did to her. Such apologies express my regretful recognition of the harm she suffered at my hands,[16] and thus also of the claims she has on my concern and respect. Although she cannot properly criticize me for the harm I did, she could properly complain if I failed to apologize, since I would then fail to show her the respect and concern due to her. Apologies for wrongdoing, however, involve more than this. They express or purport to express not just regret at the harm that I caused but remorse for the wrong that I did, my repudiation of that wrong as something I now wish I had not done, and my implicit commitment to strive to avoid doing such wrong in future (for a repudiation that involved no such implicit commitment would not be a genuine repudiation). They thus also seek forgiveness from and reconciliation with the person whom I wronged and to whom I now apologize. Even if the wrong did not threaten to *destroy* our relationship (as lovers, friends, colleagues, fellow citizens, or just fellow human beings), it was inconsistent with the normative bonds by which that relationship is defined. It created a flaw, if not a rupture, in the relationship. Such flaws can be ignored or forgotten, but they can be removed or remedied only by an apology made by the wrongdoer and accepted in a spirit of forgiveness by the victim.

It is also worth noting that apologies can have a ritual or formalized character and that—especially in less intimate relationships—an apology whose sincerity is doubtful or unknown can still have value. I might apologize to the person I wronged not because I truly repent my action, but because that is what is expected or demanded of me; and while between friends or lovers apologies are worthwhile only if sincere, between strangers it might be enough that the apology is made—that the ritual is undertaken. The point is not that we accept apologies that we know to be insincere, but that we respect the other's privacy and the limits on our relationship by acting as if they are sincere without inquiring into whether they are.

Sometimes, however, a (mere) apology is not enough. If I have done a serious wrong to another person, I cannot expect to settle or resolve the matter merely by apologizing to him: something more than that is due to him and from me. This is not because a serious wrong is likely to involve some material harm for which compensation must also be paid. Some such wrongs (serious betrayals of a friendship or a marriage, for instance) involve no such harm, while some such harms (the harm involved in a rape or in a fraud committed by a friend, for instance) cannot be made good by material compensation. The point is rather that the victim cannot reasonably be expected to forgive me, to treat the matter as closed, merely on receipt of a verbal apology, however sincere, and that the wrongdoer cannot reasonably expect to close the matter thus. The wrong goes too deep for that.[17] It goes too deep for the victim. A (mere) apology cannot heal the moral wound done by the wrong. It also goes too deep for the wrongdoer, whether or not she realizes it. To think that she could just apologize, and then return to her normal life, would be to portray the wrong as a relatively trivial matter that did not seriously damage the victim or their relationship.

Two thoughts are involved here: that the wrongdoer owes the victim something more than (mere) apology, and that the wrongdoer deserves or ought to suffer (see ch. 1.4.1) something more than (merely) having to apologize. But what is this 'more'?

This 'more' need not be something separate and distinct from an apology (hence the bracketed occurrences of 'mere' in the previous two paragraphs). The 'more' that is owed to the victim is something that will recognize and address the seriousness of the wrong he has suffered. The 'more' that the wrongdoer should suffer has to do with the pains of remorse—with what is involved in recognizing the wrong she has done and its implications for the victim, for their relationship, and for her own moral life. Their lives and their relationship have been ruptured by the wrong: the victim's life as someone who is respected and cared for in the light of the values (supposedly) intrinsic to their relationship; the wrongdoer's life as a moral agent bound by those values; their relationship as one structured by those values. What can repair those ruptures, however, is not an apology *plus* some further and separate measure, but an apology of a kind that takes and addresses them seriously. This can be achieved by some mode of reparation that itself expresses the wrongdoer's apology.

Suppose that the burglar in a criminal mediation process agrees to pay for the damage he caused or (which might be ideal but not always practicable) to help repair it himself, or that the violent husband agrees to take on some extra domestic duty that hitherto had been his wife's. These can both be reparative measures. What gives them their significance as reparation, however, is not their material content (the damage might be as well repaired by the victim's insurance; such a shift in domestic responsibilities can hardly by itself make up for the violent assaults) but their meaning as forceful expressions of apology. The wrongdoer shows that he means what he says in apologizing, that he takes his wrongdoing seriously, by undertaking this burdensome task for the victim's benefit. We might add (a point that becomes important as my argument develops) that by undertaking such reparation, the offender can also focus his own attention on the wrong he has done.

This then is the significance of reparation in a criminal mediation process. It serves, not just or primarily as material repair or compensation for such material harm as was done, but as a way of adding weight and force to the apology by which offender and victim are to be reconciled. The reconciliation that is sought, as far as the criminal law is concerned, is not reconciliation as spouses or as friends (that is not the criminal law's business) but simply as fellow citizens. Whatever happens to any more intimate relationship that existed between the offender and the victim, the central aim of the mediation process, as a process conducted under the aegis of the criminal law, is that they should recognize and accept each other as fellow citizens who can live within the polity, if not in friendship, at least in civic peace.[18]

4.3. Criminal Mediation, Punishment, and Communication

Advocates of mediation programs often portray them as essentially *non-punitive*. We must look, Christie argues (1981, 11), for "alternatives to punishment, not only alternative punishments"; and central to those "alternatives" are informal processes of mediation and reparation. Mediation is, we are told, a matter of "restorative" or "reparative" justice rather than of the "retributive" justice that punishment involves.[19] Mediation, even of the 'criminal' kind sketched above, does indeed differ significantly in its procedures and its outcomes from the modes of criminal punishment with which we are most familiar; and it sits unhappily with the punitive rhetoric (and practice) that so often dominates contemporary penality. I argue, however, that we should see such a process, subject to certain refinements, as one appropriate paradigm of punishment.

Consider first the standard accounts of what punishment is (see Introduction, sec. 1): something painful or burdensome imposed on an offender for an offense by someone with the authority to do so, and intended to communicate censure. A criminal mediation process is intentionally *painful or burdensome* in its procedure and its outcome. For while it does not simply aim to "deliver pain" (see Christie 1981), the process of being confronted with and having to listen to the victim should be painful for the offender, as is the remorse that that process aims to induce. The reparation undertaken must also be burdensome if it is to give real weight to the apology it is meant to express. Such suffering, such burdens, are integral to, not mere side-effects of, the process (cf. Christie 1977, 10). Under existing schemes, mediation is admittedly not *imposed* on offenders against their will, since they must agree to it (although, depending on the alternative, that agreement might not be wholly free). But a punishment that the offender agrees to undergo does not thereby cease to be a punishment.[20] It is (self-)imposed *on offenders* (if they did not commit the wrong, the process is pointless), *for their offense*—it is imposed because they committed an offense, and it focuses on the offense. It might not be directly imposed by a legal *authority*, but a scheme of the kind envisaged here is authorized by the law, administered by a court, and organized by an official mediator; and, as I suggest in section 5.2, below, its outcome must be approved by a court. Finally, *censure* is central to the process: the offender is to "receive a kind of blame that it would be very difficult to neutralise" (Christie 1977, 9).

However, my claim that we should see criminal mediation as a mode of punishment is not merely the conceptual claim that it (more or less) fits standard definitions of punishment. It is, rather, the normative claim that criminal mediation *can* serve the appropriate aims of criminal punishment and *should* be thus understood, organized, and justified—even if this requires us to modify conventional understandings of both mediation and punishment.

First, mediation is a communicative process. The procedure itself is communicative. It consists in communication between victim and offender about the nature and implications of the crime as a wrong against the victim. It aims to bring the offender to face up to the wrong she has done. The reparation that the offender then undertakes also serves a communicative purpose: it communicates to the victim the offender's apology for what she did. But it is a process of *punitive* communication: it censures the offender for her crime and involves intentionally burdensome reparation for that crime.

Second, criminal mediation is retributive in that it seeks to impose on (to induce in) the offender the suffering she deserves for her crime and is justified in those terms. She deserves to suffer censure for what she has done. Mediation aims to communicate that censure to her in such a way that she will come to understand why, as well as that, she deserves it. She deserves to suffer remorse for what she has done. Mediation aims to induce such suffering in her by bringing her to recognize the wrong she has done. She ought to make apologetic (and thus necessarily burdensome) reparation for that crime to its victim. Mediation aims to provide such reparation. By seeing criminal mediation as punishment, we can thus make clear and plausible sense of the retributivist idea that the guilty deserve to suffer, by showing what they deserve to suffer and why.

Third, criminal mediation is also future-directed. Its most obvious and direct aim is that of reconciliation between victim and offender through apologetic reparation by the offender, but it also aims to dissuade the offender from future crimes. To bring her to a remorseful recognition of the wrong she has done, and of the need to make reparation for it, will also be to bring her to see that and why she should not commit such wrongs in the future. Mediation can thus address the consequentialist's concern that punishment must aim to do some good if it is to be justified. However, the relationship between penal mediation and the good that it aims to achieve is not merely instrumental (as the relationship between punishment and its justifying aim is for consequentialists), since the ends themselves specify the means that are appropriate to them. The reconciliation that is to be achieved is one that must involve a recognition of and apology for the wrong that was done, and must therefore be achieved by a process that includes such recognition and apology. The offender is to be dissuaded from future crime precisely by her recognition of the wrong she has committed.

Fourth, the reparative burden that the offender undertakes can be seen as a species of penal hard treatment. It is intentionally burdensome, and while it serves a communicative purpose, it is burdensome—making demands on the offender's money or time or energies—independently of its communicative meaning. But this hard treatment is now integral to the communicative purpose of criminal mediation as a punishment. It is the means by which the offender can make apologetic reparation to the victim.

Fifth, the mediation process is clearly inclusionary rather than exclusionary. It brings the offender and the victim together, and seeks to reconcile them as fellow citizens. Rather than excluding offenders from community, it precisely treats them as being bound to their victims by the bonds of community.

Sixth, this approach avoids the problems that were, I argued (sec. 4.1, above), fatal to accounts of punishment as moral education. Apart from explaining how hard treatment is an integral part of the communicative penal process, it avoids suggesting that offenders need moral *education*. Punishment aims, not so much to teach them that or why certain kinds of conduct are wrong, but to bring them to confront and to respond appropriately to their own wrongdoing. The implication is not that they did not know that what they did was wrong, but that they did not attend to its wrongfulness as they should or were not sufficiently motivated to avoid it.[21] This approach also shows why punishment should be the means by which we pursue the goals that we aim to achieve. The reconciliation that is sought can properly be achieved only through such a process as this.

This is not to suggest that I have yet provided an adequate account either of criminal punishment or of criminal mediation as a species (let alone a paradigm) of punishment. Mediation will, for a variety of reasons, not always be either practicable or appropriate, and there are still significant differences between criminal mediation as I have portrayed it and criminal punishment as it is normally understood. A central point is that I have yet to show why we should see mediation as a criminal process dealing with *public* wrongs rather than as a civil process dealing with purely *private* wrongs (see ch. 2.4.3). It might seem so far to be essentially a matter between victim and offender, in which the wider community has no interest beyond that of helping them to be reconciled with each other.[22] All I have tried to do so far, however, is to introduce some of the central themes of my account of punishment: the idea of a kind of censure that aims to bring offenders to face up to and recognize the wrongs they have done; the idea of burdensome reparation that expresses such an apologetic and repentant recognition; the idea of a reconciliation, mediated by such recognition and reparation, between victim and offender; and—although this is admittedly not prominent in criminal mediation as so far described—the idea that the offender is thus also brought to recognize the need to avoid such wrongdoing in future.

I explain and develop these ideas in what follows, initially through another example, which comes closer to more familiar conceptions of criminal punishment—that of the English 'Combination Order', which combines probation with Community Service.

5. Probation and Community Service as Communicative Punishments

Probation has been a feature of both English and U.S. penal systems for over one hundred years, but not until section 8 of the Criminal Justice Act 1991 did English law give it the formal status of a *sentence* or *punishment*. Until then, courts had made probation orders "instead of sentencing" the offender (Powers of Criminal Courts Act 1973, sec. 2). Community Service Orders, under which the offender performs a specified number of hours of unpaid work of an approved kind, were introduced in the United States in 1966 (see Morris & Tonry 1990, 150), and in England in 1973 (Powers of Criminal Courts Act 1973, secs. 14–17). English courts can also now impose "Combination Orders," combining probation with community service (Criminal Justice Act 1991, sec. 11; see Ashworth 1995a, 281–82; Brownlee 1998, 117–19). By looking at these two kinds of sentence, we can see how—both separately and in combination—they can form appropriate modes of punishment for a liberal polity.

5.1. Probation as Punishment

For a long time probation was seen (especially by probation officers) as an *alternative* to punishment.[23] In its early prestatutory form in England, in the police court missions, this was indeed its character. Offenders who would otherwise have been imprisoned were spared from punishment by being released on recognizance to the supervision of a 'friend' who was not a criminal

justice official (McWilliams 1983; King 1969, ch. 1). The growth of the "treatment model" in the probation service's self-perception after 1945 strengthened this nonpunitive view of probation. Probation was portrayed as a mode
of therapeutic social work from which "any punitive quality . . . had been
removed." It aimed (at its most ambitious) not merely to "eliminat[e] the
probationer's anti-social conduct" but to "improve his personality" and
achieve "a more nearly perfect adjustment."[24]

The treatment model of probation, like that of punishment (see ch. 1.2.2),
came under attack in the 1970s. It was accused of denying offenders
their standing as responsible moral agents, and of disguising as benevolent
help what were in truth modes of coercive manipulation (see Bottoms &
McWilliams 1979). But no clear new conception of probation replaced the
treatment model,[25] and probation officers continued to insist that their
proper role was not a punitive one, reacting with hostility to government
moves to give them a more prominent role in administering "punishments in
the community." By thus "convert[ing] supervision from an attempt to influence constructively the offender's future behaviour into a measure deliberately designed to impose irksome restrictions as a form of punishment," and
by emphasizing "punishment rather than positive influence," such moves
"would make a clear break with the established role and values of the probation service," which are founded on "a constructive, personal and helpful engagement with offenders which helps them to face up to the need for
changes in their attitudes and behaviour."[26] Probation officers would still insist, despite the government's attempts to make "punishment . . . the central theme of the new measures, . . . that their job was rooted in social
work, using techniques designed to confront offenders with the effects of
their offending" (J. Roberts 1989).

The sharp contrast that such comments draw between 'punishment' and
the supposed aims of probation resembles that which advocates of mediation
draw between 'retributive' and 'restorative' justice (see sec. 4.3, above). It reflects an understandable response to the punitive rhetoric in which government policies are so often garbed. But it also reflects, I argue, an impoverished understanding both of what probation must be if it is to be a measure
that can justifiably be imposed on responsible citizens, and of what punishment could be.

Probation as a punishment presupposes a responsible, culpable offender.
If a defendant has not committed a crime, or was not at the time of his crime
responsible for his actions, or is not now a responsible agent who can be held
answerable for that crime (see Duff 1986, 15–28, 263–64), he is not properly
punishable–although he might be eligible for some kind of (perhaps compulsory) psychiatric treatment or protection. If he was and is a responsible agent,
then the state must treat him, as it must treat every citizen, in ways that respect his autonomy, freedom, and privacy.[27] One implication of this is that
his conviction should not be used as the 'occasion' for the coercive imposi-

tion of measures designed to bring about a general improvement in "his personality" or "adjustment."[28] He may be *offered* help with personal or social problems that he has (in equipping himself for or in finding employment, for instance, or in dealing with his marital problems). But measures that are *imposed* on him as a sentence must be justified by reference to the offense for which they are imposed (see Bottoms & McWilliams 1979, 168–75), since it is only his commission of that offense that legitimates this coercive intrusion into his life by the state.

What kinds of measure, with what aims, could his commission of the offense justify? The central aims of probation, according to the probation officers' leaders quoted above, are "to confront offenders with the effects of their offending" and thus to help "them to face up to the need for changes in their attitudes and behaviour." These are, however, also the aims of a communicative process of censure. In censuring someone for a wrong she has done, we hope to bring her to recognize the fact and implications of that wrong; and in recognizing that she has done wrong, she will also recognize that she needs to amend her behavior and the attitudes that informed it to avoid committing such wrongs in future. Furthermore, this is how we *should* seek to bring about the desirable "changes in their attitudes and behaviour" if we are to treat offenders as responsible members of the normative community. Our enterprise should be one of 'transparent persuasion' (see sec. 2.2, above) that aims to bring them to recognize the wrongs they have done and to recognize that they should take steps to avoid committing such wrongs in future.

This suggests that the proper aims of probation are not in conflict with, indeed that they match, the aims of punishment as a mode of communicative censure. We can confirm this suggestion by looking more closely at the two elements that probation can involve.

The first and basic element is supervision. The offender is required to report regularly to his probation officer. This enables her to keep a formal check on his behavior, and provides a structure within which he can seek and she can offer advice and help in avoiding future criminal conduct. It is a punishment—a burden imposed on him by the court for his offense. Implicit in it is the censure that his crime deserves. That censure, as thus communicated, makes clear the implications of his crime: for this punishment tells him that his commission of the crime cast doubt on his commitment to the community's public values (the values embodied in the criminal law), threatening to undermine the mutual trust on which the community depends; he must therefore subject himself to a kind of supervision that other citizens need not accept. But it is a punishment that also looks to the future. Through this supervision he will, we hope, come to face up to the need to amend his future conduct and be helped to see how to achieve such amendment.

Second, however, further conditions can be attached to a probation order (see Walker & Padfield 1996, 262; Morris & Tonry 1990, 178). Some of these (requirements to live in an approved hostel or to attend a probation center, for instance) may make the supervision more intensive and effective. Others (requirements to undergo treatment for drug dependency, for instance) may aim to deal with conditions directly involved in his criminal conduct. Others, such as requirements to refrain from certain kinds of association or activity, require him to remove himself from the contexts in which he offended. As I have noted, such further requirements must, if they are to be justified as appropriate responses to his offense, be justified by reference to that offense. But it is clear that they can, in principle, be thus justified. A residential or attendance requirement can be justified if it communicates and actualizes the message that the offender has shown by his crime that he cannot be trusted to live a law-abiding life without such intensive supervision. He is still a citizen, but a citizen who must reestablish his trustworthiness in this way. Requirements to undergo a treatment program can be justified if they communicate and actualize the message that the offender has shown by his crime that he cannot be trusted to deal with his problems in a way consistent with the criminal law. This nonoptional help is a condition of his continued freedom. Restrictions on his movements can be justified as temporary disqualifications. A football hooligan who is banned from attending matches, or someone guilty of drunken violence in pubs who is banned from going into pubs, is told by this punishment that he has by his crime rendered himself ineligible or unfit to take part in these ordinary activities.[29]

Such further conditions and requirements can thus also be seen as punishments that the offenders deserve to suffer for their offenses. This is not to say that they are imposed (any more than the burdensome reparation that an offender undertakes in a mediation scheme is imposed) *simply* in order to burden or pain offenders, as "mere retribution." It is rather to say that they are imposed *for* their offenses, as responses that aim to bring home to them the character and implications of those offenses as public wrongs and thus to persuade them to see that they must (and how they can) modify their future conduct.

5.2. Extending Probation

Once probation is recognized, as it should be, as a punishment (rather than as an alternative to punishment), there is no reason why it should not be extended further to include a range of additional measures. Before I discuss Combination Orders, two other possibilities are worth noting.

First, there are a large number of specialized programs focused on particular kinds of crime and criminal whose aims seem very close to those of probation as it is understood by many probation officers: "to confront offenders with the effects of their offending," to help them "face up to the need for changes in their attitudes and behaviour"—and to help them make those necessary changes. The CHANGE Project in Scotland provides an example

(Dobash & Dobash 1992, ch. 7; Morran & Wilson 1994; Scourfield & Dobash 1999). This program is aimed at domestically violent men. It seeks to challenge them, to bring them to accept their responsibility for their violence, and to help them change their ways, through confrontational group work involving both reenactment and discussion. It might again be tempting to see such programs as *alternatives* to punishment: instead of punishing the offender, we subject him to this essentially therapeutic program, which aims to deal with the causes of his offending and to cure his violent disorder. But this would be to misunderstand the character of the program, which portrays and responds to the offenders' violence not as the symptom or manifestation of a disorder requiring treatment (for which, as a disorder, it would be hard to hold the men responsible) but as a wrong for which they are responsible. It aims to bring them to recognize the nature and seriousness of that wrong, and their responsibility for it, and thus also to bring them to recognize the necessity for a radical change in their behavior and in the attitudes from which it flowed. This change they must make for themselves, though the program can help them to do so. It requires from the start a "non-negotiable abstinence from violence" (Dobash & Dobash 1992, 245), as a moral (not a therapeutic) demand that condemns their previous conduct and should guide their future conduct. It aims to bring them to recognize the force and importance of that demand, as well as to help them equip themselves to fulfill it.

Such programs should be seen not as therapy but as communicative punishments. They are imposed on (or accepted by; see p. 97, above) offenders for their offenses, as an appropriate response to those offenses. That response censures those offenses as wrongs and seeks to persuade the offenders to recognize them as wrongs (and so to accept that censure as justified). They are also deliberately burdensome or painful. The mere fact of having to attend the program is burdensome; and we should see that burden, not merely as an inevitable side-effect of therapy, but as part of the offenders' punishment—as something we impose on them to bring home to them the seriousness of the wrongs they committed. The program's content is designedly painful. It aims to confront offenders forcefully and uncomfortably with the nature of what they have done and thus to induce in them a necessarily painful repentant recognition of their wrongdoing. Such programs also look to the future—to the offenders' future commitment to refrain from violence. But (which distinguishes them from purely therapeutic programs) that commitment is to be mediated by the recognition of the wrongfulness of their past conduct, and this change in their behavior is something that they must in the end bring about for themselves.

There is no reason in principle why such programs as this should not be included in a probation order, since they serve the same (punitive) aims as probation should serve. They could also figure as one outcome of a mediation scheme. Mediation between a violent man and his battered partner, for instance, might lead to his agreement to enter such a program. This could be an appropriate kind of reparation in that while it cannot undo or provide compensation for his previous violence (nothing could do that), it can be a burden that he accepts in order to make forcefully clear his apologetic recognition of the wrong he has done and his commitment to improve his future conduct. This leads us to a second possible way in which probation could be extended, to include mediation between offender and victim, and enables me to complete the picture, left incomplete above, of mediation as a form of punishment.

An offender is convicted of a crime with a direct victim, and the court calls for a presentence report from a probation officer to help it in determining the appropriate sentence (see Walker & Padfield 1996, 24–30). Suppose that mediation is incorporated more fully within the criminal justice system, as one sentencing option. The probation officer, after discussions with offender and victim, forms the view that in this case mediation is an appropriate measure: the victim is willing to take part in the process; the offender, even if not inclined to volunteer for it, is willing to obey a requirement to take part in it.[30] The court then makes a probation order, which includes a requirement to take part in the mediation process that the probation officer will organize and conduct. The court will also have to approve whatever reparative measures are agreed in the mediation process.

We can see mediation, as thus organized, as a fully fledged punishment within the penal system. It presupposes the offender's conviction of a crime—of a public wrong. The process aims to bring home to the offender the censure that that crime deserves, and the probation officer's role, as mediator, is partly to make clear that that censure comes not just from the victim (as it might with a purely private wrong) but from the whole community in whose name she is acting, and which shares in the wrong done to the victim (see ch. 2.4.3). The reparative measures that the offender agrees to undertake also take on a public dimension. By undertaking reparative work for the victim or paying compensation, the offender communicates to the wider community, as well as to the victim, his apologetic recognition of the wrong he has done;[31] and in approving those measures the court publicly approves them as being adequate to that purpose.

Sometimes, of course, there will be no scope for reparation to an individual victim. There may be no identifiable individual victim (as, for instance, in many cases of vandalism, or of theft or fraud involving public rather than private property, and in many driving offenses), or the victim might not be interested in such reparation. In such cases, especially the former kind, Community Service Orders can be seen as punishments that involve reparation to the whole community.

5.3. Community Service Orders as Public Reparation

While some advocates of mediation and of probation portray them as alternatives to punishment, Community Service Orders are uncontroversially recognized as punishments. We can, however, best understand their meaning and point by seeing them as public forms of the kind of reparation to which victim-offender mediation can lead.[32]

This meaning is most obvious when the content of the Order, the work that the offender is required to undertake, has some obvious relation to the nature of her offense—as when a vandal's Order requires her to work at repairing the effects, if not of her own vandalism, then of others' vandalism, or in other ways improving the local environment. As a punishment imposed on her, the Order communicates to her the censure she deserves for her crime— not just a formal censure whose content is simply that she has committed an offense, but a richer and more substantive censure that seeks to bring home to her the nature and implications of that offense. By confronting her with the damage done by vandalism and the work involved in making it good, it says to her in effect "Look what you have done!" It also constitutes an apologetic reparation that she is now required to make to the community (to *her* community) that she wronged. This is what she must do, she is told, to 'make up' to the community for the wrong she committed and to reconcile herself with her fellow citizens. If she comes to accept it in these terms for herself, if it thus becomes a sincere expression of her apologetic recognition of the wrong she has done (and she might come to such a recognition precisely through carrying out the Order), then she also implicitly commits herself to trying to avoid such wrongdoing in future; and by her acceptance of this punishment she reconciles herself with her fellow citizens.[33] Even if she does not come to accept it as a mode of reparation, however, it constitutes an attempt to persuade her to face up to the wrong she has done. We could also add that, just as it may be appropriate to accept another's formal apology without inquiring into its sincerity (see p. 95, above), so her fellow citizens should accept that in completing the Community Service Order she has sufficiently apologized for her crime.

5.4. Combination Orders: Mediating between Community and Offender

We can now see how probation and Community Service Orders can appropriately fit together in a Combination Order; and indeed how they could be not just added to each other as two separate elements in such an Order, but integrated into a sentence that would amount to a kind of Community-Offender mediation scheme.

Just as in a criminal Victim-Offender mediation scheme the discussion between victim and offender includes discussion of the nature and effects of the crime and of what kind of reparation the offender should now undertake, so we could envisage a Combination Order that requires the probation officer, acting on behalf of the community, to work out with the offender what kind of community service he should now undertake by way of reparation to the community. The discussion itself, as an aspect of probation, is part of his punishment. It is a burdensome task imposed on or required of him, because of the crime he committed, which aims to bring him to face up to what he has done, to accept as justified the censure that his conviction communicated (and that the discussion reinforces), and to recognize the need for some kind of reparation. In making the Combination Order, the court specifies community service as the appropriate mode of reparation, though it is for the probation officer and the offender to work out just what form that service should take.[34]

The community service, as a burdensome task that the offender would not otherwise have undertaken,[35] now serves several related roles (apart from any material benefit it brings to the community). It constitutes a forceful public apology, which the offender is required to make, for an offense for which a 'mere' apology would not suffice (see sec. 4.2, above); it provides an authorized, publicly recognized form in which an offender who has genuinely repented her crime can express that apologetic repentance to her fellow citizens—and thus assure them of her commitment to avoid such wrongdoing in future. But it is also a means by which an offender who has not yet faced up to or repented her crime can properly be brought to do so. For intrinsic to it, as a punishment for her crime, is the censure that crime deserves. It thus seeks to focus her attention on her crime and its implications, in the hope that she will thus come to repent the crime—and therefore accept this punishment as an appropriate way of expressing her repentance.

The discussion in this and the previous section of mediation, probation, and Community Service Orders has introduced the central elements of the account of criminal punishment I defend. It is time now to make that general account more explicit.

6. Punishment as Penance

We should understand and justify criminal punishment, I suggest, as a species of secular penance. It is a burden imposed on an offender for his crime, through which, it is hoped, he will come to repent his crime, to begin to reform himself, and thus reconcile himself with those he has wronged.[36] Although the idea of criminal punishment as penance might sound strange and disturbing to liberal ears, I argue that it provides a conception of punishment that is suitable for a liberal political community—a conception of punishment as a communicative and inclusionary response to the public wrongs committed by citizens of such a polity.

I can best explain this account by discussing, first, the '*three Rs*' of punishment as thus conceived[37] and, second, the issue of *who owes what to whom* when a crime is committed.

6.1. The Three 'R's of Punishment

Punishment, on this account, aims at the goals of *repentance, reform,* and *reconciliation.* These goals are to be pursued by a communicative process of imposing penitential burdens on offenders.

Repentance is, as I suggested above (sec. 2.2), an aim internal to censure. When we censure others for their wrongdoing, our intention or hope is that they will accept that censure as justified. But to accept censure as justified is to recognize and accept that I did wrong, the wrong for which I am censured; and an authentic recognition that I did wrong must bring with it repentance of that wrong. I recognize and own it as mine—I do not deny it or seek to justify or excuse it. But I also disown it, as something that I should not have done and now wish I had not done. Repentance is necessarily painful, since it must pain me to recognize and admit (to myself and to others) the wrong I have done. In aiming to induce repentance, punishment thus aims to bring offenders to suffer what they deserve to suffer—the pains of repentance and remorse.

Censure is the appropriate way to try to bring a wrongdoer to repent his wrongdoing. What justifies the claim that he ought to repent, and the attempt to bring him to repent, is the very fact that he has done wrong. If we are to address him as a responsible moral agent, if we are to engage in an appropriate effort at 'transparent' persuasion (see sec. 2.2, above), we must therefore seek to induce his repentance by focusing our and his attention on that wrong—by censuring him for it. The kinds of punishment discussed in the previous two sections aim to do this. Part of the aim of criminal mediation and of probation, as I describe them, is to persuade the offender to recognize, face up to, and repent what he has done.

The further kinds of penal hard treatment involved in such punishments, the reparative work or the community service required of the offender, can also communicate the censure he deserves for his crime. Just as we can communicate our admiration or gratitude to one who has done some notable good not just by praising her but by giving her a reward, so we can more forcefully communicate censure by giving it such material expression. But why *should* we communicate the censure in this way, rather than merely by some formal public declaration, by what is said in the mediation process or by the probation officer, or by some purely symbolic punishment (see sec. 2.3, above)?

The answer to this question has to do partly with some familiar aspects of our ordinary human nature as fallible moral agents and partly with the nature of repentance. When I have done wrong, it is often tempting and all too easy to distract myself from that fact. I might say, to myself or to others, "Yes, I did wrong and am sorry for it." I might think that I have now repented the wrong. But all too often I have not seriously repented, because I have not thought seriously enough about, that wrong. I allow myself to think that the matter is closed when I have merely papered it over. Repentance, at least with serious wrongs, cannot of its nature be something that is achieved and finished with in a moment, however intense the feelings of guilt might be in that moment. It must go deep with the wrongdoer and must therefore occupy his attention, his thoughts, his emotions, for some considerable time. Someone who claims to have been deeply grieved by the death of a loved one, but who resumes her normal life, thoughts, and feelings after a day, thus belies her claim. Similarly, someone who claims to have repented the serious wrong he did, but who rapidly resumes his normal life and gives that wrong no further thought, thus belies his own claim. The task of facing up repentantly to the wrong I have done (to the wrong and to my doing of it) cannot be achieved in a moment. It must involve thinking through and seeking to understand what I did to the person I wronged and how I could have done it.

This then is one purpose of penal hard treatment, such as the reparative burden or the community service that might be imposed on an offender. It is a way of trying to focus his attention on his crime. It provides a structure within which, we hope, he will be able to think about the nature and implications of his crime, face up to it more adequately than he might otherwise (being human) do, and so arrive at a more authentic repentance. As fallible moral agents, we need such penances to assist and deepen repentance.

Some consequentialists might accuse me of seeking to foster an unhealthy, unproductive kind of guilt, focused obsessively on the past—when we should instead look to the future. Part of the answer to that charge is that, although guilt *can* be unhealthy or neurotic, there is nothing intrinsically unhealthy or inappropriate in seeking to face up to and to understand the wrong I have done. Indeed, a proper concern for the values against which I offended, for those whom I wronged, will express itself in my repentance and remorse. The other part of the answer to the charge is that repentance, and punishment that aims to induce repentance, are not purely backward-looking, since they also aim at reform.

Reform, more precisely a commitment to *self*-reform, is an implication of repentance. To recognize and repent the wrong I have done is also to recognize the need to avoid doing such wrong in the future. Truly to disown that wrong is also to commit myself to trying to avoid repeating it. A process of censure or punishment aimed at inducing repentance thus also aims to induce reform: not to re-form the wrongdoer as an object that we must mold to our wishes, but to persuade her of the need to reform herself.[38] Furthermore, repentance involves trying to work out *how* I should reform myself, as well as recognizing *that* I must do so—what kind of change I must make in my attitudes and behavior and how I can work towards making it. A constructive process of censure will also address this aspect of repentance. It will aim to help the wrongdoer come to see what she must do and how she can do it. This again is one of the explicit aims of probation as I described it, and of the programs (such as the CHANGE Project for violent men) that may be associated with a probation order, It is also an aim of mediation, insofar as the discussion concerns the ways in which the offender must modify his future behavior, and it is an aim to which penal hard treatment of an appropriate kind can contribute.

Programs like the CHANGE Project themselves involve a kind of penal hard treatment. Offenders required to attend such programs are deprived of their time and liberty, and are subjected to confrontational challenges that are liable (and intended) to be unpleasant or disturbing even if they do not attend to their meaning. Other kinds of penal hard treatment, such as reparative work or community service orders, can also play a role in the reformative enterprise, just as they do in the enterprise of inducing repentance—especially, but not only, when their content is related to the character of the offender's crime (as when a vandal's community service involves repairing the effects of vandalism). If the offender is thus brought to think more carefully and remorsefully about the nature and implications of his crime, about how he could have come to commit it, he will also be thinking about how he can so reform himself that he will avoid such crimes in future. Penances, as vehicles of repentance, are at the same time vehicles for the self-reform that repentance motivates.

Reconciliation is what the repentant wrongdoer seeks with those she has wronged—and what they must seek with her if they are still to see her as a fellow citizen. As argued above (sec. 4.2), when what makes reconciliation necessary is wrongdoing, some form of apology is required. And in cases of serious wrongdoing, the apology itself requires a more than merely verbal expression. This then is the third aspect of penance and of penitential punishments. They constitute a forceful and weighty kind of apology, which should reconcile the wrongdoer with those she has wronged. Such an apologetic penance can take the form of reparation, of burdensome work undertaken by the offender for the benefit of the individual victim or of the wider community, which in some material way repairs the harm (or the kind of harm) she did. This is the significance of the reparation to which mediation can lead, and of Community Service Orders. But it need not take that form. An offender can offer a suitably forceful apology by undertaking or undergoing any kind of penitential burden that expresses to those concerned her repentant recognition of the wrong she has done.

There might seem to be some sleight of hand in the previous paragraph. An apology that is to reconcile a wrongdoer with those he has wronged must surely be one that he makes for himself. A penance that is to communicate the seriousness of that apology must surely be one that he undertakes for himself. Criminal punishments, however, are typically *imposed* on the offender against or regardless of his will. How can they serve, as voluntarily undertaken penances can serve, as apologies?

Part of the answer to this question concerns the formalized ritual of public, as distinct from private, apology (see p. 95, above). Whereas between friends, or other kinds of intimate, apologies have reconciliatory value only if they are sincere, in less intimate contexts (such as our dealings with our fellow citizens) there is more room for purely formal apologies whose sincerity is not an issue. What matters is that the wrongdoer apologizes. We do not inquire into her sincerity. This point can also apply to at least some kinds of punishment: if the offender completes the work prescribed by a Community Service Order (a punishment part of whose meaning is that it constitutes a public, reparative apology), her fellow citizens should accept that, without inquiring into her reasons for doing so. She has now 'paid her debt' of apology and reparation.

It might be objected that to *require* offenders to make public apologies—either explicit verbal apologies or the kinds of symbolic apology that, on my account, reparation and Community Service Orders involve—is to fail to treat them with the respect due to them as members of a liberal polity (see von Hirsch 1993, 83–84, on "compulsory attitudinizing"). It is to require them to express attitudes of self-criticism and remorse that, as I admit, they might not feel. But if those attitudes are not authentically theirs, if they do not repent their crimes, we are requiring them to be untrue to their own understanding of what they have done—to themselves. We may communicate to them the censure their crimes deserve, and hope that they will make that censure their own in remorse. We may *offer* them a way of communicating their remorse *if* they come to repent their crimes. But to *require* them to apologize is to write their side of the communicative dialogue for them—whereas if we are to respect them as fellow citizens of a liberal polity, we must leave them free to write their own side of the dialogue.[39]

This objection would have real force if what the apology (explicit or symbolic) required of the offender was, in content or context, demeaning: if the offender was "compelled against his will to admit himself to be a *moral pariah*" (von Hirsch 1993, 84; emphasis added); if the context in which the punishment was imposed was such that the offender would in effect be groveling or humiliating himself. This is, no doubt, very often true of our existing penal practices.[40] Required public apology, however, need not in principle have this character. Its content and context (the way and the spirit in which it is required and made) can be such that I do not degrade myself merely by making it. As for the charge that to *require* someone to apologize is already to deny him the respect due to him as an autonomous citizen of a liberal polity, we must remember that he is not *forced* (how could he be?) to *mean* what he thus says. Instead, he is required to take part in this public ritual, which has other dimensions of meaning than that of apology (the first two aspects of penance discussed above) and whose apologetic dimension has a formality that is intended and known to leave the question of sincerity open.

(I am not, I confess, wholly confident that this is an adequate answer to the objection: that to tell offenders what they ought to say, by words or deeds, and to *require* them to say it, is fully consistent with a proper respect for their autonomy as citizens. However, we could deal with any remaining anxieties on this point in the following way. When the court passes a sentence on an offender—consisting, for instance, in a probation order together with a requirement to undertake some specified reparative work or community service—the offender should be given the chance to state that she is *not* undertaking the various elements of the sentence as a form of apology. Her punishment is still justified, given the first two aspects of penance, as an attempt to persuade her to repentance and self-reform. It could still become, if she is thus persuaded, an apology that she now willingly makes. She should still be treated as having 'paid her debt', since she has undertaken or undergone what would constitute an adequate apology if she came to mean it as such—and others should not inquire into whether she has come to mean it thus. But it is not now an apology that she is required to make against her will.)

Up to this point my comments apply only to punishments in which the offender is, to some extent, an active (even if unwilling) participant: punishments that are required of, but not strictly inflicted on, the offender. The offender is required to undertake a specified kind of community service or to conform with the terms of a probation order. Although there will be sanctions for the breach of such requirements (see p. 152, below), it is up to him to conform, or to fail to conform, to them. We can thus say that in conforming to those requirements he is also making a formal, public apology. Other punishments, however, most obviously imprisonment, are simply inflicted on the offender, who is taken from court to prison. It is hard to see such passive subjection to punishment as amounting to making even an apology that I make reluctantly only because I am required to make it. There is room to introduce further aspects of active participation by the offender into modes of punishment that are now purely passive (see ch. 4.2.2). But while this would give more force to the idea (implicit in my account) that offenders should be active participants in their own punishments, there are limits on how far we can take this. And punishments will in the end be simply inflicted on any offenders who refuse to obey penal requirements for themselves.

To meet this point, we can refer to the other aims of punishment as an attempt to induce repentance and self-reform. A punishment inflicted on an unwilling offender can in principle serve these aims. We can hope to persuade him to attend to the communicative content of his punishment and to attend in what becomes a repentant spirit to his crime. If he is brought to repent his crime and to see the need for some reparative apology to reconcile him with those he has wronged, he will also come to accept his punishment as the formally prescribed way in which that apology is to be made. What began as a punishment inflicted on him in order to induce repentance becomes a punishment (a fully fledged penance) that he accepts or wills for himself as an expression of that repentance. This is the proper aim of punishment as penance. The offender comes to recognize and repent his crime as a

wrong and to realize that he must, and how he can, so reform himself as to refrain from such crimes in the future. He also comes to accept his punishment
as a justified response to his crime—as an appropriate means of inducing that
repentance and as an appropriate way in which he can express that repentance to others (cf. Winch 1972d, 217–20).

6.2. Who Owes What to Whom?

There is still much to explain and justify in this account of criminal punishment. I have yet to show how punishment as thus conceived is consistent
with or expressive of the values of a liberal polity, how this account applies to
different kinds of punishment and to different types of offender, what sentencing principles or policies flow from it, and how it relates to the actualities
of our existing penal practices. I undertake these tasks in what follows. But I
should first attend to the objection that, even if we accept all I have said so
far, it does not yet come close to justifying a system of criminal punishment.

Suppose we accept that criminal punishment can, in principle, achieve the
goods of repentance, reform, and reconciliation; and that a liberal polity
could recognize these as *public* goods, which are of proper interest to the
state (see sec. 8, below). It does not follow that a liberal state would be justified in creating a system of punishment to secure these goods. We must
also ask whether these goods are important enough (and likely enough to be
achieved) to justify allocating the resources that such a system requires and
to outweigh the costs and drawbacks that such a system will involve (see
Husak 1992b; also Murphy 1985). Punishment is expensive in both material
and human terms. It inflicts serious hardships on those subjected to it. Even
in a reformed and improved penal system, it will quite often fail to achieve
the goods of repentance, reform, or genuine reconciliation, and will be prone
to error or abuse. Can I really argue that these goods are important enough to
justify accepting these costs and drawbacks of a penal system?

To meet this objection, I need to show that criminal punishment is not
just a source of *goods* such as repentance, reform, and reconciliation, but that
it is something that is *owed*—something that a liberal state has a *duty* to do. To
see why this is so, we must ask what is owed by whom and to whom in the
context of crime.

We can begin with the obvious point that the state owes it to its citizens to
protect them from crime—from the kinds of wrong that are defined as public
wrongs. This is a central aim of the criminal law (see ch. 2.4.3). It owes this to
all its citizens as potential victims of crime, either as direct victims of directly
victimizing crimes or, collectively, as a community whose public interests
may be affected.[41] There are many ways in which this protection can be provided, including educational policies, policies aimed at remedying crimo-
genic social or economic conditions, measures of situational crime prevention, the criminal law itself as a source of authoritative declarations and

definitions of public wrongs, other kinds of public exhortation—and, of course, criminal punishment.

If we think only of what is owed to potential victims of crime, we might see punishment simply as a means of preventing crime and justify it insofar as it is an efficient means. This would be to understand and justify it in consequentialist terms. But the state owes something too to its citizens as potential *criminals*—as citizens who are liable to be tempted to commit crimes and to give in to such temptations. What it owes them is to treat and address them as members of the normative political community. That means treating and addressing them as citizens who are bound by the normative demands of the community's public values, who must thus be called to account and censured for their breaches of those values, but also as citizens whose membership of the community must be preserved and whose autonomy, freedom, and privacy must be respected (see sec. 1, above). The protection from crime that it provides for its citizens as potential victims of crime must therefore be a kind of protection that also shows them, as potential criminals, the respect and concern due to them.

It follows from this that criminal punishment cannot be justified as an instrumental means of preventing crime by such techniques as deterrence, incapacitation, or reform. Such techniques do not treat those on whom they are imposed, or against whom they are threatened, as responsible members of the normative community (see sec. 1.2, above). But punishment *can* in principle be justified if it is understood and administered as the kind of secular penance I describe. Penitential punishment that censures criminal wrongdoers, aiming to persuade them to repent their wrongdoing and to embark on the necessary task of self-reform, constitutes a mode of moral communication that addresses them as autonomous moral agents. It aims, not to coerce them into conformity with the law, but to appeal to their consciences—to their moral understanding. Like any mode of rational communication, it leaves it in the end up to them to be persuaded (to accept the message it communicates) or to remain unpersuaded. It also respects their privacy in that it focuses on the offenses they committed, which, as public wrongs, cannot be said to belong in the realm of the private (see further sec. 8, below). Finally, such punishment aims to reconcile offenders with those whom they wronged—with their direct victims and with the whole community: it seeks to maintain and reaffirm their membership of the normative community. Punishment is thus justified as a method of protecting citizens from crime that also shows potential and actual criminals the respect and concern due to them as citizens.

We must also ask what is owed, by whom and to whom, when a crime is committed. What the offender owes the victim is an apology that recognizes the nature and seriousness of the wrong done. This is owed to the direct victim of the crime, if there is one, but also to the wider community—both for crimes that injure the community *rather than* any individual victim and for directly victimizing crimes: for the wrong done to the individual victim is also a wrong against the community, which shares that wrong and whose values have been flouted. Punishment can constitute such an apology, to the victim (as when the penal hard treatment consists in some direct reparation) and to the community as a whole.

But does the community owe it to the victim to *extract* such an apology from the offender by requiring the offender to undergo such punishment?

The community certainly owes it to victims to recognize the wrongs they have suffered. That is part of what it is to share those wrongs. Such recognition can include various kinds of 'victim support,' not just aimed at remedying whatever material harm was caused by the crime (that could be done through a system of private or national insurance that did not distinguish harms caused by crime from other kinds of harm), but offering moral support and reassurance to those who have been wronged. It will also properly be manifested in what the state, as the legal embodiment of the political community, does to or about the offender. If Henry and Shona are my friends and Shona does Henry some serious wrong, it would be morally inconsistent for me to sympathize with Henry about the wrong he has suffered but not to allow that wrong to make any difference to my conduct to Shona. I owe it to him, as her victim, to criticize her for what she has done and to urge her to apologize to him. Furthermore, if I am both to respect her as a responsible moral agent and to care for her as a friend, I also owe it to her to criticize her conduct rather than to ignore it, and to urge her to reconcile herself with Henry by apologizing to him. Similarly, if a community is, through the legal organs of the state, to take seriously the public wrong done to a citizen, it must not only sympathize with the victim but also censure the offender. It owes it to the victim, whose wrong it shares, and to the offender as a member of the normative community, to try to get the offender to recognize that wrong and to make a suitable apology for it. But that is a central aim of criminal punishment as I have portrayed it.

There is also the question of what, if anything, the victim owes either to the offender or to the community as a whole. As far as the community is concerned, the victim owes it to her fellow citizens to assist in the offender's detection and prosecution. This is an implication of seeing the crime as a public wrong, which flouts or attacks the community's public values and which is not merely the victim's own business (see ch. 2.4.3). She also owes it both to them and to the offender to be ready to be reconciled with the offender through his punishment: to treat him as a fellow citizen who has paid his penitential debt.[42] This is not to say that she should be expected to maintain or restore any intimate or personal relationship that she had with the offender— as a friend, for instance, or as a spouse. It is to say only that she should be ready to be reconciled with him as a fellow citizen (see p. 96, above).

Does the victim also owe it, either to the offender or to the wider community, to *seek* such reconciliation: to be ready, for instance, to take part in a mediation process or in some kind of program that aims to get offenders to confront their crimes? Given how painful and distressing such a process can be, it would imply a very demanding conception of the duties of citizenship to hold that the victim *ought* to do this. But we could say that she should be willing to do so if the process would not be too distressing, and that she would be displaying an admirable commitment to the ideal of citizenship if she was willing to do so even when the process would be distressing and difficult.

My argument so far is that punishment as I portray it should be seen, not merely as a source of goods that the state might pursue, but as something that is owed as a matter of the state's duty to its citizens. This is not to say that we can therefore ignore the costs and the drawbacks of punishment (see Husak 1992b)—the human and material costs involved even in a properly functioning system of penitential punishments, and the dangers of error and abuse to which any human system will be prone. We must ask whether the duty to punish is stringent and important enough to justify incurring these costs and these dangers, and how effective punishment is likely to be in protecting citizens from crime and in securing the goals of repentance, reform, and reconciliation. For while my account is nonconsequentialist, in that it does not make the justification of a penal system depend upon its contingent efficiency as a means to some independently identifiable end, it is not a purely retributivist account that justifies punishment *solely* in terms of its relationship to the past crimes for which it is imposed. Punishment is justified as a legitimate attempt to protect citizens from crime and to preserve the political community by persuading offenders to repent their crimes. Such a justification cannot be independent of the extent to which that attempt is likely to succeed.

First, however, success as thus conceived is not all that matters. We owe it to victims and to offenders to make the attempt to secure repentance, self-reform, and reconciliation. But that attempt is worth making even if it is often likely to fail, since in making it we show that we do take crime seriously as a public wrong and address the offender as someone who is not beyond redemption (see further sec. 7.4, below). Second, we are not dealing here with an all-or-nothing question. We do not have to choose between making *every* effort to achieve those goals, by detecting and punishing *all* offenders, and abandoning *any* attempt to pursue those goals. The question is, rather, if we agree that a penal system is worth maintaining at all, how many resources should be devoted to it? I do not pretend to have an answer to this question. But I hope I have said enough to show how punishment, as portrayed here, is an important enough duty owed by the state to its citizens to justify, in principle, the creation and maintenance of a penal system.

7. Different Kinds of Offender

Punishment should be understood, justified, and administered as a mode of moral communication with offenders that seeks to persuade them to repent their crimes, to reform themselves, and to reconcile themselves through punishment with those they have wronged. We can understand such punishments as probation and Community Service Orders in these terms, as well as what I call criminal mediation schemes. I discuss some other familiar modes of punishment, in particular imprisonment and fines, in Chapter 4. In this section, to clarify my account and meet some objections to it, I discuss the different kinds of offender with whom any penal system will have to deal.

Offenders differ both in the nature and seriousness of their crimes, and in their reactions to those crimes and to the punishments they receive. It is the latter kind of difference that concerns us now, since that affects the way in which punishment, intended as a mode of penitential communication, impinges on them—and thus the way in which such punishment can be justified. We can distinguish several ideal types of offender.

7.1. The Morally Persuaded Offender

This account of punishment applies most easily to the offender who before her punishment is unrepentant, but who is brought by her punishment to repent her crime, to accept her punishment as an appropriate penance for that crime, and to try to reform herself and to reconcile herself with those she has wronged. Two points are worth emphasizing about this type.

First, what matters is not just that, but how, she is brought to repent her crime. If she is simply bullied or coerced into submission, she might come to a kind of repentance, but her punishment has not succeeded as a mode of moral communication. If her punishment is to address her as a member of the normative community, it must appeal to her own moral understanding: she must come to see and understand for herself that and how her conduct was wrong. For this to be possible, she must have the moral capacity to be thus persuaded: she must be within the reach of the values against which she offended and to which her punishment appeals. Perhaps she offended through weakness of will and deceived herself, to some extent, about what she was doing: but her punishment makes her face up to what she did. Or perhaps she was not committed or was only half-heartedly committed to the values embodied in the law: but through her punishment she comes to realize their importance, to accept them as hers, and to judge and condemn her own criminal conduct in their light.

This is not to deny that her punishment is coercive. It is inflicted on her or she is required to undergo it, whether or not she is willing to be punished: she is confronted by a probation officer who insists on talking to her about her crime or by a victim who insists on telling her just what she did. It addresses her forcefully, seeking to get her attention, to make her attend to what she has done. We can even hope that she will be 'compelled' to face up to what she has done and to recognize it as a wrong (see Bickenbach 1988, 779). But this is a matter of moral or rational compulsion, as when a person cannot avoid recognizing a truth that stares her in the face or forces itself on her attention. It still addresses her as an autonomous agent who must in the end accept or reject the message communicated by her punishment for herself, in the light of her own conscience; and it still leaves her free to reject it (see further sec. 7.4, below).

Second, the success of her punishment as a mode of moral communication depends on others, as well as on her. It depends on the spirit in which the punishment is administered: that it is administered in such a way that it does genuinely constitute an attempt to address her as a fellow citizen and to appeal to her conscience. It also depends on the willingness of others to be reconciled with her—on the way in which they respond to her repentance. I say more about these points in Chapter 5 (secs. 1 and 3).

7.2. The Shamed Offender

Distinguishable analytically, though often in practice not clearly, from the morally persuaded offender is the offender who is *shamed*, rather than brought to repentance and remorse, by punishment.[43]

The distinction between shame and remorse is between a response to my past conduct that is essentially mediated by the actual or imagined reactions of others, and one that is not thus mediated but embodies my own authentically first-person judgment. In remorse, I judge and condemn my own conduct for myself. That condemnatory judgment might in fact (as with the morally persuaded offender) be induced by the anger or censure of others, but it becomes my own judgment, reflecting my own values. I condemn myself even if others would not condemn me. What pains me is the wrong that I see for myself I have done. To be shamed, by contrast, is to be pained by the actual or imagined judgments of others, whose judgments might not embody my own values. What shames me is not (just) that I did wrong but that others think or would think badly of me for what I did.

Braithwaite and Pettit make much of shame (of 'reintegrative' rather than 'stigmatizing' shaming) as a proper aim of punishment (see Braithwaite 1989; Braithwaite & Pettit 1990; ch. 1.1.3, above), and it is clear that punishment can induce shame. What pains me about my trial, conviction, and punishment for shoplifting may be not so much the material burden it imposes on me, but the fact that I am exposed to the censorial or contemptuous judgment of others. Shame is also closely connected to remorse or the possibility of remorse. For while one who is shamed does not (yet) feel remorse for himself, he cannot be wholly lacking in moral sensibilities. He must care about others' moral judgments on him (for it is their moral condemnation, not merely their hostility, that pains him) and must thus have some regard for the values in the light of which they condemn him (if he despised those values, he would not be shamed).[44] Shame perhaps comes closest to remorse when it is induced, as it can be, by the *imagined* condemnation of others who will in fact never know what I have done. It is then almost as if I condemn myself in their voice.

Now shame can be a stage on the path to remorse. What begins as shame at the censure of others can be transformed into genuine remorse if I come to condemn myself in my own voice, rather than merely in their voice—if their censure ceases to be essential to my self-censure. However, remorse rather than shame is essential on my account. To address the offender as an autonomous moral agent, as a member of a normative community with autonomy as one of its central values, is to appeal to him to judge his own conduct for himself in the light of values that he has made his own. It is to try to persuade him to repent and feel remorse for his wrongdoing rather than merely to shame him. Furthermore, Braithwaite & Pettit locate shame within a strictly consequentialist perspective, as a useful technique for achieving the goods at which punishment should aim. But the value of remorse on my account is not a consequentialist value. The offender should feel remorse because that is an appropriate response to the wrong he has done; and while his remorse will also serve the goals of self-reform and reconciliation, it is not an instrumental means to those ends. It is, instead, the intrinsically appropriate way in which those goals should be pursued.[45]

(It is also worth noting that shame can blur the distinction between prudential deterrence and moral persuasion. The threat of punishment can deter people from crime because they fear the shame that conviction and punishment would bring, as well as the material burdens—the loss of money or freedom, for instance—that punishment would involve. Now this is certainly a matter of prudential deterrence: what dissuades the person from crime is the discomfort that shame brings, not the thought that such conduct would be wrong. But it is more than a matter of simple deterrence, involving purely prudential, nonmoral incentives to refrain from crime. The threat of shame can deter only those who care about being shamed, and I care about being shamed only if I have *some* regard for the moral opinion that others have of me and for the values that inform that opinion.)

7.3. The Already Repentant Offender

Suppose that an offender has already, before her conviction and punishment, repented her crime. She has faced up to the fact and character of her wrongdoing. She feels the pangs of remorse. She is determined to reform her future conduct. It might seem that on my account she cannot now be justifiably punished. For she has already done for herself the work that punishment is supposed to do—of inducing repentance. She is already suffering what she deserves to suffer—the pain of remorse. So surely her punishment is now unnecessary and would simply impose additional, excessive suffering on her (see Bickenbach 1988, 781; Ten 1990, 203–4; von Hirsch 1993, 10).

This objection presupposes that even those who have already repented *should* still be punished—as indeed they normally are. But so they should be on my account. Two points are relevant here.

First, repentance is not something that can be achieved and completed in a moment (see pp. 107–8, above): At least with serious wrongs, it requires time and effort. The initial horror or distress at what I have done, which might indeed strike me in a moment, must be deepened and strengthened into an understanding of my action as a wrong—an understanding that will stay with me. This is part of the purpose of punishment as penance, and it is one reason why even the offender who has begun to repent should still be punished.

Second, there may be (less common) cases in which the offender has not just begun to repent, but undergone a more complete and thorough penitential process for herself. Perhaps she is detected, or gives herself up, only some years after the crime. She has spent much of the intervening time in repentant contemplation of her crime, and even in punishing herself by a self-imposed penance. Or perhaps she has already suffered, without human intervention, some harm as a result of her crime that she saw and responded to as a punishment for what she did—as a penance she must undergo and in undergoing which she comes to repentance (see Winch 1972c, 197–200).[46] Or perhaps she has already been informally punished by others. She has suffered public criticism, social ostracism, perhaps the loss of her job or her friends, and has accepted this as a penance for her crime (cf. Husak 1990). Must I not say in such cases that the offender has already been punished enough, and should not suffer further, legal punishment?

The crucial point to bear in mind in thinking about such cases is that punishment, on my account, serves the aims of reconciliation with those the offender has wronged (the direct victim and the community as a whole), as well as of repentance and reform, and that reconciliation is achieved through penal hard treatment that constitutes a forceful and public apology. The criminal law, through the sentence of the court, specifies the appropriate form and content of the reparative apology the offender must make. Now in the first two examples mentioned in the previous paragraph, there is no such public penance by the offender. What she has done or undergone might suffice to reconcile herself with God or with her conscience, even with her individual victim if she made some private reparative apology to him. But she has not done what is required to reconcile herself with the political community whose laws and values she has infringed. That is why she must still be punished—why she should, if she recognizes her crime as a public wrong against the community, submit herself to the criminal process of trial, conviction, and punishment.

The matter is not so straightforward in the third example, of someone who has accepted her informal punishment as penance, since we could imagine the offender's informal punishment, and her response to it, being a genuine informal analogue of the punishment to which she would have been liable through the formal criminal process. In that case, however, there surely is good reason to exempt her from formal punishment now, on the grounds that she has already been punished enough (as Husak 1990 argues). (There is also, of course, good reason for the law itself to discourage, or in extreme instances to count as criminal, such informal kinds of punishment, since they are all too likely to be misdirected or excessive.)

Even if an already repentant offender should still be subjected (should indeed be willing to subject herself) to penitential punishment, must I not hold that she should be punished less severely than one who is not yet repentant—that her repentance should serve as a mitigating factor in sentencing?[47]

Now it is true that repentance can figure in current penal practice as a mitigating factor or as grounds for early release from punishment. An offender who pleads guilty at his trial might receive a lighter sentence. A possible rationale for this reduction in sentence is that the plea manifests his remorse (although a more plausible explanation is that this encourages offenders to save the state the expense of a longer trial and victims or other witnesses the distress of having to give evidence; see Ashworth 1995a, 136–40). An offender who has already 'voluntarily' made reparation to the victim might receive a lighter sentence (Ashworth 1995a, 141). An offender's release on parole from a prison sentence depends in part on whether he has shown "that he is willing to address his offending" (Walker & Padfield 1996, 197, quoting the Home Secretary's 1992 directions to the Parole Board): evidence of repentance, that is, can shorten his sentence. Such provisions are also, however, morally problematic if they are meant to reward or encourage repentance. They provide an incentive to a dishonest pretense of repentance. They can bear harshly on the innocent, who may be pressured into pleading guilty to avoid a harsher sentence if they are mistakenly convicted or who may, if wrongly convicted, be denied parole if they continue to assert their innocence.

However (subject to one qualification), my account does not imply that repentance should entitle the offender to a lighter sentence, for two reasons.

First, a principle of proportionality between the seriousness of the crime and the severity of the punishment is intrinsic to my account. If punishment is to communicate the censure that the offender deserves for the crime, it must communicate the appropriate seriousness or degree of censure. It must neither exaggerate nor depreciate the seriousness of the crime. But the seriousness or degree of censure is expressed by the severity of the punishment. A harsher sentence portrays the crime as more serious, a lighter sentence portrays it as less serious (see von Hirsch 1993, 15–17). To impose a lighter sentence on a repentant offender is thus to imply that repentance renders the crime less serious. But this is not normally true.

(The qualification is this: sometimes an offender's *immediate* repentance can cast a different light on her crime by showing it to have been a momentary aberration. She attacked another person but at once repents the attack, is horrified by what she has done, and tries to help and apologize to her victim. We can now see the attack itself in a different light—not as a vicious assault to which she was wholeheartedly committed, but as an aberration for which she already condemns herself. Her immediate repentance is then a proper mitigating factor: it mitigates the seriousness of her crime.)[48]

Second, the purpose of punishment on my account is to communicate repentance forcefully and adequately to others, as well as to induce and strengthen it. By undergoing her punishment as a penance, the offender makes clear to the victim and to the community as a whole that she really does repent her crime and seeks to make apologetic reparation for it. Now this would commit me to counting repentance as a mitigating factor if it portrayed the punishment of a not-yet-repentant offender as involving two distinct, successive stages—a first stage that aims to induce repentance, and a second stage that enables her to express that repentance. The first stage would be unnecessary if the offender had already repented. But that is not the picture I am offering. Instead, the *whole* sentence serves the dual purpose of inducing and expressing repentance. It should consist in a mode and severity of punishment that is adequate as apologetic reparation to those the offender has wronged. For an already repentant offender it has that meaning from the start, while for a not-yet-repentant offender who comes to repentance it acquires that meaning only later and partly in retrospect—she comes to understand and accept the punishment she has been undergoing in those terms. The difference between them is not that one requires or deserves a lighter punishment than the other, but that one is quicker than the other to understand and accept her punishment as an appropriate penance.[49]

7.4. The Defiant Offender

Some offenders, of course, will finish their sentences still unrepentant. Such cases might seem to pose further problems for my account. Am I not committed to saying that we should then extend their punishments in an attempt to induce repentance? But doing so would again bring my account into conflict with the principle of proportionality, and would turn punishment into an attempt to coerce offenders into submission rather than to appeal to them as autonomous moral agents. Furthermore, must I not admit that the punishment of an offender who is not thereby brought to repentance has been a failure and that, if we are confident in advance that he will not be brought to repentance, we cannot justifiably punish him?[50]

We should distinguish different types of unrepentant or defiant offender. Some will not even listen seriously to the message their punishment aims to communicate. Others do listen but are unpersuaded. Some will not listen or are not persuaded because they do not care about the (public) rightness or wrongness of their conduct. Others will not listen or are not persuaded because they are committed to values opposed to those embodied in the law.

Amongst the latter kind of principled dissident, some will be committed to values that those who share the values embodied in the law can at least respect. Others will be committed to values that are repugnant to those who share the community's defining values.

One point we should note is that what the law says (and thus what punishment says) to a principled dissident whose values the community should respect will be different from what it says to other kinds of dissident (see pp. 64–65, above). Suppose, to take a sympathetic example, that someone kills a terminally ill friend, in the honest belief that this is morally justified (or even required), although the law counts it as murder. The law still says to her, as it says to all citizens, that such killing is wrong, and her punishment still aims to bring her to see and accept that it was wrong. But it now portrays that wrongfulness to her as more like a *malum prohibitum* than a straightforward *malum in se*. Even if, for respectworthy reasons, she dissents from the content of the law, she ought to obey it out of respect for the law and as a matter of her duty as a citizen. Her punishment must therefore embody this more complex message, and will properly be lighter than that imposed on someone whose crime did not flow from respectworthy values.

More generally, however, my account would not sanction extending the punishment of the defiant until they repent. One reason is again that it requires the severity of the punishment to be proportionate to the seriousness of the offense; and just as later repentance does not mitigate the seriousness of the offense, the offender's defiance does not aggravate it. The other reason (which also shows why we should not treat the offender's defiance itself as a further offense for which he merits further punishment) is that punishment must address the offender as a member of the liberal polity whose autonomy must, like that of any citizen, be respected. Such respect is consistent with an attempt (even a forceful attempt through hard treatment punishment) to persuade him to repent his crime and to accept the values that condemn it. We present him with, or even try to force him to hear, an interpretation of his conduct as a public wrong that he should repent. But it is up to him to accept, or to continue to reject, that interpretation. What is crucial, however, is that such an exercise in forceful moral persuasion is, like any exercise in rational communication, necessarily fallible: not just because it might in fact fail to persuade him, but because it must itself leave that possibility open. If I am trying to persuade another person to accept a moral principle that I think she should accept, I will try to find arguments or ways of presenting the issue that she will find morally or rationally compelling. My attempt must, however, consist in an appeal to her own conscience and understanding, which requires me to leave it to her to come in the end to accept *or to reject* what I say. So too with punishment as a mode of moral communication: if it is to consist in a proper attempt to persuade a responsible, autonomous agent to repent his crime rather than in an improper attempt to bully or manipulate him into submission, it must leave him free to reject its message.[51]

If the offender remains unpersuaded, his punishment has been to that extent a failure: it has failed to bring him to recognize the wrongfulness of what he did. It could still have been *partially* successful if it brought him seriously to listen to and think about the message it sought to communicate. It would then have succeeded at least in engaging him in a serious moral consideration of what he had done. But sometimes even this will not be achieved: the offender will not even listen to the moral message that his punishment seeks to communicate. We might also have good empirical reason to believe in advance that he will not listen. But, for the reasons noted above, we must not extend his sentence in an attempt to make him listen. Must I then admit that in such cases punishment utterly fails to achieve its proper goals and that if we can foresee that failure, we cannot justifiably punish the determined dissident?

Punishment certainly now fails to achieve the further goals that are intrinsic to it as a communicative enterprise. It fails to persuade the offender to repent his crime or even to think seriously about it. It thus fails to persuade him of the need for self-reform. It thus also fails to achieve the kind of authentic reconciliation through repentance and apology to which it aspires. However, it can still be justified, even if we are sure that it will thus fail, since we are sometimes justified in making an attempt that we are sure is doomed to fail.

What justifies such an attempt is partly what is owed to the victim and to the community that shares in the victim's wrong and whose values have been flouted. To take that wrong seriously is to be committed to censuring the wrongdoer and to attempting to persuade him to make the kind of apology he should make. We display our concern for the wrong done by trying to secure an appropriate reparation for it from the wrongdoer. But the attempt is also justified by what we owe to the offender. To refrain from punishing him (or to subject him instead to merely deterrent or incapacitative measures) on the grounds that punishment will not persuade him to repent would be to give up on him as a moral agent, as a member of the normative community. It would be to treat him as being beyond moral redemption, beyond the reach of the community's values. But that is not how we should treat a fellow citizen. We owe it to him to continue to treat him as someone who is not irrevocably cut off from the values he has flouted, who *could* still redeem himself— even if he will not do so. And we display that continuing regard for him as a fellow citizen by punishing him.

But how can his punishment reconcile him to his victim or to the wider community if it is obvious that he is unrepentant and unapologetic? Although, if his punishment was simply inflicted on him, he might not even have gone through the motions of apologizing (see pp. 111–12, above), we can extend the idea of an apologetic ritual to cover this kind of case. The offender has been subjected to what would constitute an appropriately reparative apology if he undertook it for himself. His fellow citizens should therefore now treat him as if he had apologized. This is not a matter of pretending what they know to be false—of pretending that he has apologized when they know he has not. Instead, it is another aspect of treating him as someone who can redeem himself—as someone who can, and to whom we owe it to hope that he will, refrain from crime in future. He might not have *paid* the apologetic debt that he owed, if his punishment was simply inflicted. But something like that debt has been exacted from him, and those who exacted it should now treat him as if the debt has been paid (but see further ch. 4.4.2).

One final point should be noted about the defiant offender. It is predictable that some of those who remain unpersuaded by their punishment as a mode of moral communication will nonetheless see the prospect of such punishment as giving them prudential reason to refrain from crime—that punishment will operate for them as a prudential deterrent. This does not by itself undermine the justification for punishing them. Indeed, the freedom they must have as autonomous moral agents includes the freedom to respond to their punishment in this way. However, there might be a temptation to *rely* on such a deterrent effect in justifying their punishment: to think that it is still worth punishing them and that their punishment can still be an effective way of protecting citizens against crime, because even if they are not morally persuaded, they (or others like them) might nonetheless be deterred. We must resist this temptation if we are to take seriously the conception of punishment as an enterprise of moral communication and the objections to using punishment as a deterrent (see secs. 1.2, 3, above). So long as their punishment is intended and designed as a mode of moral communication, the knowledge that they might treat it merely as a prudential deterrent does not undermine its justification. It still addresses them in the appropriate terms, as members of the normative community, and still seeks an appropriate response from them. However, if we begin to rely on that deterrent effect, it becomes part of what is intended by their punishment. We intend now to persuade them morally or, failing that, to deter them. But that is to use punishment (if necessary) as a deterrent; and using punishment as a deterrent is inconsistent with a proper regard for actual and potential offenders as members of the normative political community.

A communicative system of penitential punishment can express the values of a liberal political community. Such a system is inclusionary rather than exclusionary. It addresses actual and potential criminals as members of the normative community—as people who are both bound and protected by the community's public values and who need to be reconciled with their fellow citizens. It takes their crimes seriously as wrongs, but does not take those wrongs to exclude them from community. It addresses them as autonomous moral agents, thus embodying the central liberal value of autonomy: for though it seeks to induce repentance and reform, these goals are to be achieved by persuading them to recognize for themselves that they have done wrong.

Some liberals will no doubt be unpersuaded by this argument and will insist that such a conception of punishment cannot belong in a polity founded on liberal values. Indeed, they might argue that a qualifiedly deterrent system of punishment (see sec. 3, above) is more consistent with those values than is a penitential system of the kind I advocate. By meeting this objection, I can also make my own account clearer.

8. Penitential Punishment and the Liberal State

Even if I am right to argue that penitential punishment does not (if administered in the right way and the right spirit) infringe the offender's autonomy, liberals might still argue that it infringes the *privacy* that a liberal state must allow its citizens (see Lipkin 1988; Baker 1992a; von Hirsch 1993, 72–75, 1999).

Penitential punishment, as an attempt to persuade offenders to repent their crimes, seems to presuppose or to try to create a rather intimate community between the punished and the punisher (the idea of penance, after all, seems most at home in the context of a close-knit, spiritually demanding religious community). It attempts to reach, to break through to, "the inner citadels of [the offender's] soul" (Lucas 1968–69, 215). It intrudes coercively into the deepest aspects of his moral character. Now such insistent concern for a wrongdoer's moral condition might be appropriate within a close friendship or a family or a religious community. It is surely not, however, a proper task for the penal institutions of a liberal state. Even those "perfectionists" who think that the state has some proper interest in "making men moral" (see George 1993) can argue that it should not use criminal punishment as a direct means to this end (George 1993, 42–47, 75–76; Murphy 1985). The law declares certain kinds of conduct to constitute public wrongs; through conviction and punishment it seeks to communicate the censure that such wrongs deserve to those who commit them. It thus offers citizens moral reasons for refraining from crime, in the *hope* that they will heed and be moved by those reasons; and it *invites* offenders to attend to the wrongfulness of what they have done. But penitential punishment goes further, seeking to *invade* the offender's conscience and moral character. This is something that a state concerned to respect its citizens' privacy should not do, because it is something that the offender's fellow citizens should not, simply as fellow citizens, do. As fellow citizens of the political community, they are not *mere* strangers. But they are not his friends or family. They should maintain a suitable distance from him, unless he chooses to enter into a more intimate relationship.

By contrast, a qualified deterrent system of punishment of the kind sketched in section 3, above, maintains a respectful moral distance from the offender. It gives her the *option* to treat her punishment as a penance, but leaves her free to regard it simply as a prudential deterrent and the laws under which she is punished simply as external demands on her conduct. It does not attempt a coercive invasion of her moral character. It thus respects the privacy of her moral personality, as penitential punishment does not.

Now penitential punishments are certainly demanding, and may be seen as intrusive by those who resent them, in a way that merely deterrent punishments are not. If I am caught for drunken driving, I accept that I will receive a fine and lose my driver's license. My punishment might be seriously inconvenient, and gives me good prudential reason to obey the law. But suppose instead that my punishment involves attending meetings with victims of drunken driving, visiting accident units dealing with such victims, and watching films portraying the effects of car crashes—with the aim of confronting me with the effects of such wrongdoing and challenging me to face up to what I have done. This might not be more burdensome than a fine and the temporary loss of my driver's license, in that it need not involve greater costs to me in money, time, or energy, but it might be more disturbing and less welcome, because it involves a demanding moral challenge. I might prefer to accept a fine and the temporary loss of my license, which do not in the same—as I see it, intrusive—way strike at my conscience and invade my moral being. So too, other more serious offenders might prefer the harsher punishments that a sophisticated deterrent system would impose to kinds of punishment that seek to induce a repentant confrontation with the character and implications of their wrongdoing.

Such concerns about the intrusive character of penitential punishments might not be allayed by a reminder of the limits that a liberal society will set on the scope and depth of the criminal law (see ch. 2.4.5): that the law and its penal institutions must be concerned only with actions that attack or threaten important values or interests and with the attitudes directly manifest in such actions. This does distinguish my account from some conceptions of 'restorative' or 'informal' justice, according to which crimes (or 'conflicts') must be dealt with by an open-ended and unconstrained discussion from which nothing is excluded, since on my account the offender's trial and punishment can properly insist on addressing only those aspects of her conduct or attitudes that constituted her crime. But liberals might still argue that I allow the criminal law to take an improperly intrusive and coercive interest in the offender's moral condition.

Nor might such concerns be allayed by a reminder that while penitential punishments are coercive, imposed on offenders regardless of their will, they must not aim to coerce the offenders' understanding or moral attitudes. While offenders are forced to *hear* the message that punishment aims to communicate and to undergo a penal process intended to persuade them to accept it, they are not forced to *listen* to that message or to be *persuaded* by it—they are left free to reject it or to refuse to attend to it in the repentant spirit that it aims to induce. Apart from the danger that what are officially intended to be exercises in forceful moral persuasion will turn out to be oppressive attempts to coerce offenders into moral submission, liberal critics might still insist that moral beliefs and attitudes, like all matters of conscience, are not the proper concern of the criminal law—that they belong in the private sphere of individual freedom that the state must respect.

But what justifies this conception of the 'private'? The 'private' is not a metaphysical *given* (see p. 45, above). What counts as 'public' or as 'private' depends on the nature of the community in which the distinction is drawn. Those who object that penitential punishments invade the 'private' realm of conscience therefore cannot ground the objection on some a priori conception of the 'private' according to which such matters *must* count as private. They must rather claim that a liberal polity *should* define such matters as private. But why should it?

Freedom of conscience, of thought and belief, of speech are indeed crucial values for a liberal community. My conscience, thoughts, and beliefs are 'private' in the context of my dealings with my fellow citizens unless and until I choose to make them public by publishing them; and even when published in speech they generally remain 'private' as far as the law is concerned. Even here, of course, there are familiar (if controversial) limits to privacy. Some kinds of speech, some kinds of expression of attitude and belief, properly concern the law. However, a familiar way to express the liberal concern about the implications of penitential punishment is to say that the criminal law should generally be concerned only with (external) conduct, not with (inner) attitude; and to cite the 'Harm Principle' that the criminal law should be concerned only with conduct that harms protected interests (see Feinberg 1984–88). On a standard understanding of this principle, 'harms' of the kind that concern the criminal law are always identifiable independently of the human actions that might cause them (thus the harm that concerns the homicide laws is that of death). The law's interest in prohibiting and preventing harmful conduct is therefore an interest in conduct as causing or liable to cause harm as thus understood, not in whatever intentions or attitudes might lie behind such conduct. It should refer to the agent's intentions or attitudes only in order to determine whether he can properly be held responsible for his harmful or dangerous conduct.

What the law owes its citizens, as potential victims of crime, is that it seek to prevent harmful or dangerous conduct. What it owes its citizens, as potential victims of its coercive attention, is that it pursue those harm-preventive aims by means that respect their standing as autonomous agents. Now penitential punishments can protect citizens as potential victims against future crime. An offender who is brought to repentance is less likely to offend again. But this method of pursuing the aim of preventing crimes is, the objection runs, inconsistent with respect for the offender's privacy and autonomy. Penitential punishment might also be of moral benefit to the offender. It might be for her good, as a member of the community, that she repents the wrong she has done and reconciles herself to her fellow citizens. But even if the state can have *some* proper concern for its citizens' moral good, it should not pursue that concern through the coercive, intrusive methods of criminal punishment.

This argument founders, however, on its inadequate conception of harm (see Duff 1996b, 363–74). The harm suffered by the victims of central *mala in se* crimes (such as murder, rape, theft, violent assault) consists not just in the physically, materially, or psychologically damaging *effects* of such crimes but in the fact that they are victims of an *attack* on their legitimate interests— on their selves. The harmfulness and wrongfulness of such attacks lie in the malicious, contemptuous, or disrespectful intentions and attitudes that they manifest, as well as in their effects. The agent's intentions and practical attitudes (those directly manifest in his conduct) are thus relevant as conditions of liability—conditions for holding him liable for conduct that causes or threatens to cause harm. But, more than that, they are an important aspect of the wrongfulness of that conduct—of what makes such conduct a proper concern of the criminal law.[52] That is why I argued (p. 68, above) that the criminal law is properly concerned with *actions*—'action' being understood to include the intentions and attitudes that it directly actualizes.

What the law therefore owes the citizens, as potential victims of crime, is protection against wrongful actions of various kinds. It is concerned not merely with 'conduct' externally conceived in terms of its actual or likely consequences but with actions as thus more richly conceived. Its response to crimes must also be a response to them as wrongs of this kind: not merely as extrinsically harmful conduct but as wrongful actions. It owes such a response both to the victims, as a response that recognizes the character of the harm they have suffered, and to the offender, as a response focused on that about his conduct that made it and him a proper object of the law's attention. Likewise, what offenders owe their victims and fellow citizens are apologies that recognize the wrongs they have done. Compensation can help to make up for the material harm caused, but only apology, a public expression of repentance, can begin to make up for the moral harm done.

The offender therefore cannot claim that the intentions and attitudes manifested in his criminal action are 'private'—that they are no business of the criminal law. The rapist's action manifests a contemptuous disregard for his victim's sexual integrity, viciously actualized in his attack on her; a drunken driver actualizes in his conduct a culpable disregard for the safety of other road users. Penitential punishment focuses on these kinds of (practical, actualized) attitude because they are culpably harmful to the offender's fellow citizens. He is answerable for them to his fellows through the courts; he is censured for them by his conviction; and his punishment aims to bring him to recognize and repent their wrongfulness. What justifies this focus is not the claim that the state can properly take, through the criminal law, a coercive interest in its citizens' general moral character, but the claim that it can properly hold them answerable for and demand that they themselves attend to those attitudes which, as manifested in their criminal conduct, flout the central values of the legal community. Those attitudes, as thus actualized, cannot be said to belong in the 'private' realm of individual thought or conscience in which the law has no proper interest.

I conclude, therefore, that a system of communicative, penitential punishment does not improperly invade offenders' privacy. It is consistent with and expressive of a proper regard for the offender as a member—albeit perhaps a recalcitrant or unwilling member—of a liberal political community.

9. But Yet . . .

On my account, criminal punishment should be conceived of as a communicative enterprise that aims to communicate to offenders the censure they deserve for their crimes, and thus to bring them to repent their crimes, to reform themselves, and to reconcile themselves with those they have wronged. This account, I claim, provides a morally plausible rationale for penal hard treatment as part of this communicative enterprise—as a secular penance, which itself serves the aims of repentance, reform, and reconciliation. It does justice to the central retributivist concern that punishment must focus on and be justified by its relationship to the crime for which it is imposed. It also does justice to the consequentialist concern that punishment must be justified by some good that it aims to achieve, and to the abolitionist concern that we should aim not to 'deliver pain' to offenders but to achieve such goods as restoration, reparation, or reconciliation. But it does justice to such concerns by revising or reinterpreting them. In relation to retributivism, it explains the meaning of the idea that the guilty deserve to suffer, but does so partly by insisting that punishment cannot be purely backward-looking. It must also aim to achieve some future good. In relation to consequentialism, it identifies the goods that punishment should aim to achieve, but insists that punishment is not to be justified as a contingently efficient instrumental means to those ends. It is justified as a method that is intrinsically appropriate to those ends, once they are properly understood. From this it also follows that punishment can be justified as a proper attempt to pursue those ends even when we have good reason to believe that it will fail to achieve them (see sec. 7.4, above). In relation to abolitionism (and accounts of 'restorative' justice, of mediation, and of probation that portray their aims as essentially nonpunitive), it agrees that we should aim at such ends as restoration and reconciliation, but insists that in the kinds of case that properly concern the criminal justice system, what makes these reparative aims necessary is the fact that a wrong has been committed and that restoration and reconciliation are then properly achieved precisely by punishment—understood not as mere pain delivery but as a secular penance.

Punishment as thus conceived is consistent with, indeed expressive of, the defining values of a liberal political community. It addresses offenders, not as outlaws who have forfeited their standing as citizens, but as full members of the normative political community; it is inclusionary rather than exclusionary. It treats them as citizens who are both bound and protected by the central liberal values of autonomy, freedom, and privacy. It holds them answerable, as responsible moral agents, for the public wrongs they commit. But it also respects their own autonomy (since it seeks to persuade rather than merely to coerce), their freedom (since it constitutes a legitimate response to their wrongdoing and leaves them free to remain unpersuaded), and their privacy (since it addresses only those aspects of their lives and actions that properly fall within the public sphere).

But yet . . . : there are (at least) two crucial respects in which my account is still radically incomplete, and both raise questions about its plausibility or viability.

The first issue concerns its implications for sentencing. Criminal mediation, probation, and community service may be appropriate modes of penitential punishment, but what role (if any) could such familiar modes of punishment as imprisonment and fines (not to mention capital punishment) play? And how should sentencers determine either the mode or the severity of an offender's punishment? Without some discussion of these matters, my account is radically indeterminate. It is not yet clear whether it can generate a morally plausible picture of a penal system.

Second, despite my drawing on some examples of existing penal practice (on examples of mediation schemes, on the use of such sentences as probation and community service), it is not yet clear just how my account can relate to the actualities of our existing systems of criminal law and punishment. It depends on an ideal(ized) conception of liberal political community, but we must ask how far our existing political societies come near to actualizing such an ideal—and what the implications are if they do not. It portrays punishment as an attempt to engage offenders in an authentic enterprise of moral communication, aimed at repentance, reform, and reconciliation, but we must ask how far our actual penal practices could either be or become what on this account they ought to be—and what the implications are if they cannot. We must ask, that is, whether this ideal(ized) account of punishment can provide a plausible ideal towards which our actual penal practice could aspire—and what the implications are if it cannot.

I explore these two sets of issues in chapters 4 and 5.

4

Communicative Sentencing

A NORMATIVE THEORY OF PUNISHMENT MUST EITHER INCLUDE, OR BE ABLE to generate, a theory of sentencing—an account of how particular modes and levels of punishment are to be assigned to particular kinds of offense and offender. Only then can it guide or even connect with the actual practice of punishment. Normative theorizing must begin with an account of the ends that punishment should serve, of the values to which it must answer and by which it must be structured. But until it starts to show how sentences are to be determined in the light of those ends and values, it has not yet provided a theory of punishment as a possible human practice. For sentencing—the determination of the precise modes and levels of punishment to be imposed on particular (kinds of) offenses and offenders—is central to the practice of punishment.

I cannot offer a complete theory of sentencing here.[1] But I do discuss four sets of sentencing issues, which should show how the general account of punishment developed in chapter 3 can generate a practicable and morally plausible account of sentencing.

One set of issues, discussed below in section 1, concerns the role that a principle of 'proportionality' should play in sentencing and what such a principle should mean. Another, discussed in section 2, concerns the material mode of punishment rather than its severity (on which the principle of proportionality focuses): what forms can punishment appropriately take, either in general or for particular kinds of offense? A third set of issues, discussed more selectively in section 3, concerns the allocation of responsibility for sentencing: the roles that legislatures, sentencing councils, or similar bodies, and individual sentencers, as well as victims and offenders, should play. Finally, in section 4, I discuss 'persistent' and 'dangerous' offenders, who seem to pose a particular problem for a communicative account of punishment like mine.

1. Punishing Proportionately

Any normative theory of punishment includes some principle of proportionality, requiring that punishment be 'proportionate' to what justifies it. For pure consequentialists, for instance, punishment must be 'proportionate' to, that is, not more harmful than, the harm it aims to prevent. Discussions of 'proportionality' in punishment, however, typically focus on one particular kind of proportionality—that between punishment and the crime being punished. Thus the familiar objection to purely consequentialist theories that they cannot find room or a firm enough foundation for a principle of proportionality is the objection that they cannot do justice to the idea that punishment must be proportionate to the crime being punished. A familiar constraint posited by side-constrained consequentialist theories is that punishment must be proportionate, or not disproportionate, to the crime (see ch. 1.2.1).

Some such principle of proportionality has strong intuitive appeal, as is evidenced by the frequency (and fervor) with which people complain that certain sentences are too lenient or too harsh for the crimes for which they are imposed. Some such principle is also intrinsic to the idea that punishment must be *for* an offense. If punishment is to be for an offense, its character and severity must surely be determined by the offense for which it is imposed. Some such principle is also intrinsic to any version of retributivism. If punishment is to be justified as what an offender deserves for an offense, it must be proportionate to that offense. My concern here, however, is with the role that such a principle should play, and its meaning, within a communicative account of punishment of the kind developed in chapter 3.

A requirement of proportionality is intrinsic to any theory on which the, or a, primary purpose of punishment is to communicate the censure that offenders deserve for their crimes (see ch. 3.7.3, above; also von Hirsch 1992, 69–71; 1993, 15–17). We must determine not just that an offender deserves censure but how severe that censure should be: the more serious the crime, the more severe the deserved censure. That censure is communicated by penal hard treatment, and severity is a dimension of penal hard treatment as it is of censure. Thus the severity of the penal hard treatment will communicate the severity of the censure: the more severe the hard treatment, the more severe the censure it communicates. But it is then a simple requirement of justice (and of communicative honesty) that the severity of the offender's punishment (as penal hard treatment) be proportionate to the seriousness of her crime. To punish her with disproportionate severity, or leniency, is to communicate to her more, or less, censure than she deserves. This is, however, dishonest and unjust, since it is to punish her more, or less, severely than she deserves.

However, these initial statements fall far short of showing either what 'proportionality' is or just what role such a principle should play in a communicative system of punishment.

1.1. Relative or Absolute Proportionality?

A principle of penal proportionality is clearly at least a principle of *relative*, or 'ordinal', proportionality.[2] It requires at least that an offender's punishment be proportionate (or not disproportionate) *relative to* the punishments imposed on other offenders. Offenders who committed comparably serious offenses should be punished with comparable severity, and those who committed more serious crimes should be punished more severely than those who committed less serious crimes. To punish one offender more severely than another is to censure him more severely, which is to portray his crime as more serious; and that portrayal must be justified.[3]

However, a requirement of relative proportionality can be satisfied by penal systems of very different general levels of harshness. A system, for instance, whose lightest sentence was a one-dollar fine and whose heaviest was a year in prison would satisfy the requirement. So too would one whose lightest sentence was a year in prison and whose heaviest was death. The requirement can help us determine sentences within an existing scale of penalties, but it cannot help us determine the upper and lower limits of the scale or what material modes of punishment the scale should include. To find guidance on these issues from the idea of proportionality, we would need to appeal to a notion of *absolute*, or 'cardinal', proportionality. We would need to be able to judge that a certain level or mode of punishment is proportionate to a certain crime, not just *relative to* the sentences imposed on other crimes or offenders, but *intrinsically*.

Before exploring whether we can say that certain material modes of punishment are appropriate or inappropriate for certain kinds of crime, we must focus on the issue of severity: for the principle of proportionality, as orthodoxly understood, concerns the relation between the seriousness of the offense and the severity of the punishment.

Such intuitions as we have about proportionality do seem to include intuitions about absolute, as well as relative, proportionality. Five years' imprisonment would be a grossly disproportionate sentence for a parking offense, and a fine of 10 dollars a grossly disproportionate sentence for a brutal murder. Such judgments do not, I think, depend only on comparing such sentences with existing sentencing practices. Such sentences would be disproportionate in any penal system, and a system within which either of them was relatively proportionate would be an absolutely disproportionate system. What underpins such judgments is some valuation of the interests or goods infringed by the offense and by the punishment. To think that an offense that causes only relatively minor inconvenience is appropriately punished by the deprivation of five years' liberty, or that the deliberate taking of a life is appropriately punished by a trivial financial penalty, would display a grotesquely distorted valuation of the interests and goods involved or of the people whose interests and goods they are (and see von Hirsch 1993, 36–37).

Whatever the rational force of such intuitive judgments, however, they clearly cannot take us very far towards fixing a determinate scale of penalties. We can, in extreme cases, judge certain sentences to be absolutely (and grossly) disproportionate. But we cannot make determinate judgments about which kinds of sentence would be absolutely proportionate.

We can make *some* progress by asking what kinds or levels of punishment would serve the proper communicative goals of punishment. Thus von Hirsch argues that if penal hard treatment is to provide merely a "prudential supplement" to the law's moral appeal, it should not be so harsh that it drowns out, rather than supplementing, the law's moral voice. This, together with a commitment to penal parsimony, should lead us to adopt the "decremental strategy" of progressively reducing sentence levels—perhaps towards a system in which the maximum sentence for homicide was five years' imprisonment and the maximum for any other offense was three years' imprisonment (von Hirsch 1993, ch. 5; see ch. 3.3.2, above). My account, however, which gives penal hard treatment a more ambitious, penitential purpose, does not give even this much guidance. If we ask what levels of punishment would be appropriate as secular penances, no determinate answer is forthcoming. We can rule out *modes* of punishment that are cruel or degrading or unduly intrusive—that do not address the offender as a member of the normative community or are inconsistent with the values of that community (see, e.g., Murphy 1979d; von Hirsch 1993, ch. 9). But this still leaves a wide range of possible modes of punishment open, and does not help us determine appropriate levels of penal severity.

We must recognize, I think, that any attempt to work out a penalty scale (either its anchoring points or its content) from scratch is doomed to failure. There is no archimedean point, independent of all existing penal practice, from which we could embark on such an enterprise.[4] We can only begin from where we are now, with a penalty scale whose content and upper and lower limits have been determined by a host of historical contingencies. If we care, as we should, both about the burdens that punishment of its nature imposes and about the danger that those burdens will be excessive or harmful, we should accept a principle of penal parsimony, which requires us to impose punishments no harsher (in mode or amount) than is strictly necessary for the aims that punishment is to serve. This will then generate the "decremental strategy" of gradually reducing the general levels of penal severity: of looking for less coercive, less exclusionary, and less potentially oppressive modes of punishment (thus preferring, where possible, noncustodial to custodial forms of punishment; see sec. 2.2, below) and of gradually reducing the general levels of punishment within each mode.

The point of such a strategy will be to see how far we can lower our conceptions of what modes and levels of punishment will be adequate to communicate an appropriate kind and degree of censure to offenders, in a way that might induce repentance and self-reform, and adequate to communicate to others the offender's reparative apology. Given that punishment should aim not to *exact* repentance but only to persuade offenders in a way that leaves them the freedom to remain unpersuaded (see ch. 3.7.4), and given that what we will count as 'adequate' depends on conventions and on understandings of penal severity that are modifiable, such a strategy should lead to significant reductions in general levels of penal severity. We cannot predict how far we will be able to take such reductions, especially since the meaning of different kinds or levels of punishment depends crucially on the wider social context (of attitudes to the law and to punishment itself, and of the social relationships between citizens) in which they are set. But I see no reason to believe that they could not in the end be very significant.

My discussion in section 2 of modes of punishment also bears on the question of absolute levels of punishment. First, however, further questions must be raised about the notion of relative proportionality.

1.2. Proportionality of What to What?

Penal proportionality, as orthodoxly understood, is a relation between the seriousness of the crime and the severity of the punishment. Judgments of relative proportionality depend, therefore, on our ability to rank crimes in terms of their seriousness and sentences in terms of their severity. There are familiar problems involved in trying to work out either of these rankings. I mention these only briefly here, since my main concern is with whether we should even aspire to develop complete, unitary rankings of all crimes on a single scale of seriousness and of all penalties on a single scale of severity. If we give the principle of proportionality a central, dominant role in sentencing, so that the first task of sentencers is to ensure that they impose proportionate punishments, we will need to develop such rankings. But, I argue, even if this can be done, the costs of doing it are too high.

Criminal seriousness is usually taken to be a function of harm plus culpability. To rank crimes in terms of their seriousness, we must thus identify and rank criminal harms, identify and rank kinds of criminal culpability, and then combine these two rankings into a single scale of criminal seriousness. In carrying out these tasks, we must ask whether what matters is only the harm intended or expected, or also the harm actually caused (this is one aspect of the controversy between 'subjectivists' and 'objectivists'; see Duff 1996b, chs. 6–8). We must ask whether we can always identify 'harm' and 'culpability' separately, or whether the harm suffered by the victim of a criminal attack is partly *constituted* by the culpable character of the attack (see p. 128, above). We must ask how 'harms' are to be measured and ranked. (The 'living-standard' analysis [see von Hirsch and Jareborg 1991], which attends to the interests affected by the crime and the importance of those interests for normal living standards, can help with this question as far as directly victimizing crimes are concerned.) And we must ask how culpability is to be defined and ranked—how adequate

the standard Anglo-American categories of intention, knowledge, recklessness, and negligence are—and how we can then combine the measures of
harm and of culpability into a single measure of seriousness.[5]

I do not suggest that these problems are utterly insuperable. We do after
all manage to make some comparative judgments of seriousness between different crimes, and sentencing councils do manage to produce more complete
rankings of crimes. But an attempt to rank *all* crimes on a *single* scale of seriousness incurs certain costs. We will need to treat both harm and culpability
in rather general terms. Harm will be understood, for instance, in terms of
setbacks to a list of standard interests, which will themselves be ranked by
reference to their importance for normal living standards, and culpability
will need to be analyzed in terms of a limited set of fault concepts (intention, knowledge, recklessness, negligence, for instance), which can then be
ranked relative to one another. The cost of this is a kind of generalization, of
abstraction from the concrete particularities of different kinds of crime,
which threatens to separate the law's definitions of crimes from extralegal
moral understandings of them as wrongs. Those moral understandings are
more complex, particularized, and concrete than are the understandings
available within such a legal framework. They preclude any unitary ranking
of all crimes on a single scale of seriousness, since they connect the wrongfulness of different kinds of crime to different kinds of value that cannot without distortion be rendered rationally commensurable.[6] This, I argue below, is
a cost we should not be willing to pay.

Penal severity looks like a simpler matter. For whereas in judging criminal
seriousness we have to deal with the two dimensions of harm and culpability,
penal severity has only one dimension—the impact of the punishment on
the offender. We might hope that a living-standard analysis will help us here
too (see von Hirsch 1993, 34–35)—that we can gauge the severity of punishments by asking which interests they affect and how important those interests are for normal living standards. Still, however, there are problems to be
faced and a general question to be asked.

The problems have to do with what counts as the relevant 'impact'. How
far should we attend to the different impacts that what is in some sense the
'same' sentence would have on different offenders, given their different situations and sensibilities (see Tonry 1994, 69–73; Ashworth & Player 1998)?
How far, if at all, should we attend to the further effects that the sentence
will have on the offender—for instance, on her employment prospects—or
on others—for instance, on her family (see Walker 1991, 106–10)?

The question has to do, again, with how ambitious we should be. Should we
aim to rank all sentences on a single scale of severity? This will involve certain
costs. It will require us to set strict limits on the range of sentences available to
the courts in order to ensure that all sentences are (at least roughly) commensurable. We can rank terms of imprisonment by their length (albeit imperfectly, given the different conditions of different kinds of prison) and fines by

their amount (relative to the offender's means); and we might try to decide whether and when a sufficiently harsh fine is more severe than a brief term of imprisonment. Matters become more problematic with noncustodial punishments such as Community Service Orders and probation. Although we can rank these in terms of their length, it becomes harder to render them commensurable with imprisonment and fines. Furthermore, length (the number of hours of community service, the number of months on a probation order or of hours spent with the probation officer) seems a radically incomplete measure of severity, given the very different kinds of work that Community Service Orders can involve and the very different conditions and requirements that may be attached to probation orders (but see Bottoms 1998, 70–77). But even if we can—at the cost of a degree of artificiality and abstraction—include some such 'intermediate sanctions' along with imprisonment and fines on a single scale of penal severity, we will need to set strict limits on their form and content. We cannot allow them to be too diverse in their content, or allow sentencers to construct individualized sentences with very different kinds of content for particular offenders, or allow sentences to be negotiated through a mediation process. Such flexibility will render commensurability, and a unitary ranking of all penalties in terms of their severity, impossible.[7] This cost, I argue, is also too high.

1.3. Positive or Negative?

Some theorists, such as von Hirsch, read the principle of proportionality as a *positive* principle, which requires sentencers to impose *proportionate* sentences. Their first task is to determine what level of sentence is proportionate and to impose a sentence with that degree of 'penal bite'. Only when two or more sentences with equivalent or comparable penal bite are available can they properly appeal to considerations other than proportionality to decide which sentence to impose.[8] Others, like Morris and Tonry, read it as a *negative* principle (as a feature of 'limiting retributivism'). It forbids courts to impose *disproportionate* sentences. But within the limits set by that constraint, they should appeal to other considerations (of efficient crime prevention, of penal parsimony) in determining the precise level and mode of punishment (see Morris 1974; Morris & Tonry 1990, ch. 4; Tonry 1994, 1998; Frase 1997).

So long as the negative version of the principle is taken to set lower as well as upper limits on sentences (to forbid disproportionately lenient as well as disproportionately harsh punishments),[9] it might seem that the two versions cannot differ. A sentence must be either proportionate or disproportionate: to forbid disproportionate punishments is therefore to require proportionate punishments. There can of course be disagreement about just how determinate the demands of proportionality are (about how precisely we can measure and rank both criminal seriousness and penal severity) and this will lead to disagreement about how much room there is for other kinds of consideration to come into play once the demands of proportionality have been satisfied. But these are disagreements about the implications of the (univocal) principle of proportionality, not about whether that principle should be read in positive or in negative terms. The difference between the positive and negative formulations is a merely verbal one.

There is *some* truth in this. The disagreement between von Hirsch and Morris and Tonry does in part concern the extent to which the demands of proportionality can be made precise and determinate, without artificially distorting our conceptions both of criminal seriousness and of penal severity. Furthermore, if the upper and lower limits that limiting retributivism sets on sentencing leave sentencers the discretion to choose between sentences of different degrees of severity (as they seem to), then it allows sentencers to impose *disproportionate* punishments: for they will be allowed to impose sentences of differing severity on offenders whose crimes are of comparable seriousness. Limiting retributivists must then be read as arguing, not that proportionality sets only negative constraints on sentencing, but rather that the demands of proportionality can sometimes be *overridden* by other considerations—so long as the sentences imposed are not grossly disproportionate (see Duff 1996a, 59–61).

However, we can find (or construct) a more interesting difference between 'positive' and 'negative' versions of the principle of proportionality, involving the principle's meaning. An analogy can bring this difference out.

In discussing practical reason, philosophers sometimes distinguish 'optimizing' from 'satisficing'. The optimizer seeks 'the best' course of action: the action that, out of all the available options, will most efficiently bring about the most good. The satisficer, by contrast, is less ambitious (and perhaps more realistic). She seeks only a course of action that is 'good enough' or 'satisfactory'. She will not take a course of action that is obviously worse than some alternative, but she will not even try to rank all the available options on a single scale of goodness in order to determine which is 'the best'.[10]

Somewhat analogously, proponents of 'positive' proportionality (as I use the term) insist that the first task of sentencers is to impose *the* proportionate quantum of punishment. This requires us to provide unitary rankings of crimes in terms of their seriousness and of penalties in terms of their severity. This also requires us to operate with somewhat abstract and general criteria of seriousness, and with a limited range of modes of punishment that can be rendered commensurable as to their severity (see sec. 1.2, above). Only when this task has been discharged can the sentencer appeal to other considerations, to decide between two or more sentences of equivalent severity.

By contrast, proponents of 'negative' proportionality do not look for *the* proportionate quantum of punishment. They will, instead, identify a range of possible sentences, involving different modes of punishment, all of which are 'good enough' as far as proportionality is concerned, that is, none of which is clearly disproportionate. They will then choose between those sentences on grounds other than proportionality, without even trying to ask whether one is more precisely proportionate than the others. Nor need they try to rank all crimes on a single scale of seriousness or all penalties on a single scale of severity. If we are committed to positive proportionality, we will need to be able to compare any two crimes in terms of their seriousness and any two penalties in terms of their severity, since otherwise we will not be able to check that the demands of proportionality are being satisfied across the whole spectrum of crimes and punishments. We must therefore provide complete unitary rankings of criminal seriousness and of penal severity. If we are committed only to negative proportionality, however, we need not make such comparisons for *all* crimes and *all* penalties. When they can be made, when one crime is evidently more serious than another or one penalty more severe than another, we must respect the demands of proportionality. We must punish the more serious crime more severely and reserve the harsher punishment for a more serious crime. But such comparisons will not, as we can now recognize, always be possible, since some crimes and some penalties are incommensurable. Nor should they always be the main focus of our attention. What matters about crimes is not just their seriousness but their character as public wrongs. What matters about punishments is not just their severity but their character as responses to such wrongs. Negative proportionality thus gives sentencers more room to attend to the concrete particularities of the crime, without worrying about rendering it commensurable with all other crimes in terms of its seriousness, and to choose between a wider range of penalties, without worrying about rendering them all commensurable in terms of their severity.

A communicative system of penitential punishment, I argue below (in sec. 1.5), should be structured by a negative rather than by a positive principle of proportionality. Such a principle does give proportionality its due.

1.4. Overriding or Defeasible?

Whatever version of the principle of proportionality we adopt, we must ask how binding or stringent it should be. There are three possibilities.

First, we could treat it as a *categorical* and *indefeasible* principle, which requires us to impose proportionate (or not-disproportionate) punishments and which can never justifiably be overridden.

Second, we could treat it as a *categorical* but *defeasible* principle. It demands that we impose proportionate punishments, and that demand is normally or presumptively absolute. But in *exceptional* circumstances it can be overridden by other urgent considerations, which justify the imposition of a disproportionately harsh or lenient sentence.

Third, we could treat it as just one consideration among others that bear on sentencing (though perhaps a weighty consideration). In determining sentences, sentencers must attend to proportionality, but also to various other considerations, such as the principle of penal parsimony and consequentialist considerations of efficient crime-prevention. Although the demands of proportionality might often outweigh such other considerations when they conflict, there is no presumption in their favor. They can be straightforwardly outweighed.

The explanation of proportionality given at the start of this section rules out the third of these possibilities. The principle of proportionality is a categorical principle of justice: it specifies, not a good to be weighed against other goods, but a demand of justice that must, at least presumptively, be satisfied. The question then is whether we should see that demand as being, in exceptional circumstances, defeasible or as being indefeasible (see Robinson 1987a; von Hirsch 1993, ch. 6).

We should, I suggest, treat upwards and downwards deviations from proportionality differently. The demands of proportionality should be indefeasible in the former context but (exceptionally) defeasible in the latter.

Upward deviations—the imposition of disproportionately harsh punishments—cannot be justified. Punishment must, as punishment, be *for* an offense. It must communicate the censure the offender deserves for his offense, but it cannot then in justice be harsher than the offense deserves. This might seem too hasty a response to any suggestion that, for the sake of public protection, we should provide special measures of extended preventive detention for persistent, dangerous offenders. But I am not yet arguing that such measures cannot be justified. My claim so far is only that if they are to be justified, either they must be justified *as punishments*, by arguing that the offender's persistent and dangerous criminality makes a categorical difference to the seriousness of his current offense, so that an exceptionally long term of imprisonment can be proportionate; or they must be justified and administered as *nonpenal* measures of civil detention. I do not think that the latter kind of justification is ultimately plausible.[11] But I say more about the former kind of justification in section 4.2, below.

Downward deviations, the imposition of disproportionately lenient punishments, can be justified at least in cases in which mercy is appropriate: when, given what the offender is already suffering, it would be inappropriate to insist on focusing our and his attention on his crime (see ch. 3, n. 46). I also think, however, that these are the only cases in which downward deviations can be justified. In all other cases offenders should receive sentences proportionate (or not disproportionate) to their crimes. This might sound unreasonably harsh. There will surely be cases in which to punish offenders as severely as they admittedly deserve will not only do no more good than would be done by a lighter punishment, but will actually do (unnecessary and thus unjustified) harm (see e.g. Tonry 1994, 72–73; on which see Brownlee 1994). This criticism would be justified were I trying to justify the modes and levels of punishment imposed under our existing systems of criminal justice. But it has much less force against the modes and (lower) levels of punishment that would be imposed under a properly communicative and penitential penal system. The reasons I give (see ch. 3.7.3) for punishing the already repentant offender also apply here. To which we can add that, if sentencing is subject to the constraints of negative rather than of positive proportionality, sentences can be more flexibly and thus less harmfully tailored to the offender's particular situation (see further sec. 3.2, below).

My suggestion is, then, that the principle of proportionality should be *negative*, in the sense explained in the previous subsection, but also relatively *strict*—indefeasible as far as upward deviations are concerned and only exceptionally defeasible as far as downward deviations are concerned. I need now to justify my claim that we should prefer the negative to the positive version of the principle, both by explaining what such a negative principle amounts to and by showing why it is more appropriate to the communicative aims that punishment should serve.

1.5. Beyond Proportionality

A positive principle of proportionality, of the kind favored by von Hirsch, embodies a particular reading of the familiar thought that the punishment should "fit the crime": 'fit' is interpreted as a formal relationship between criminal seriousness and penal severity. If we also take the principle (as von Hirsch does) to be either indefeasible or only exceptionally defeasible, we will hold that sentencers' primary task is to determine the appropriate, that is, proportionate, *quantum* of punishment—the level of penal severity that will communicate the degree of censure appropriate to the seriousness of the crime. Only when more than one of the available sentences satisfies this requirement may sentencers choose between sentences on grounds other than proportionality. This then requires us to understand crimes in rather abstract and general terms, so that we can rank them all on a single scale of seriousness, and to set strict limits on the modes of punishment available to sentencers, so that we can rank them all on a single scale of severity.

Now this understanding of the meaning and importance of proportionality fits with the modest communicative aims that von Hirsch posits for criminal punishment, and with the liberal limits that he wants to set on the penal powers and ambitions of the state (see ch. 3.3.2). If punishment should communicate deserved censure but should not intrude into the offender's soul, if it must preserve the kind of respectful distance from the offender that a liberal state should display in its coercive dealings with its citizens, then it seems appropriate that its communicative content should consist primarily in the somewhat formal and abstract message that the offender committed a wrong of a certain degree of seriousness; and that the choice of modes of punishment should be constrained by the requirement that they be suited to the communication of this kind of message about the seriousness of the crime.

Matters are very different, however, on my more ambitiously communicative account of punishment as secular penance. Punishment aims now to do more than simply communicate—as it were, at arm's length—a certain degree of formal censure. Punishment aims to persuade offenders to face up to what they have done—to the substantive moral character and implications of their crimes as public wrongs. Likewise, penal hard treatment, the material burden that punishment involves, is intended to further the penitential aims of punishment as penance, rather than (as on von Hirsch's account) to provide an additional prudential incentive to refrain from crime. If the punishment is to "fit the crime" on this account, it must be apt, not only to communicate a proportionate degree of censure, but to serve these richer, more ambitious communicative goals. There must be a more *substantive* 'fit' between punishment and crime, such that the punishment can bring offenders to face up to the character and the significance of what they have done, and serve as apologetic reparation for the crime.

Before pursuing this idea of a 'substantive fit' between punishment and crime, I should say something more about its relation to the principle of proportionality—about the role a negative version of that principle will play on my account, and about the constraints it sets on sentencing.

In arguing that the requirement of proportionality should be read in negative terms, I am not arguing that it merely sets side-constraints on our pursuit of penal aims in which proportionality plays no part. That is how side-constrained consequentialists might understand the role of proportionality. The goal of crime prevention, they might say, does not in itself require that punishments be proportionate to crimes and might be efficiently served by disproportionate punishments, but the pursuit of that goal is constrained by the requirement that we must not inflict disproportionate punishments (see ch. 1.2.1). On my account, however, proportionality is intrinsic to the *aims* of punishment as penance. Punishments that are to communicate the censure that offenders deserve for their crimes—and are to constitute adequate apologies for those crimes—must be proportionate to those crimes. Disproportionate sentences cannot serve the proper goals of punishment (see sec. 1, above).

Why then should I not accept a positive principle of proportionality of the kind that von Hirsch advocates? Because proportionality, as a relationship between the seriousness of a crime and the severity of its punishment, is only one dimension of the proper relationship between crime and punishment on a communicative conception of punishment as penance. A communicatively appropriate punishment should communicate, not just a degree of censure proportionate to the seriousness of the crime, but a more substantive understanding of the nature and implications of the crime as a wrong. Such an understanding is hindered rather than assisted by the attempt to rank all crimes on a single scale of seriousness that a principle of positive proportionality requires, and such a communicative enterprise is hindered by the strict limits that such a principle sets on the range of modes of punishment that should be available to sentencers.

Rather than saying (as advocates of positive proportionality say) that a communicatively appropriate punishment must, above all, be proportionate to the crime, we should therefore say that a communicatively appropriate punishment must, among other things, not be disproportionate to the crime. This still sets *strong* constraints on sentencing, since it forbids punishments that are disproportionately severe or lenient (unless mercy is appropriate; see sec. 1.4, above). But the constraints are not as *narrow* as those imposed by a principle of positive proportionality, since a wider range of different types of sentence can satisfy a requirement that punishment not be disproportionate (or be 'proportionate enough') than can satisfy the requirement that punishment be proportionate, or as precisely proportionate as possible—just as a wider range of actions can satisfy the requirements of satisficing than can satisfy those of optimizing (see sec. 1.3, above). Within that range, sentencers will then be able to select the particular kind of sentence that is substantively apt as a communicative penance for the particular crime.[12]

How narrow or broad will that range be? How can we give practicable form to such a principle of negative proportionality, in a way that will effectively guide and constrain the decisions of individual sentencers? I cannot provide detailed answers to these questions here, though I say something more about them in the following two sections. The guiding idea, however, should be this. Other than in those (relatively rare) cases in which imprisonment should be mandatory (see sec. 2.2, below), sentencers should have a range of non-custodial sentences available to them, and should look within that range for a sentence that is communicatively appropriate to the offender's crime. Negative proportionality is an essential dimension of communicative appropriateness. Insofar as crimes can be ranked as more or less serious, and sentences as more or less severe, the severity of the sentence must not be disproportionate to the seriousness of the crime. But it is only one dimension, and its requirements will in most cases leave sentencers with a choice between a range of different sentences. That choice is then to be guided by considerations of 'substantive fit': what mode of punishment is apt to communicate an appropriate understanding of the particular crime and its implications?

To explain the meaning and implications of this notion of 'substantive fit', I turn in the following two sections to two further sets of issues: one concerning the meaning of different modes of punishment, the other concerning individualized sentencing.

2. Punishments and Their Meanings

To talk of a 'substantive fit' between punishment and crime is not to say, as some versions of *Lex Talionis* suggest, that punishment should inflict on offenders something resembling what they did to their victims. Waldron (1992) argues that *Lex Talionis*, interpreted as requiring an offender's punishment to "possess some or all of the characteristics that made the offense wrong" (35), can play a role in a system of punishment that aims, among other things, to induce "awareness of wrongdoing and repentance" (31). It follows from this, he thinks, that the communicative and educative purposes of punishment could, in principle, be served by sentencing a rapist to be sexually attacked. By inflicting on him an "invasion" similar to that which he inflicted on his victim and "calculated to traumatize him and reduce his dignity," Waldron argues, we can "drive home to the sexual offender exactly what made his action . . . wrong." We will rightly object to such a punishment. But this is because of what it would do to those who had to impose it, not because it is "in principle inappropriate" (38; see Garvey 1998, 775–91). This argument is, however, misguided. Nor is it one to which my account of punishment commits me.

It might sometimes be tempting to think that we can get a wrongdoer to recognize what he has done by doing something similar to him: "now he'll know what it's like to be raped." But, first, an action intended to inflict on him the "trauma, indignity and degradation" that he inflicted on his victim (Waldron 1992, 37) is not a *communicative* action that addresses him, as punishment must address the offender, as a member of the normative community. It therefore cannot even "in principle" be an appropriate punishment. It might have the effect of changing his understanding of what he did, depending on how he later thinks about what he has suffered. But it does not address him as a rational moral agent—it simply seeks to traumatize and humiliate him (cf. Murphy 1979d, 233–34). Second, we cannot make the kind of separation that Waldron needs to make between the "deontic" features of an action—its wrongfulness—and those features on which its deontic features supervene (1992, 34–35). He must separate them, because the punishment imposed on an offender cannot itself be a *wrongful* action if is to be justified; but it must share as many as possible of the features in virtue of which the crime was wrongful if it is to accord with *Lex Talionis*. We cannot, however, separate them, because the fact that an action is intended to inflict "trauma, indignity and degradation" on its victim is not a property on which the action's wrongfulness supervenes. Instead, it *constitutes* the action as essentially wrongful. Furthermore, insofar as we can make such a separation, the punitive action loses it communicative force. If a law officer secretly takes a thief's property without his consent, she might reproduce the essential non-deontic features of his crime. But just because her action is (supposedly) legitimate, as a punishment, and is not dishonest, it is ill-suited to communicate to the thief what it is like to be the victim of a theft—of a dishonest and illegitimate taking.

This discussion of Waldron's suggestion should ward off any suspicion that my account of punishment suggests or favors such a version of *Lex Talionis*. Offenders' punishments should indeed aim to communicate to them an understanding of the wrongfulness of their crimes. But we do not do that by inflicting something similar on them.

How then do we do it? The examples given in chapter 3 provide the start of an answer to this question: probation, Community Service Orders, and criminal mediation and reparation programs (see ch. 3.4–5) are appropriate punishments because they are suited to the aim of persuading offenders to face up to and to repent their crimes, to begin to reform themselves, and to make apologetic reparation to those whom they wronged. What makes such sentences obviously appropriate as communicative punishments is in part the fact that, especially with probation and mediation, their communicative content is direct and explicit. In her meetings with the offender, the probation officer tries to get him to think and talk about his crime and about how he needs to change. In a mediation process the offender is confronted by the victim's angry or distressed account of the impact of the crime (see also the CHANGE program at ch. 3.5.2). An offender's Community Service Order might bring him face to face with the effects of crimes like his (see ch. 3.5.3).

Even these kinds of sentence, however, have an important symbolic dimension: not just in the fact that they mark the political community's claim, through the law, to authority over the offender—though that is a crucial dimension of all criminal punishments—but also in the more particular meanings that they have as particular modes of punishment. Probation, for instance, tells the offender that her crime put her trustworthiness as a citizen in doubt. The imposition of a Community Service Order shows the offender that she owes something to the community by way of reparative apology—by way of some burdensome work through which the moral implications of her crime can be communicated to her and she can communicate her apologetic repentance to the community.

This dimension of meaning—not just the meaning of punishment as punishment, but the meanings of particular modes of punishment—is important for a communicative account of punishment, though it is too little discussed by penal theorists.[13] We must ask what modes of punishment are appropriate, either in general or for particular kinds of offense. And while answers to this question depend in part on noncommunicative considerations of humanity and practicability, they must also depend on the meanings of the different possible modes—on what they say to and about offenders, on how they portray offenders' relationships to the political community and to the law. This point about the meanings of punishments becomes more important for an ambitiously communicative account like mine: for we must now ask, not just how different modes of punishment can serve the general aim of communicating censure to offenders, but also how they can help to communicate a more substantive understanding of the wrongfulness and the implications of particular kinds of offense.

I can illustrate this general point, and fill in some of the gaps in my discussion of sentencing, by considering three other modes of punishment.[14] Two of them, fines and imprisonment, are central to our existing penal practices: given their meanings, they can still play roles—albeit severely reduced roles—in a communicative system of punishment. The third, capital punishment, retains a controversial role in some contemporary penal systems but should not figure in a properly communicative system.[15]

2.1. Monetary Punishments

Fines are the most widely used form of noncustodial punishment in Britain.[16] Their attractions are many. They are relatively economical and easy to administer. They can be proportioned to offenders' means by a system of 'unit' or 'day' fines,[17] and can thus be rendered both commensurable and proportionate. They preserve a certain distance from the offender—the law takes her money but does not really touch *her*. And (for better or worse) they sit happily with a culture of commodification in which everything, including crime, has its monetary price. This last point, however, should also lead us to wonder whether fines are really appropriate for the whole range of offenses for which they are or may be imposed, or whether in relation to at least some crimes they do not have the wrong kind of meaning.

Young (1994) argues this point in relation to rape. If we ask why a fine should be seen, as it generally is, as an inappropriate punishment for rape, the answer is not, Young argues, that a fine is too lenient. It would be in principle possible to impose a fine so stringent that the offender would have to devote all his resources for many years to paying it. The answer is, rather, that it is the wrong *kind* of punishment for rape. It suggests that rape could be 'paid for' in monetary terms, and thus distorts the character of rape as a kind of wrong that cannot be compensated (hence the controversy aroused by the English judge who ordered a young rapist to pay his young victim compensation of 500 pounds so that she could take a holiday).

This argument might seem unpersuasive. We have become used to monetary payments that serve as compensation or damages for civil wrongs, and while that trend might be criticized as manifesting a morally corrupting kind of commodification, this is surely also often the only practicable form that reparative apology can take. A monetary payment to someone I have wronged cannot itself, as monetary payment, repair or make up for that wrong. But it might be the only practicable way in which I can express my apologetic repentance to my victim. So too with fines as punishments. Once we recognize that moral reparation need not take the form of material compensation for the harm done (which might be uncompensatable), and that fines (like monetary reparations) cost wrongdoers something they care about, we can surely see fines as a proper method of communicating censure to offenders, and as a proper way for them to express their apologies to those whom they wronged, for at least very many kinds of crime.

Nonetheless, I think there is force to Young's argument. First, fines are liable to be misleading. We are so used to paying taxes, to purchasing goods or services, to making monetary compensations of various kinds, that a monetary punishment could easily suggest that the crime can be adequately 'paid for' in this way.[18] Second, a fine does not seriously address the substantive character of, for instance, the rapist's crime. It does not seek to confront him with what he has done, as a substantive wrong against both his victim and the whole community, or to bring him to consider its meaning and implications. A fine might communicate formal censure, telling the offender that he has committed a wrong of a certain degree of seriousness, measured by the size of the fine. But it is not suited to the richer communicative purposes that I argue punishment should serve.

What then is an appropriate punishment for rape? I comment on imprisonment, which is in fact the usual sentence for rape, in section 2.2. But we should note here the way in which such punishments as probation, Community Service Orders, and criminal mediation procedures are generally more suitable than fines for the purposes of substantive penal communication. This is partly because probation and mediation include a direct and challenging discussion of the offender's crime; but also because all three kinds of sentence allow for flexible kinds of penal content, which can be adapted to the particular character of the offender's crime. The conditions that may be attached to a probation order can include programs, such as the CHANGE project, that directly address the offender's crime or restrictions that can bring home to him the implications of his crime (see ch. 3.5.1–2). Community Service Orders (or reparation undertaken as part of a criminal mediation procedure) can have contents that make them apt to serve as reparative apologies (see ch. 3.5.3).

This is not to say that there are no offenses for which a fine is an appropriate sentence. It is most obviously appropriate for crimes of material greed, especially when they are crimes against the community as a whole rather than against an individual victim (tax evasion, for example). By requiring the offender to make this additional, punitive payment to the community, we directly address the financial greed that her crime manifested. By making such a payment, the offender who comes to accept her punishment can communicate her own disavowal of that greed. It is to say, however, that a communicative system of penitential punishments should make far less use of fines than our own systems do.

This view might provoke two objections from liberal advocates of a positive principle of proportionality. First, the very flexibility of these other kinds of sentence is inimical to a positive principle of proportionality (see sec. 1, above). Whereas fines can, if their monetary value is determined by the offender's means, be administered in a way that satisfies the demands of positive proportionality, it becomes impossible to ensure the commensurability required by positive proportionality if we allow sentencers such flexibility in determining the content of probation or community service. Second, if they are allowed such flexibility, in order to impose sentences whose content is substantively appropriate to the offenders' crimes, they might be encouraged to impose sentences that are improperly intrusive and oppressive, in an attempt to get through to the offender or to address his supposed moral failings.

The first of these objections is met by arguing, (see sec. 1, above) that sentencing should respect a negative rather than a positive principle of proportionality. The sentences imposed on offenders should not be clearly disproportionate in their severity to the seriousness of the crimes for which they are imposed, since they would then communicate an inappropriately harsh, or lenient, censure. We can achieve this by ranking probation orders in terms of their length, by distinguishing 'simple' from 'intensive' probation (see Morris & Tonry 1990, ch. 7), and by ranking Community Service Orders in terms of the number of hours work required: but we need not try to achieve any strict commensurability of content between them.

The second objection is met by recalling the limits that my account sets on the scope and depth of the criminal law and of criminal punishment (see ch. 3.8). While punishment aims to address and challenge not merely the offender's behavior as understood in external terms, but the criminal attitudes manifest in her conduct, it must address only those aspects of her conduct and life that are directly implicated in her crime. It must also address her as an autonomous moral agent who is both bound and protected by the values of the liberal polity. *She* might see her punishment as 'intrusive', and we must always recognize the danger that punishment, which should be a mode of respectful moral communication, will in fact be administered in ways that makes it improperly intrusive or oppressive (see further ch. 5.1). In principle, however (and I am talking so far at the level of principle), such punishments need not intrude into what properly counts as 'private'.

2.2. The Meaning of Imprisonment

What of imprisonment? There are in fact various possible forms of custodial or quasi-custodial sentence, of which detention in a prison for a continuous period of months or years following immediately on sentencing (the most familiar form of imprisonment) is just one. Instead of being taken from court to prison, offenders can be required to present themselves to serve their prison term on some date after they have been sentenced (as happens in the Netherlands), or be sentenced to 'intermittent' imprisonment, involving weekend custody for instance, or be required to spend time (daily or residentially) in some institution other than a prison (a hostel or treatment center, for instance),[19] or be put under a curfew order forbidding them to leave their home during specified hours (see Walker & Padfield 1996, 143–44, 266–67; also Ashworth 1995a, 275–76). The feature common to all these different forms is that they consist centrally in a sharp restriction on the offender's liberty: he is restricted to a particular place—the prison, the hostel, his home.

They differ not just in the number of hours, days, or months for which he is restricted (although this, and the conditions under which he must live while restricted, are of course important aspects of the sentences) but in whether the restriction is one that is simply *inflicted* on him or one to which he is *required* to subject himself (see p. 111, above). They also differ in whether he is restricted to somewhere that is part of his normal life (such as his home) or to somewhere utterly removed from his normal life (such as a prison), and in whether the removal from normal life is short or intermittent enough for him to continue with much of his normal life (as with weekend detention) or so long and continuous that his normal life is radically interrupted (as with ordinary imprisonment).

We can begin with ordinary imprisonment, continuous detention in a prison for a period of time lasting at least, say, a month. The most salient aspect of imprisonment is that it *excludes* the offender. It cuts him off from his normal life and relationships, from participation in the normal life of the community. How then can imprisonment be justified on an account that aims, as my account aims, to render punishment inclusionary rather than exclusionary? Part of an answer to this question is that imprisonment must not be permanent: the offender must be restored to normal life and community after he has served his term.[20] But a more adequate answer (since even temporary exclusions are still exclusions) is that imprisonment must not be *mere* exclusion. It must itself, even while excluding the offender from normal community, be a way of reconciling him with the community. By this I mean, not just that prisoners must be offered help during their prison term to equip them for life on their release, but that their imprisonment itself, as imprisonment, must be understood and administered as a way of reconciling them with those they have wronged.

How could imprisonment serve such a purpose? It could do so if it serves as a penance, rather than merely as exclusion: if its meaning is that the offender has, by his crime, made the maintenance of normal community with him impossible but that community can be restored if he undergoes this penance. His imprisonment then gives material form to this implication of his crime—it seeks to bring him to recognize that his crime has rendered the maintenance of normal community impossible. But it also constitutes the penitential burden through which he can, if he does repent, express his repentant and apologetic understanding of crime, or by which, even if he does not repent, he is restored to normal community as if he had repented (see ch. 3.7.4).

By seeing imprisonment as a species of penance, we can also make sense of the way in which it does more than just exclude the offender from ordinary community in a kind of temporary exile. It *subjects* him to a particular regime. A temporary exile is left to make his own way outside the community from which he is exiled, whereas imprisoned offenders are required or forced to live within a prison, under the rules by which it is organized. Of course, exile is not normally a practicable possibility. It is unlikely that other states would willingly take in a criminal exile. Nor can a liberal polity expel its citizens to the homeless condition of utter outcasts. But if punishment is to serve as a penance, it is anyway appropriate that the offender should be imprisoned rather than exiled: the prison should provide a regime that is suitable to that penitential purpose.

There is of course much more to be said about what kinds of prison regime are suitable to this purpose. I am certainly not suggesting that the regimes typically found in our existing prisons are suitable. All I can say here is, first, that I am not advocating a return to the kind of 'penitentiary' favored by some of the early advocates of imprisonment who thought that criminals could best be brought to repentance by *solitary* confinement. Such confinement was intended to remove them from all corrupting influences, including (or especially) those of their fellow prisoners (see Ignatieff 1978; Sowle 1994– 95). That might be an appropriate regime for a Protestant religious community for whom sin is a matter between the individual offender and God, but not for a liberal political community dealing with public, social wrongs. Second, it is crucial that the prison regime treat those subject to it, as far as is possible consistently with their detention, as members of the normative community—as citizens, not as outcasts.[21] Third, imprisonment clearly provides an opportunity for many of the provisions or programs that can be attached to probation (see ch. 3.5.1–2). But it is important to preserve the distinction between measures that are *imposed* on offenders as part of their punishment, which must therefore be directed only at their criminal conduct, and measures that may be *offered* to them in order to help them with other problems but that must not be imposed on them.

The main point I want to emphasize here, however, is that given what imprisonment means, it must (on a communicative account of punishment as penance) be reserved for the most serious kinds of crime. The message of imprisonment is that the offender has not just damaged or threatened, but has *broken*, the normative bonds of community. He has made it impossible for us to live with him in the ordinary community of fellow citizenship unless and until he has undergone this penitential punishment. The other modes of punishment so far discussed are punishments "in the community":[22] offenders can preserve their ordinary place in the community while being punished. Imprisonment precludes this, removing the offender from the ordinary community. It can be justified only if that removal actualizes the moral implication of his crime. Now this is, in general, a reasonable response to some kinds of wrong—that they are *destructive* of the bonds of the community in which they are done. (Think, for instance, of the implications of plagiarism by an academic researcher or of a long and intimate adulterous affair by a spouse). This is also the element of truth in the argument that criminals have 'forfeited' their rights or standing as citizens (see ch.1.3.1). But, first, it is a reasonable response not to all wrongs but only to the most serious wrongs, which directly flout the community's most central or essential values. This is one reason why we should not say that *all* criminals forfeit their standing as citizens. Second, to argue (as I do) that punishment should be inclusionary rather than exclusionary is in part to say that punishment should itself be a way of negating or denying that 'forfeiture'. We *could* see those who commit such serious crimes as having forfeited their standing as citizens, but we *should* not do so. We should instead still see them as fellow citizens to whom we owe it not to allow their crimes to destroy the bonds of community, and it is precisely by punishing them that we preserve those bonds.

To say that imprisonment should be reserved for the most serious crimes is not novel. It is by now almost a commonplace amongst penal theorists, although sadly not amongst penal policy makers, that we should drastically reduce the range of crimes for which imprisonment is the normal sentence. I simply suggest a new reason, based on a communicative and inclusionary conception of punishment, for this conclusion. Nor does it yet tell us *which* crimes should be punished by imprisonment—which crimes should be seen as so serious that imprisonment is necessary to mark their implications. We cannot give a determinate or fixed answer to this question. Any answer depends on the community's understanding of what kinds of wrong make community impossible. But that understanding can change, and itself depends not merely on the character of the wrongs involved but on the willingness of other members of the community to live with those who commit them. All we can do, again, is embark on a "decremental strategy" (see sec. 1.1, above), which seeks both to reduce the range of crimes that are to be punished by imprisonment and to reduce the length of prison terms, without knowing in advance how far this strategy will take us. Once we recognize, however, both how severe any prison sentence is, given its meaning, and that a prison sentence of, for instance, three years is a *very* harsh punishment, whatever the conditions under which it is served, we can hope that such a strategy would lead to radical reductions of both kinds.[23]

My comments so far apply to continuous prison sentences of a length that seriously interrupts the offender's ordinary life. Matters are rather different with home curfews and with intermittent sentences involving a series of brief (for instance, weekend) detentions. As far as the former are concerned, we should perhaps compare them not with imprisonment in a penal institution but with other more limited kinds of restriction on offenders' movements, such as when someone convicted of football hooliganism is banned from attending matches for a specified period. What could justify requiring an offender to stay at home through evenings and nights is not that she must, given her crime, be temporarily removed from her ordinary community (for she is not thus removed) but that she should be as it were temporarily disqualified from that range of social activities in which citizens, including her, can normally engage outside working hours. As for intermittent sentences, they resemble continuous imprisonment in involving detention in some kind of prison, but are radically unlike such imprisonment in that they do not involve the complete rupture of the offender's normal life and community. They can thus (especially if combined with appropriate programs during the brief periods of detention) find a place among other intermediate sanctions—for instance, as indicating that the offender's crime threatened the bonds of community.

One further issue about imprisonment should be mentioned here: its role as the ultimate "back-up sanction" for failures to comply with the requirements of noncustodial sentences—for fine default (see Ashworth 1995a, 268), or for failures to comply with Community Service Orders or probation requirements (see Ashworth 1995a, 282–84; Brownlee 1998, 131–33). On one hand, it seems that imprisonment must be available as the ultimate sanction, since it might be the only sanction that can be *enforced* against those who fail to comply with other sanctions—and the law cannot allow offenders to escape punishment simply by refusing to comply with the requirements of their sentence. On the other hand, especially if we are to reserve imprisonment for the most serious crimes, we cannot simply imprison all those who default on a noncustodial sentence. Their initial offense was, *ex hypothesi*, not serious enough to warrant imprisonment, and we cannot plausibly say that their default itself is so serious an additional offense as to warrant imprisonment. We can go some way toward resolving this problem by distinguishing willful defaulters from those whose default is due to incompetence or lack of resources, or to the fact that their original sentence was not realistic or feasible (see Carlen 1989). We can then seek to help rather than punish the latter: by making serious efforts to persuade or enable defaulters to comply, by not being too quick to activate default sanctions, and by providing only a modestly increased sanction as the initial penalty for default (see von Hirsch, Wasik & Greene 1989, 609–10; von Hirsch 1993, 63–64; Tonry 1998, 294). We must still make provision, however, for the (perhaps very rare) offenders who willfully fail to comply with *all* the other sanctions required of them; and it is hard to see what alternative to imprisonment there would be in such cases. But perhaps when an offender's defaulting becomes that persistent, a (relatively short) prison term would be an acceptable and proportionate punishment. Such a persistent refusal to comply with what is penally required becomes a serious enough breach of the conditions of community to warrant imprisonment.

2.3. Capital Punishment

I would have liked to avoid discussing the death penalty: to say simply, with von Hirsch and Ashworth, that "[a] civilized state . . . should not have this vile sanction at all, so there should be no occasion for the courts to have to decide [or for theorists to have to discuss] when and why it should be imposed" (von Hirsch & Ashworth 1998, vi). But death is still used as a punishment in too many jurisdictions, and is still seen as in principle an appropriate punishment by too many theorists, for me simply to ignore the question whether it could be, or why it cannot be, a possible penalty within a communicative system of punishment.

My discussion is, however, brief. I do not discuss the complex empirical question whether the death penalty can be a more efficient deterrent than other available modes of punishment; or the related question whether, even if its deterrent or otherwise preventive benefits are doubtful, it can still be argued that we are justified in inflicting certain death on murderers for the sake of some uncertain saving of the lives of potential victims. On my communicative account, the justification of any particular mode of punishment, like that of punishment in general, does not depend on its preventive efficiency; it depends on whether it is an appropriate response to the offender's crime. Nor do I discuss the wide variety of retributivist answers to this question. The truth in retributivism, the sense in which crime 'deserves' punishment, is that punishment communicates the censure that crime deserves. Thus my question is whether the death penalty could, in principle, serve this communicative role. Nor, accordingly, do I discuss objections to the death penalty based on the possibility (the certainty) that some innocents will be mistakenly convicted and executed, or on other kinds of injustice (such as racial bias) that affect its administration. Such objections are not intended to address the basic question of principle that concerns me here—whether death can be an appropriate punishment for any crime.[24]

It might seem that on my account the answer to this question is obvious. The infliction of capital punishment could *in principle* communicate with the criminal, as well as with the wider community. This is one difference between the death penalty and torture, for instance, which cannot even in principle be a mode of communication with a responsible moral agent (cf. Murphy 1979d, 233–37). But capital punishment cannot, surely, constitute a penitential process through which offenders can come to understand and repent their crimes, to reform themselves, and to reconcile themselves with their fellow citizens. Death precludes reformation and reconciliation. My account thus has no room for the death penalty, which is the ultimately exclusionary punishment. The matter is not, however, that simple.

Someone has committed a terrible crime and comes to realize just what he has done. He is horrified and distraught. But what can he do? He *might* see suicide as the only course open to him. Now suicide in such a context could have very different meanings: it could be an act of despair—he cannot face the life that is now left to him; it could reflect a rational decision that, given how others will treat him and how he will feel, life is no longer worth living. But it could, instead, reflect a moral understanding of the implications of his crime. By his crime, he thinks, he has rendered himself unfit for, cut himself off from, human life: from human life itself, rather than merely from ordinary social life (which would suggest self-exile to a hermitage or a willing acceptance of life imprisonment). Furthermore, he might see suicide, as well as actualizing this understanding of the implications of his crime, as a way of reconciling himself with those whom he wronged: for reconciliation is possible, not merely *despite* death, but *through* death (even for those who do not believe in life after death). The wrongdoer might hope to make his peace with those whom he wronged through his suicide—his self-execution; and his fellow citizens, when they realize why he has killed himself, may come to see and respond to him differently—he is restored to community with them in their thoughts and memories.

Now I would not want to say that a person who responds in this way to a truly terrible crime is wrong or irrational. Indeed, if I ask myself how someone who had committed such a crime could live (with himself, with others) in the full realization of what he had done, I might come to respect his action. Must I then agree that death is in principle an appropriate punishment, if not for all murders, at least for the most terrible murders? I am agreeing that death inflicted by the wrongdoer on himself can reflect and communicate a moral understanding of the implications of his crime, that it can express his repentance and a kind of self-reform (he is reformed by that very understanding of what he has done), and that it can reconcile him with his fellows. I have also argued that punishments imposed by others can serve these aims. They can aim to induce a repentant recognition of the crime and its implications, and to become penances that the offender accepts as appropriate vehicles for repentance, reform, and reconciliation. So must I now admit that, since death can be a penitential punishment that a wrongdoer imposes on himself, it could also be an appropriate punishment for others to impose on him?

I cannot avoid this conclusion by noting that the death penalty as it is in fact currently administered could not be reasonably expected to serve these proper aims of repentance, reform, and reconciliation. The same is true of imprisonment, which I argue could in principle be an appropriate sentence for some crimes; and my concern here is anyway with the question of principle, not (yet) with the question whether or how ideal principles could be translated into actual practice. The repugnance that many people feel, and that I feel, at the death penalty is no doubt partly and justifiably grounded in the actualities of its current practice. But my question now is whether it could be justified even in ideal theory. There are, however, three stronger reasons for concluding that it should not even in principle have a place in a system of communicative, penitential punishment.

The first reason concerns the difference between first person and third person: between what a person can properly think that she ought to (or must) do and what others can properly claim that she ought to do—let alone require her to do or force onto her. I say that I could respect the action of someone who sees suicide as the only possible response to his terrible crime. I do not say that I would think (let alone say to him) that he ought to do it. That is, I think, a judgment that only he can make. Similarly, whatever we might think collectively about a wrongdoer's response to his crime, it is not for us to judge that he ought to suffer death—let alone to tell him this, to require him to kill himself, or to kill him if he does not do so. But why should I say this, if I allow that imprisonment may be inflicted on offenders who do not offer themselves for imprisonment or think that they ought to suffer this punishment? Is it just that I am not sure that death is the appropriate penalty for the most terrible crimes, or not as sure as I am about the appropriateness of imprisonment? That is part of the answer. But the answer also has to do with what it is to kill a person, especially when the killing takes the form of a legal execution (see Orwell 1965; Cockburn 1991). I focus here on the implications of the banal fact that death is final. These implications constitute the second reason for excluding the death penalty from a communicative system of punishment.

To execute someone is to say to him (and to ourselves) that he has wholly removed himself from human community—from the possibility of a continuing human life. He might be able to reconcile himself, in death, with his fellows, but he can do so only by removing himself or being removed from any continuing life (other than the shadow of life he may have in the memories of others). It is one thing for a person to make and act on such a judgment about his own life and deeds. But it is not, I believe, a judgment that we can ever properly make and act on about another person. Just as we can never properly see another as being beyond redemption (see p. 123, above), so we can never properly say that he can be redeemed only by death.

The third reason for excluding the death penalty concerns the unrepentant or defiant offender (see ch. 3.7.4). We can justifiably punish an unrepentant offender in the hope that she will come to repent. Even if she remains unrepentant at the end of her punishment, this does not render the attempt to persuade her pointless or unjustified. Now for any punishment other than death, we can still hope that she will come to change her views later: that she will come to look back on her punishment as a justified penance that she is now glad she was required or forced to undergo. This might not be a realistic hope, but it is a crucial aspect of the attitude we should have towards the offender as someone who is not beyond redemption. Capital punishment, however, precludes any such hope. If the offender remains unrepentant or does not come to see his execution as an appropriate (or morally necessary) response to his crime, his punishment can *never* become what it must aim to be—a penance that he willingly accepts. To execute such a person is to *place* him beyond redemption—beyond the very possibility of redemption. We can never be justified in doing that to a fellow citizen—or indeed to a fellow human being.

3. Who Decides?

A communicative system of sentencing should be constrained by a negative principle of proportionality, and must attend to the meanings of the material modes of punishment that it imposes. But how, and by whom, should sentences be decided?

One central controversy, which has loomed large in recent debates about penal policy, concerns the proper scope of judicial discretion: how far should individual sentencers be left free to determine the appropriate sentence for the case at hand; how far should their decisions be constrained or determined by sentencing guidelines or rules laid down by legislatures or sentencing commissions?[25] This is the topic of the next subsection. Another question, which is not widely discussed but is raised by my account of the proper aims of punishment, concerns the role (if any) of the offender in determining her sentence. This is the topic of section 3.2.

3.1. 'Doing Justice': General versus Particular

Those who insist on a positive principle of proportionality typically take a 'just deserts' view of punishment and sentencing: the primary aim of punishment, and so the primary task of sentencing, is to give offenders their 'just deserts' by imposing on them sentences whose severity is proportionate to the seriousness of their crimes. Such theorists also typically argue that individual sentencers' discretion in determining sentences should be tightly constrained by guidelines that specify, if not mandatory sentences, at most a small range of sentences for each offense. They oppose highly individualized sentencing practices that allow sentencers a wide discretion to decide what sentence is appropriate for each case that comes before them.

It might not be clear why a demand for positive proportionality should thus bring with it a rejection of wide individual discretion in sentencing. If the primary aim in sentencing is to determine a sentence proportionate to the seriousness of the offender's crime, why should we not leave sentencers to determine sentences in the light of all the relevant features of the offense—especially because those features, insofar as they concern the offender's culpability, will be hard to capture adequately in any set of general sentencing rules?

Part of the answer to this question is that the principle of proportionality is a principle of *relative* proportionality (see sec. 1.1, above). Doing justice to individual offenders is therefore a matter of doing justice *between* offenders. We punish *this* offender justly by ensuring that her sentence is proportionate to her crime, relative to the sentences imposed on *other* offenders. We thus need some mechanism by which we can try to achieve such relative proportionality and prevent relative disproportionalities. Sentencing guidelines are one such mechanism. This is only part of an answer, however, since it is not in general true that we can achieve this kind of relative proportionality only by general guidelines that tightly constrain individual discretion. The grading of students' work, for instance, is subject to the demands of relative proportionality. What makes the grade given to a particular essay just is crucially, if not entirely, its relation to the grades given to other essays by other students. We must try to ensure that essays of comparable quality receive the same grades, that better essays receive better grades, and so on. Now we can try to produce general grading guidelines, indicating what kinds of essay should receive an A, a B, a C, and so on, but such guidelines are inevitably extremely vague (even if they avoid utter vacuity). Grading depends in the end on the particularized judgments of individual graders, and what secures relative proportionality is not their adherence to a set of substantive and determinate guidelines but (apart from their own trained experience) their use of a system of selective monitoring of the grades given to individual essays. Why then should the demands of proportionality in sentencing not be satisfied by a system that leaves individual sentencers wide discretion to decide the appropriate sentences for the individual cases that come before them, subject to monitoring by an appellate court?

One partial answer to this question is that we cannot trust individual sentencers to do justice in this way. Another partial answer is that we need to ensure that justice is not only done but clearly seen to be done, and this is most easily achieved by a system of published sentencing guidelines.[26] But I think that support for a system of sentencing guidelines also reflects the familiar liberal concern that the law should preserve a suitable distance from the citizens. A system that allows individual sentencers extensive discretion might be justified by the argument that this is necessary if they are to do justice to the concrete particularities of each case, determining offenders' sentences in the light of all the relevant features of their crimes. Any system of general guidelines will be too crude to cope with the many subtle aspects of the offense (and the offender) that should be relevant. But such a system will also require or allow sentencers to inquire rather closely into the details of the particular offense, of its context, of the offender's motivation and background; and such inquiries could soon intrude into matters that should not concern the law (see ch. 3.8). To protect citizens from such over-intrusive inquiries, we need a system of strict sentencing guidelines, that define and limit the factors (aggravating or mitigating) that are to be relevant to sentencing. This will admittedly involve a degree of 'abstraction'. We will need to define crimes in rather general terms that abstract from the particularities of individual cases and omit many of the subtler features that would be relevant to thorough *moral* judgments on offenders and their offenses. But such abstraction is necessary to protect individuals against overintrusive judicial inquiries, to ensure that we can properly rank all crimes in terms of their seriousness, and to ensure that all offenders are fairly sentenced under rules that are applied to them all.[27]

Now those who advocate a negative rather than a positive principle of proportionality can in fact accept much of this line of argument. They will differ about the need to rank all crimes and all sentences on single scales of seriousness and of severity. They will differ perhaps about which aspects of the offense and the offender can be of proper interest to the law, as 'public' rather than 'private' matters, and about just how we should weigh the demands of fairness between offenders against those of doing justice to the particularities of individual offenders. (The latter, on my account, include the demand that sentences should be substantively apt to particular offenders.) But they can agree that individual sentencers' discretion should be constrained by general guidelines. They can do so because they can agree that we cannot always trust individual sentencers to do justice, and that if justice is to be seen to be done the law must give a clear, public indication of the kinds of sentence that will be imposed on different crimes. They can also agree that there must be limits on how closely the courts should be able to inquire, or the law should be able to intrude, into offenders' lives. The difference between advocates of positive and of negative principles of proportionality is not that the former support sentencing guidelines while the latter oppose them. It rather concerns how precise the guidelines should be and how much discretion they should leave to individual sentencers. Advocates of a positive principle of proportionality are likely to favor relatively precise sentencing guidelines, leaving sentencers with a relatively limited discretion to choose between levels and modes of punishment. Advocates of a negative principle of proportionality, in contrast, are likely to favor less precise guidelines, which leave sentencers a larger discretion in determining the level and mode of punishment.

I cannot pursue this issue further here,[28] or discuss who should produce such guidelines (legislatures, sentencing commissions, appellate courts?) or what form they should take (numerical sentencing grids, as used in Minnesota, for instance, or detailed principles to be applied by the courts, as in the Swedish sentencing law of 1988?).[29] As my argument in this chapter reveals, I would want such guidelines to be loose enough to allow individual sentencers more discretion than von Hirsch, for instance, would allow them to choose between a range of material modes of punishment. Perhaps a system more like that proposed by Tonry (1997, 1998), which would contain six overlapping "zones of discretion," would be appropriate. The guidelines would allocate offenses to one of the six zones, and could also specify "dispositive presumptions" within each zone, but would still leave sentencers a fairly wide discretion to choose between sentences within the zone.[30]

My account might, however, seem to have a more radical and disturbing implication: that sentences should be *negotiated* between the offender and the court (or between offender and victim). I now turn to this issue.

3.2. Negotiated Sentences?

Punishments, in our existing systems of criminal justice, are typically *imposed* by the court on the offender. Offenders might be able to secure a lighter sentence by a plea bargain, but it is for the court to decide what sentence to impose. Neither the offender nor, typically, the victim has any formal role in the decision.[31] It might seem entirely right that offenders should be the recipients of, not participants in, sentencing decisions: for as wrongdoers, their role is surely to submit themselves to the authority of the law; and they are not well placed to form an impartial judgment on what kind of punishment they deserve. This is one focus of the abolitionist claim that the criminal law "steals" the "conflicts" that it defines as "crimes" from those to whom they properly belong (see Christie 1977; ch. 1.5.2, above). But, we might think, once we recognize crimes as public wrongs (see ch. 2.4.3), we should also recognize that the appropriate punitive response to them falls to be decided by the court, acting on behalf of the law and the community.

On the other hand, I have argued (ch. 3.4.2–3) that a criminal mediation process, involving reparation by the offender to the victim, provides a paradigm of communicative punishment; and negotiation is central to that process, since offender and victim must (with a mediator's assistance) negotiate the type and amount of reparation. More generally, it might seem that I should favor a system of negotiated sentences, whether negotiated between the offender and the victim or between the offender and the community (through the criminal court). Punishment, on my account, aims not merely to communicate with the offender, but also to provide a means by which *she* can communicate apologetically with her victim and the community. One who is required to engage in such a communicative exercise must surely, if she is to be treated as a responsible agent, be allowed a say in determining just what and how she should communicate. But this suggests either that my account is not, after all, an account of *punishment*—that it is rather an account of a *non*-punitive practice of restorative, as distinct from retributive or punitive, justice (see ch. 3.4.3)—or that if it is meant to be an account of punishment, it is open to the objection that a system of negotiated sentences will be inconsistent with even a negative principle of proportionality (see, generally, Ashworth 1993b; von Hirsch & Ashworth 1998, 300–311; also Zedner 1994).

Now I do not think that my account *demands* a system of negotiated sentences. Citizens are required to accept the authority of the substantive criminal law—to refrain from conduct that it defines as criminal even if they do not themselves see that conduct as wrong. The law, in claiming such authority, still communicates with them as responsible members of a liberal polity, so long as there is some suitable forum in which they can question and seek to change its content (see ch. 2.4.4). They can also be expected to accept the authority of the law in sentencing: to accept the sentences that the law, through the courts, imposes on the crimes they commit, so long as there is some suitable democratic forum in which the general levels and modes of punishment and the guiding principles of sentencing can be debated and decided. Furthermore, when what is required is a public apology for a public wrong, it is not unreasonable that the law should prescribe the form and content of that apology. Offenders ought to apologize. But what will count as an adequate apology depends on the character and seriousness of the crime, and on the meanings of the various modes and levels of apologetic reparation. Since these are public rather than private matters, depending on the community's understanding of the crime and of the modes of reparation, the law can reasonably prescribe not just that, but also how, offenders should apologize. Nor does this prevent the apologies' being authentic—ones that offenders genuinely make for themselves (if they come to repent their crimes). If I see that I ought to make apologetic reparation for the wrong I have done, I can also accept and make my own the particular mode of reparation that the law prescribes.

However, it is also true that my account *favors* a system of negotiated sentencing. First, a liberal polity that values autonomy should in general prefer participatory to passive modes of citizen involvement in its activities. Its institutions should where possible be such that those affected by them can have an active role in determining their operations. Second, as far as punishment in particular is concerned, its communicative efficacy would surely be enhanced if offenders could take part in determining their own sentences. We are more likely to bring offenders to understand the nature and implications of their crimes and to make their punishments their own as genuine modes of apologetic reparation if they are involved in a discussion of what kind of reparation the crime requires.

We can see more clearly what a system of negotiated sentences might involve, and how it could meet the objections that it is liable to provoke, by asking what is to be negotiated, between whom, and subject to what constraints.[32]

As to what is to be negotiated, one matter that is not up for negotiation is that the offender committed a wrong (see ch. 3.4.2). Sentencing, whether negotiated or not, presupposes conviction for a specified crime. While the negotiation in which the offender would then be expected to engage with the victim or with a probation officer or both would properly include a discussion of the meaning and implications of the crime, its nonnegotiable starting point is that the offender committed that crime.[33] Another matter that is not up for negotiation is that the offender must undertake or undergo a punishment that is (negatively) proportionate to the seriousness of the offense. This point follows from the argument of this and the previous chapter, that offenders must be punished and that their punishments must be (negatively) proportionate to their crimes.

What is to be negotiated is the precise form and content of that punishment, subject to the constraints of negative proportionality and to further constraints concerning the mode of punishment. One such constraint concerns imprisonment. It must be for the court to decide whether the offender's crime was so serious that the sentence must involve a prison term. Other constraints concern the kinds of noncustodial sentence that should be available. Although sentencers should have quite a wide discretion in determining the mode of punishment (a discretion that will feed into the negotiating process), that discretion should not be unlimited. Sentences must be practicable—both feasible for the offender and such that they can be practicably monitored and enforced. They must not involve measures that are inhuman, degrading, or improperly intrusive (see von Hirsch 1993, ch. 9). They must have an appropriate kind of meaning in relation to the crime. The obvious way to apply these constraints is for the law to specify the general range of types of sentence (including imprisonment, community service or reparative work done for the victim, probation orders with a range of possible conditions to be attached to them, and fines). The court will specify a range of possible sentences for the particular crime (subject to such sentencing guidelines as it is bound by), with this specification to include any necessary elements of the sentence (such as imprisonment). The negotiation will then concern the precise form and content of the sentence within that range, and the outcome of the negotiation will be subject to approval by the court.[34]

In thinking about the appropriate mode and level of punishment, we must distinguish compensation from punishment. Compensation is for the material harm done by the crime. It typically involves a financial payment that meets at least some of the material costs incurred by the crime (the costs of replacing or repairing stolen or damaged property, of medical treatment for injuries, and so on). What compensation, if any, is required thus depends on the actual effects of the crime; it will not necessarily be closely related to the seriousness of the crime (compare an offense of negligence that causes very expensive harm with a failed attempt at murder that causes no material harm). What compensation, if any, the offender can pay will depend on her means. Now punishment does, on my account, involve reparation. The reparation required, however, is for the *wrong* that was done, which is not to be identified with the material harm actually caused. What kind or degree of reparation is required thus depends on the character and seriousness of the offense, and not on the harm actually caused if that does not affect the seriousness of the offense (this meets the problem posed by Ashworth 1993b, 290–91).

We could mark this crucial distinction by making compensation a matter of civil law,[35] leaving reparation as the sole concern of criminal punishment. This would be too simple, however, since reparation can take the form of compensation. An offender can sometimes make apologetic reparation for the wrong he has done by making a monetary payment that helps to compensate the victim for the harm caused by the crime.[36] Compensation and punishment are nonetheless analytically distinct, even when punishment takes the form of reparative compensation. In deciding what kind and level of punishment is appropriate (even if the punishment involves paying compensation), we must ask what would constitute an appropriate reparative apology for the wrong done, not what compensation is required for the material harm caused.

Between whom should the negotiation take place? If the crime was committed against an identifiable victim, it is appropriate that he should be involved and that the negotiation should focus at least in part on what reparation the offender should make to him. This is not because the crime is a 'private' rather than a 'public' wrong (cf. Cavadino & Dignan 1998, 353). It is a public wrong in which the community as a whole takes a proper interest (see ch. 2.4.3); and just as the community speaks, through the court, on behalf of the victim whose wrong it shares, so the victim should speak in a criminal mediation process on behalf of the whole community as well as on his own behalf. His involvement in the process is appropriate because it is right that the offender should be thus confronted by the victim and try to make some reparative apology to him; and because the victim himself can thus help to hold the offender to account. Even when there is a victim who is willing to take part in the process, however, it must involve other voices than those of offender and victim. In particular, since the process is dealing with a public wrong and with what is owed to the community as a whole as well as to the individual victim, it must be conducted under the aegis of the law and in accordance with the constraints (noted above) properly imposed by the law.[37] This condition requires the participation of an official mediator, whose responsibility it will be to facilitate the discussion between offender and victim, to indicate which kinds of reparative measure would or would not be appropriate, and to help formulate the proposal that will then be submitted for the court's approval. A particular task for the mediator will be to intervene in cases in which the victim is too demanding or too undemanding—in which he exaggerates or underrates the seriousness of the wrong in his claims about what reparation is due. Since the wrong is a public wrong, which concerns the whole community and for which reparative apology is due to the community (even if it is made directly to the victim), the victim's view of what reparation is required cannot be dispositive.

Sometimes, of course, such a criminal mediation process between offender and victim will not be possible, because there is no individual victim who could take part in the process, or because the victim is unwilling to do so. In such cases, the negotiation must be between the offender and the community as a whole (whereas in victim-offender mediation schemes the negotiation is indirectly with the community, through the victim) or, we could say, between the offender and the law, since the law speaks for the community in relation to such public wrongs. Here then is an obvious role for the probation officer: to meet the offender after conviction, to discuss what the punishment should be (subject to whatever guidance the court has given), and to formulate a proposal to submit for the court's approval (cf. Bottoms & McWilliams 1979, 184–87; Raynor 1985, 117–22, 180–204). We could indeed give probation officers a central role in *all* sentencing negotiations (expanding and modifying the role they now play in producing presentence reports). Once the offender has been convicted, a probation officer would be assigned to her case: his initial task would be to arrange a discussion with the offender (involving, where possible and appropriate, the victim as well) with a view to producing for the court a sentencing proposal in whose construction the offender would play an active role, though subject still to the kinds of constraint noted above. More precisely, since the very discussion of her offense with the probation officer (and the victim) is a punitive process (see ch. 3.4.3; ch. 3.5.1), the offender's sentence in all but the most minor cases would be to take part in this discussion (which also aims to confront her with the wrongs she has done), *plus* whatever further measures the court approves as a result of the discussion.

The probation officer's further role would then be to supervise and manage the measures that are approved (except for imprisonment). This is to suggest that probation should be the normal sentence for all but the most serious, and the most minor, crimes. But 'probation' would now be significantly enhanced to include not only its traditional roles (see ch. 3.5.1) but also the negotiation and supervision of all except the most trivial noncustodial sentences. This would require probation officers to see themselves, more clearly than many now wish to see themselves (see ch. 3.5.1), as officers of the criminal law engaged in administering punishments: but that is how they should understand their role.[38]

(Provision would of course need to be made for offenders who refuse to take part in the discussion or refuse to make or accept reasonable proposals. In such cases a sentence would need to be imposed, as it is under our current systems.)

Such a system of negotiated sentencing would no doubt, despite the constraints to which it would be subject, produce disparities between cases that would disturb proponents of a positive principle of proportionality. Disparities would appear both in the precise mode and content of the sentence, which would make it hard to check whether the sentence was proportionate relative to those agreed for similar offenses, and in levels of penal severity, where those could be compared. These disparities would appear because the courts would be (rightly) reluctant to turn down proposals that were consistent with the appropriate constraints and that had been agreed by the offender and the probation officer (and the victim). But, first, the sentence would conform to the requirements of a negative principle of proportionality (since that is one of the constraints on the process), which I have argued is the version of the principle we should accept. Second, we must bear in mind the claims of procedural justice as well as those of outcome justice. What makes a sentence just is not merely that it is proportionate or fitting to the offender's crime, but that it is the result of a just sentencing procedure; and a just sentencing procedure, I suggest, is a procedure that allows offenders and victims a voice.[39]

4. Criminal Record and 'Dangerous' Offenders

Some readers will no doubt find the account of criminal punishment offered in this and the previous chapter quite implausible, even as an ideal account of what punishment ought to be. I do not think I can say anything more to try to persuade them. Others might find my account plausible or attractive as an *ideal* account, but think it so remote from our existing systems of penality that it lacks application to our actual world. I address such concerns in the next chapter. Others, however, might find it plausible in relation to *some* kinds of offense and offender, but argue that it fails to address the problems posed by other kinds of offense and offender. This concern forms the topic of this section.

A communicative system of punishment, imposing sentences that are relatively mild compared with those imposed under our existing systems and aiming thereby to persuade offenders to repent their crimes, to begin to reform themselves, and to reconcile themselves with their fellow citizens, might be appropriate for offenders who are, or whose crimes do not show them not to be, within the reach of this kind of moral communication. These are offenders who might, we can sensibly hope, listen to their punishment and be persuaded by it, and with whom we can hope still to live in community. Such offenders will not always be persuaded to repent, or even if they are persuaded, some will slip back into crime again. Such a system *might* be less effective than a harsher, deterrent system in dissuading potential offenders from crime.[40] But so long as their crimes are not *seriously* destructive of the goods or interests of the community and its members, perhaps this is a price we should be ready to pay in order to maintain a civilized liberal polity that treats all its citizens as full members of the normative community. A critic might argue, however, that there are other kinds of offender, for whom such a system of communicative punishment is utterly inappropriate: offenders whose crimes show them to be deaf to all such attempts at moral communication, or are so seriously destructive that we cannot regard them as a price that we must pay for the sake of a liberal civility.

Which kinds of offense or offender raise this worry? Sometimes, in the mouths or minds of politicians (and, they suppose, of their voters), such concerns seem to be aroused by *any* offender who commits more than two felonies—as with the various "three strikes and you're out" law in the United States—or who commits a specified type of felony more than twice—as with the mandatory sentencing provisions introduced in England in 1997.[41] Such extensive provisions as these, however, can have no place in a liberal polity. Quite apart from their very doubtful efficacy as crime-preventive measures (see Tonry 1996, ch. 5), they mark too quick a readiness to exclude offenders from the normal rights and protections of citizenship and, in the case of mandatory life sentences, to exclude them permanently.

The same is true of proposals for 'selective incapacitation', which aim for cost-effective crime prevention by finding suitable sets of 'indicators' that will identify special categories of high-rate offenders and subjecting offenders falling within those categories to extended terms of incapacitative imprisonment (while reducing sentences for other offenders).[42] Quite apart from the doubtful accuracy of such 'indicators' and the doubtful efficacy of such measures even in achieving their stated aims, a liberal polity should not be so ready to exclude whole categories of offender (such as persistent burglars) from the normal rights and protections of citizenship.

There are, however, other kinds of offender who might raise a more serious problem for my account—in particular, those whom we might properly count as 'dangerous'.

The 'dangerous' offender comes in various guises. These include the terrorist, committed to a campaign of violence aimed at securing political ends that he cannot achieve by democratic means; the professional 'hard man' or the member of a criminal organization, committed to a career of crimes involving serious violence against the person; the 'thug' who is not a career-oriented criminal, but who habitually engages in serious violence (often against members of particular groups); the sexual predator who persistently attacks women; and the pedophile who commits persistent, serious (sometimes fatal) sexual assaults on children.

There are of course questions to be asked about these images of dangerousness: about the extent to which they are products of moral panics, and the extent to which some such offenders (especially pedophiles) are responsible agents who are in control of themselves and their actions. We might also hope that in a political community (very different from our own societies) in which a communicative system of penitential punishments could be fully justified (see ch. 5), there would be very few such offenders. However, I assume that there are, and will be, some offenders whom we can properly call 'dangerous' and who pose a problem for my account of punishment: in particular, offenders whose dangerousness consists in their persistent commission of crimes of serious violence against the person, that is, in their persistent serious *attacks* on their fellow citizens.[43]

The problem they pose is this. It is one thing to say in general terms (as liberals do say) that a liberal polity must accept a certain level of crime. It must eschew methods of crime prevention that, even if they would achieve a reduction in crime, are inconsistent with its defining values. But suppose we are faced with an offender who has persistently engaged in serious criminal attacks on others, who has been unresponsive to his previous punishments, and of whom we can plausibly predict that he will commit further such attacks if he gets the chance to do so. Even on my account, he is likely to be sentenced to a (relatively) long term of imprisonment for each successive crime (see sec. 2.2, above). But we can predict that once released (and even if required to accept some special supervision thereafter) he will commit further such crimes. What then can we say to his next victim or to the family of a victim he now kills? Can we honestly say to those whose lives have been destroyed that this new crime is a price that we (and especially they) must pay for the sake of maintaining a liberal polity? Might they not reasonably reply that this is to denigrate *their* rights to protection against this kind of predictable attack, that we owed it to them to keep the offender in prison if we could have been reasonably sure that he would commit such a crime if released?

I have some sympathy with such a reply—as I think any penal theorist must. But what then can I say?

It might be tempting to propose a policy of "bifurcation" (see Bottoms 1977, 87–91; Cavadino & Dignan 1997, 23, 26). We should preserve a system of communicative, penitential punishments for 'ordinary', 'nondangerous' offenders who are likely either to be amenable to such punishments or not to do too much harm if they are not. But we should subject dangerous, persistent offenders to a much harsher penal regime, which we can hope will either deter them (addressing them in the only language to which they will listen) or incapacitate them.

This would be to treat such offenders as partial outlaws: to say that by their persistent, serious, violent criminality, they have excluded themselves from the normative community within which punishment can function as I argue it should. It would also be to qualify quite severely the claims I have made for my account. It would be to admit that the criminal law of a liberal polity cannot address *all* its citizens in inclusive terms, as full members of the normative community. Some must be excluded, or be taken to have excluded themselves, from such membership and be subjected to deterrent or incapacitative punishments that no longer address them as citizens sharing in the community's defining values (see ch. 3.1.2). Even if there would be few such offenders, this would be a serious and morally disturbing retreat from my claim to be offering a genuinely and fully inclusionary account of punishment.

To see whether I can either justify or avoid such a conclusion, I briefly discuss two issues that bear on this question and that have figured prominently in recent debates in penal theory. This also enables me to identify more clearly the kind of offender who is seriously problematic for my account (a rather small class, as I show).

The two issues to be discussed are, first, the role of prior criminal record in sentencing and, second, the question whether 'dangerous' offenders could justifiably be subjected to extended periods of incapacitative imprisonment. I argue, following von Hirsch, that an offender's prior criminal record should not by itself make a significant difference to the sentence she receives for her current crime. The class of those who might justly be subjected to special penal measures under a policy of bifurcation is thus much narrower than the class of those with prior criminal records—even when those records include serious crimes. I then discuss, with rather less confidence, the question whether we can identify a narrower class of genuinely 'dangerous' offenders who could justly be subjected to such measures.

I should emphasize one initial point, however: the central question must be whether we can *justly* exclude any offenders from full membership of the normative community, not whether it might be consequentially useful or cost-effective to do so. This point follows both from the retributivist dimension to my account of punishment (punishment must be just, as being deserved, if it is to be justified) and from my account of a liberal polity's relationship to its members (if the rights and standing of full membership can be lost at all, this can only be because we can justly treat the person as having forfeited them by her own conduct). This means that the question should not be whether we can justifiably *deviate* from the demands of proportionality, by subjecting some offenders to penal measures more severe than they deserve. It is, rather, whether an offender's prior criminal record, or his 'dangerousness', can make such a significant difference to the seriousness of his crimes that such measures would not be disproportionately harsh (see sec. 1.4, above).

My focus in what follows is thus on repeat or persistent offenders. There is also the question, noted in chapter 3 (nn.18, 42), whether a *single* crime could be so serious that the person who commits it can justly be taken to have thereby excluded himself from the community. In line with my comments on the 'defiant' offender and on capital punishment (ch. 3.7.4; sec. 2.3, above), I am inclined to think that it could not: that while I could respect an offender who formed and acted on such a belief about the implications of his own crime, that is not a judgment that we should ever make or act on about another person.

4.1. The Relevance of Prior Criminal Record

The mere fact that an offender who is now convicted of a crime has a prior criminal record can make no justified difference to his sentence. The fact, for instance, that someone now convicted of theft was convicted of wounding five years ago provides no good reason to impose a harsher punishment for the theft, since it provides no good reason to judge either the current offense or the offender more harshly. The question of prior record becomes a serious one only if the prior offenses were relatively recent, and more so if they were of the same kind as the current offense.[44] Suppose, then, that a defendant is convicted of burglary, and it turns out that he has been convicted and punished for burglary twice in the past three years.[45] Do we have any reason, on my account of punishment, to say that though he has already been punished for the previous two burglaries, the fact that this is his third justifies punishing him more severely—that he now deserves a harsher punishment, expressing a harsher censure?[46]

If my account portrayed punishment as a matter of moral *education*, this might seem to follow. If a pupil shows that she has failed to learn what she ought to have learned, it might be reasonable to subject her to a further, more strenuous teaching process to try to get her to learn it, and thus if the offender has failed to learn from his previous punishments, we should now try something new and more severe.[47] But punishment is not, on my account, a matter of moral education (see ch. 3.4.1), and the necessary fallibility of communicative punishment, the offender's essential freedom to remain unpersuaded (see ch. 3.7.4), rules out any idea that we can properly keep increasing the sentence each time until he is persuaded. Nor, I think, can we say that the fact that his previous punishments failed to persuade him to repent and to reform himself renders his current offense more serious, since he has shown himself to be determinedly committed to wrongdoing. The mere fact of such previous convictions does not show this, since it is equally consistent with the offender's being weak willed, and any attempt to determine the correct interpretation of his conduct would involve an improper intrusion into his general moral character (but I comment below on the "first offender discount" and on the persistent dangerous offender).

Another possibility might be to argue that the repeat offender's current offense is more serious and thus deserving of harsher punishment because, in addition to the wrong intrinsic to the particular offense, he now displays a culpable lack of respect for the law. Not only has he again infringed his victim's rights: he has closed his ears to the authoritative voice of the law as it spoke to him through his previous punishments. Now a liberal polity should seek to foster a proper respect for the law and its authority among the citizens, and can properly punish as public wrongs actions that seek or threaten to undermine the law's institutions (as with offenses such as perverting the course of justice). But it should not punish 'disrespect' as a wrong distinct from or additional to the particular substantive crimes in which it may be manifested. Either the offender's particular crimes are themselves genuine *mala in se*—in which case the wrong for which he is punished should not be 'disobedience to the law' but the substantive wrong that the law defines as a public wrong—or they are *mala prohibita*—in which case the wrong intrinsic to the current offense is already the wrong of disobedience to or lack of respect for a law that he ought to obey (see ch. 2.4.4, above; also Fletcher 1982, 57; von Hirsch 1985, 79–80).

Perhaps, however, we can see some modest relevance in the offender's prior record if we invert the question. We might ask, not whether the offender with a record should be punished more severely, as if her record *aggravated* her current offense, but whether one without a record, who is thus (as far as the law is concerned) a first offender, should receive a lighter punishment—whether her lack of a record should be a *mitigating* factor. This is von Hirsch's argument (von Hirsch 1991; see also Ashworth 1995a, 156–60). A first offender should receive a penal discount, partly as a sympathetic recognition of human fallibility—of "the all-too-human weakness that can lead to a first lapse" (von Hirsch 1991, 55)—but also because she has not yet had the chance to respond or to fail to respond to the forceful censure that punishment would communicate to her. That mitigation, however, is progressively lost as she commits further offenses. She has now been confronted, by her previous punishment(s), with a forceful public censure, which aimed to persuade her to recognize the wrongfulness of such conduct. She cannot now mitigate her offense, as she might have been able to mitigate her first offense, by saying that she had not really grasped or taken to heart its character as a wrong, since her previous punishment(s) gave her the chance to do precisely that, and she has culpably failed to take it.

This argument does, I think, make sense of the intuitively plausible thought that, in the criminal law as in other contexts, the fact that this is the offender's first offense should be a modestly mitigating factor. It would thus justify punishing the third-time burglar more severely than he was punished for his first burglary. First, however, first, this cannot plausibly be applied to *every* crime (see von Hirsch 1991, 56). The more serious the crime, the more obvious its utter wrongfulness ought to have been to anyone with even a modest regard for the rights and interests of others, the less room there is for this kind of mitigation of a first offense. Second, it does not allow criminal record to carry very much weight in sentencing. The mitigation provided by the fact that this is the defendant's first offense can only be quite modest, so that the increase in severity of sentence as it is lost will itself be quite modest; and once the mitigation is lost (if not with the second offense, at least after rather few further offenses), the argument provides no justification for further increases in the severity of the sentence for further offenses. The fact that this is an offender's twentieth burglary does not justify a harsher punishment than was imposed for the tenth burglary.

It is true that we might come to see the offender, not merely as a *repeat* offender, but as a *persistent* offender. By this I mean that we can no longer see his successive burglaries as a series of discrete aberrations, but can only see them as part of a persisting pattern of conduct manifesting a persisting criminal attitude of complete disregard for the values he flouts (see Duff 1998a, 161–62). It is also true that as the offenses multiply, the offender's successive punishments might take on something of a ritual air. The sentencer, or the probation officer who discusses the sentence with the offender, might try a different mode of punishment, to see whether that will get through to him. But those involved might increasingly have the sense that they are simply going through the motions of punishment with an offender who is not going to be persuaded to repentance and self-reform. Nonetheless, to treat the offender as a moral agent is to treat him as someone who *could* come or be brought to repentance—which means that we must not give up such successive efforts to persuade him, however futile they might seem. To treat him as a fellow citizen, as a fellow member of the normative community, is to treat him as someone who has through his punishment made apologetic reparation for his crime—which means that we must treat him at least *as if* he is to be trusted again (see ch. 3.7.4).

However, it is one thing to say this about the persistent burglar or thief, but can I really say the same about a persistent offender whose crimes are individually much more serious—about the kinds of 'dangerous' offender mentioned earlier?

4.2. 'Dangerous' Offenders

By a 'dangerous' offender I mean someone who has defined or constituted himself as a serious danger to others by his persistent commission of crimes of serious violence against the person (see Duff 1998a, 141–42, 151–56). The judgment that he is dangerous is justified solely by his own criminal conduct, not by whatever set of 'indicators' we can find to be empirically closely correlated with the commission of the relevant kinds of crime. Nor is it justified merely by the fact that he has been convicted of several crimes of violence over the years—that he is a *repeat* offender, whose crimes could be seen merely as a series of discrete aberrations in an otherwise value-sensitive life. He must be a *persistent* offender—one whose criminal career can only be interpreted as manifesting an utter and continuing disregard or contempt for the values that he flouts and for those whom he attacks. We can thus say, not (merely) that *we* judge him to be dangerous, but that *he* has defined or constituted himself as dangerous. By his own persistent criminal conduct he has defined himself as someone who will, unless he undergoes a radical moral conversion (which his previous punishments have certainly failed to achieve) or is prevented, continue to commit serious attacks on others.

It is tempting to say of such an offender that when he is convicted of his latest serious crime of violence, he should be subjected to an extended period of secure imprisonment to incapacitate him from committing further such crimes: not just because, on consequentialist grounds, this will be a cost-effective method of preventing serious crimes, but because this would be a justified, deserved, response to his crimes. We might argue that here at least the model of punishment as societal defense is applicable (see ch. 1.3.2). He has shown himself to be engaged in a *continuing* attack on or war against others, and we can properly take what steps are necessary to prevent him from carrying it through. Or we might argue that even if offenders do not generally forfeit the rights or moral standing of citizenship (see ch. 1.3.1), there comes a point when they do. One who flouts the basic requirements of citizenship so persistently and seriously cannot claim and does not deserve the respect and restraint that should normally govern the state's dealings with its citizens. But what can the account of criminal punishment that I defend say about such an offender?

If that account applies to him as it applies to other offenders, he will certainly be liable to a (relatively) severe sentence of imprisonment for his latest crime. It is a serious crime for which imprisonment is an appropriate sentence (see sec. 2.2, above), and he has long lost any mitigation that the lack of a criminal record could provide. But it will be a determinate prison term, probably somewhat shorter than those currently imposed for serious crimes, after which he will be entitled to be restored to normal community with his fellow citizens, as someone who has paid his penitential debt. And his fellow citizens, while they might not want to seek or maintain any closer relationship with him, will owe him the respect, concern, and trust that define their shared membership of the normative community. His punishment, each of his successive punishments, must still address him as a member of that normative community. It must still constitute an attempt—however futile the attempt may come to seem—to persuade him to repent his crimes and to embark on the process of self-reform. It must leave him the freedom to remain unpersuaded and unrepentant. It must be seen by his fellow citizens (if not by him) as reconciling him with them as fellow members of the polity.

But can I really believe this? More to the point, could I honestly say to the offender's next victim, and to his next victim's family and friends, that while they have indeed suffered a terrible wrong (a wrong in which I share as their fellow citizen), and while it was wholly predictable that he would commit such a wrong (since it marked simply the continuation of the course of serious crimes by which he had defined himself as dangerous), nonetheless this was the price that we—and especially they—must pay in order to treat the offender as a fellow member of the normative community (and that he must again be restored to full community after his punishment for this latest crime)?

I have argued elsewhere (Duff 1998a) that there may come a point at which we need not and should not say this. Other kinds of community can justly exclude a member permanently from the community, on the grounds that her persistent and serious flouting of the essential values on which the community depends renders her continued participation impossible. A university, for instance, can properly expel a member who persistently plagiarizes others' work or who persistently treats other members in ways quite inconsistent with the defining values of an academic community; a religious community can expel or excommunicate a member who persistently denies or flouts its central values. Somewhat similarly, people can be excluded or disqualified from various kinds of activity (for instance, from driving or from the practice of medicine or the law) on the grounds of their persistent and serious misconduct. These kinds of expulsion or disqualification serve a protective purpose. They protect others from the harm that the excluded person would otherwise, as her persistent wrongdoing has shown, be liable to cause. But they can also be justified as punishments, whose severity is proportionate to the seriousness of the offender's wrongdoing. By her persistent and serious wrongdoing she has rendered herself unfit for, in effect disqualified herself from, continued participation in that community or that activity. Now unless we believe that citizenship, as involving the right to participate in the normal life of a political community, is *unconditional*, it seems that we can offer an analogous argument for excluding the dangerous offender from the normal political community. By his persistent, serious criminal wrong-doing he has made reconciliation—the maintenance or restoration of civic fellowship—impossible. He has disqualified himself from continued partici-pation in the community's normal life. We can thus justly subject him to an extended, indeed if necessary life-long, period of imprisonment, both to protect others from his continuing depredations and as a proportionate punishment for his crime. What makes it proportionate, although it is very much more severe than the punishments imposed on other, nonpersis-tent offenders who committed crimes similar to his latest crime, is that his crime, as part of a pattern of persistent serious criminality, is categorially more serious than theirs. In the context of that pattern, it is no longer a single, isolated attack on others but a further stage in a *continuing* attack, a continuing *campaign* of attacks, on the community's members and its central values.

Much more needs to be said about the practical implications of this argu-ment: about just how we could identify those (few) offenders who should be li-able to such extended periods of imprisonment, about the organization and conditions of their imprisonment, and about the provisions that would need to be made for them to secure their release by showing that they were no longer dangerous. (Even if their imprisonment, their exclusion from the ordinary community, should be *presumptively* permanent, it should not be *irreversibly* permanent; we would owe it to them, as moral agents who could still redeem themselves, to allow them a way back to community.) My concern now, how-ever, is with the principled foundations of the argument rather than with its practical implications: with the question whether such a system of extended imprisonment would be *in principle* justifiable, rather than whether the diffi-culties and dangers involved in implementing such a system would be so great as to render it in practice unjustifiable (though that is a real question).

I remain uneasy with the argument and its conclusion. Even if such im-prisonment would only be presumptively permanent and would be served under conditions far more humane and constructive than those that charac-terize too many of our existing prisons, we would still in effect be saying to the offender, "You can never again live with us in political community, and must live out your life (unless you reform) in prison." Even if that is not to give up entirely on the offender as someone who is capable of redemption, it comes close to doing so. That unease is strengthened by the following objection.[48]

Expulsion from other kinds of community is just that: the person is ex-pelled, and is left free to make her own life, to find her own way, outside that from which she is excluded. This might be hard: an academic who is perma-nently excluded from the professional academic community, a doctor permanently disqualified from practicing medicine, might find it materially and psychologically very hard to (re)construct a life for herself. But there is life outside the academy, outside medical practice; the person who is expelled is not thereby deprived of all opportunities to find or maintain a place for herself in other communities and to decide for herself where and how to live. The presumptively permanent imprisonment to which the dangerous offender is liable to be subjected is, however, radically disanalogous in two related ways. First, he is excluded from far more—from participation in any kind of life, in any community, outside the prison. Second, and even more crucially, the offender is not just excluded. He is not simply *exiled*, to find his own way in the world outside. He is forced to live in a particular place, under particular and heavily constraining conditions. To justify such imprisonment, we therefore need to justify his *subjection* to such detention, as well as his *exclusion*. The analogy with exclusions from other kinds of community does not provide such a justification.[49]

Nonetheless, it still seems to me that to reject this argument we would need to be able to believe that all offenders have, as citizens, an *unconditional* right to be restored to ordinary community after a normal term of imprisonment, whatever the nature of their crimes. This would also be to believe that all citizens have a duty to accept the risks and harms that that involves. I am not sure that I can believe that in the kind of case that concerns me here: that of an offender who has, by his persistent, serious, and violent criminal conduct, defined himself as someone engaged in a continuing career of violent attacks on his fellow citizens.

Perhaps I am overstating the problem here. First, there would be very few offenders who would, even on my argument, be eligible for presumptively permanent imprisonment. We should at least be very slow to judge that an offender has rendered reconciliation—the restoration of civic fellowship—impossible, and we might be able to make noncustodial provisions (such as extended periods of supervision) to protect potential victims against at least some 'dangerous' offenders after their release. Second, even presumptively permanent imprisonment need not exclude the offender completely from participation in the ordinary life of the political community (from citizenship) or from other communities to which he belonged. He could retain the right to vote and to participate in political debates. He could be allowed and encouraged to maintain at least some connection with or participation in other communities, such as his family. Third, such imprisonment need not involve abandoning any attempt to persuade or help those imprisoned to repent their crimes and redeem themselves. It could indeed retain some of the central characteristics of punishment as penance. It would still communicate an appropriate message to the offender about the nature and implications of his persistent crimes. It could, if he repented, become an accepted penance through which he is restored to full community (for the imprisonment must be only presumptively, not irreversibly, permanent).

Might these points be enough to render presumptively permanent imprisonment, for a very small class of 'dangerous' offenders, morally acceptable?

I am still, I confess, uneasy with this conclusion. I am uneasy, not just about the dangers involved in an attempt actually to implement such a measure (though those are serious enough to warrant the rejection of any suggestion that it should be a feature of our existing penal systems), but about whether it is even in principle acceptable as a feature of an ideal penal theory. The fact remains that such a measure would keep some people locked up until they died. It would mark a kind of giving up on them, even if there is some scope and help for them to redeem themselves. I am not sure that a liberal polity should be ready thus to give up on any of its members.

For the reasons given above, however, I cannot confidently reject the argument that leads to this conclusion, and thus I remain in a state of uncomfortable uncertainty. All I can say here is that I think that such an uncertainty is not simply a product of my particular account of punishment. I have not, I think, simply created a problem for myself that could be avoided by abandoning my ambitious account of punishment as communicative penance. The problem of 'dangerous' offenders is, rather, a significant—if not intractable—problem for anyone who takes seriously the question: What does a liberal polity owe to all its citizens, both as actual or potential victims and as actual or potential offenders?

5

From Theory to Practice

CRIMINAL PUNISHMENT, I ARGUE, SHOULD BE UNDERSTOOD AND JUSTIFIED as a communicative, penitential process that aims to persuade offenders to recognize and repent the wrongs they have done, to reform themselves, and so to reconcile themselves with those they have wronged. I now tackle some questions about the relationship between this theory of punishment and actual penal practice.

1. Ideal Theories and Actual Practices

My account of punishment is a normative, ideal account of what punishment ought to be, or must be if it is to be adequately justified. That account is not wholly detached from our existing penal practices: it cannot be, if it is to justify a recognizably human practice of criminal punishment (see Introduction, sec. 2); and it draws on some particular features of our existing practices in explaining the proper purpose and meaning of punishment. However, it is not intended either as a description or as a justification of our existing penal practices. We cannot plausibly say that those practices are generally designed and administered to serve the communicative and penitential goals that punishment on my account should serve. Nor can those practices be justified in terms of this account.

This radical lack of fit between normative theory and actual practice, between criminal punishment as the theory says it ought to be and criminal punishment as actually practiced, does not by itself constitute an objection to the theory. Indeed, it is a feature of any plausible normative theory of punishment. A normative theory of a human practice does not offer a comforting justification of the status quo. It offers a critical standard against which we must judge our existing practice, an ideal account of what that practice ought to be, towards which we can aspire, but in whose light we must recognize the (perhaps radical) deficiencies in our actual practice. The gap between theory and practice marks (for those who find the theory persuasive) not the theory's inadequacy but the practice's imperfection.

However, while even a radical gap between ideal theory and actual practice does not, in itself, constitute an objection to the theory, it does raise problems for a theory that aspires to guide practice.

The most obvious problem is how we can get from here to there: how we can so reform our existing practice that it comes closer to the ideal portrayed by the theory. The wider the gap between theory and practice, the more difficult this problem becomes. Not only do 'we', who advocate the theory, have to work out how to persuade policy makers and practitioners of its merits. Even if 'we' include those with the power to reform the practice, we must work out how it can be thus reformed or transformed. This already presents major problems. Even if penal policy makers and practitioners could be persuaded that criminal punishment should become a communicative, penitential process of the kind I have described, the changes required in penal institutions and policies, in practitioners' attitudes and activities, would be vast. But even if we attend only to the institutional structures and operations of criminal punishment (and I show in sec. 2, below, that we cannot do this), there might be a more serious problem than this.

We must also ask whether the theory is even in principle practicable: whether, that is, it describes a practice that human beings like ourselves should even aspire to actualize. In one way, the theory can be a plausible ideal theory only if it is thus minimally practicable, since to find it plausible as an ideal is to recognize the practice it describes as one in which—if we could actualize it—we would be morally at home. In another way, however, a plausible ideal theory can fail the test of practicability, and not just because we might reasonably believe that we could never *fully* actualize the ideal. Fallibility and imperfection are general features of human life, and the fact that we will not achieve perfection does not undercut the force of the injunction "Be ye therefore perfect"[1]—which requires us to aspire towards ideals that we will admittedly never attain, and humbly to recognize the extent to which we fall short of attaining them. Sometimes, however, we might have to recognize that an attempt to aspire directly toward an ideal will not just fall short of the ideal but be *destructive* of the very values that the ideal embodies. Our situation then is rather more difficult.

This is certainly a feature of our individual moral lives. I might realize that someone else is in distress and see that ideally I should (that someone with the appropriate kind of moral concern and sensitivity would) step in to offer sympathetic help. But I might be sufficiently aware of my own inadequacies—my lack of imagination, sensitivity, and tact—to realize that if I tried to help I would probably make matters worse by a predictably crass and insensitive intervention, and that I therefore should not even try directly to help.[2] Something similar can also frustrate the collective pursuit of political ideals. We might recognize, for instance, that criminal punishment should ideally be the kind of communicative, penitential enterprise that I describe: but also believe that if we tried to actualize that ideal by transforming our existing penal practices in that direction, we would probably end by betraying rather than serving the very values that inform the ideal.

Why might we believe this? Part of the answer lies in the ambitious character of the ideal, according to which punishment, as a mode of forceful moral communication, must address and respect the offender as a fellow member of the normative community. It must seek to persuade (but not to coerce or manipulate) him to repent his crime and to accept his punishment as a penance for that crime, while leaving him free to remain unpersuaded and unrepentant. It is hard enough in our individual dealings with others to ensure that what is intended as an exercise in forceful moral persuasion does not become a morally disreputable exercise in bullying or manipulation that ceases to respect the other as a moral agent. It is hard enough to ensure that what is supposed to be an attempt to address her moral understanding, with reasons whose force we hope she will come to see for herself, does not become an attempt simply to coerce her into conformity with our wishes. It is very much harder to guard against those dangers if such attempts at moral persuasion are made by the officials of a system of state punishment, given the sheer power that such a system exercises over those subjected to it. The greater the would-be persuaders' power over those whom they would persuade, the greater the danger that persuasion will turn into oppression and bullying. It is harder still to guard against those dangers when such attempts involve the imposition of penal hard treatment—given how easy it is for such impositions to become the exercise of an oppressive and vindictive power.

Furthermore, criminal punishment on my account is a mode of communication that is imbued with emotion. It seeks to induce remorse in the offender—which, depending on the nature of the crime, might involve horror, disgust, or contempt for what he sees that he has done. It seeks to communicate to the offender the indignation or anger that his crime aroused in his victim and in others. Indignation and anger, however (especially if felt to be righteous or justified), can easily be or become corrupt. They might not always be irrational or corrupt: they can be informed by an appropriate grasp of the moral character of what arouses them. But they can all too easily become irrational—in particular, irrationally excessive. They can all too often be corrupt, as the hypocritical or self-deceptive disguises by which we seek to conceal our baser emotions of malice or envy. They can all too often lead us to actions that are brutal, vindictive, and oppressive.[3] This gives us further reason to fear that if we allow such emotions a role, as my account does allow them, in a system of criminal punishment, that system will not be one that administers communicative punishments to offenders who are still seen and respected as fellow citizens; that it will instead be one through which the self-righteously law-abiding vent their anger on those whom they see as outlaws.

Such worries might give new force to some of the liberal objections to my account that I discussed in chapter 3 (sec. 8). Even if a communicative system of penitential punishment could, in theory, be consistent with the values of a liberal polity, in practice it could too easily be destructive of those values—bullying and demeaning those whose autonomy it should respect, excluding those whom it should include, intruding into what should remain private. Such worries might thus also make some of the accounts of punishment that I reject look more attractive, particularly those that make the communication of censure a central purpose of punishment but explain the hard treatment dimension of punishment in deterrent terms (see ch. 3.3). For the censure that is to be communicated on such accounts need only be a kind of formal, somewhat detached censure that does not seek to force itself into the offender's soul; and deterrent punishments can be portrayed as preserving a certain moral distance from the offender—as not seeking to invade "the inner citadels of his soul" (Lucas 1968–69, 215).

Such worries are indeed serious. But they do not, by themselves, undermine my account of punishment as an account of an ideal we should aspire to actualize.[4] First, they do not weaken my objections to using punishment as a deterrent (see ch. 3.1.2; ch. 3.3)—and systems that combine censure with deterrence will of course be vulnerable to their own kinds of corruption. Second, my account favors levels and modes of punishment that should reduce the dangers of serious oppression and coercion. It favors a decremental strategy, of reducing general levels of punishment. It would radically reduce our reliance on imprisonment (which is perhaps the most fertile ground for penal corruption). It favors modes of punishment (such as probation and community service) that are less likely to be oppressive. This is not to say that these dangers are not still real: any attempt to actualize such an ideal theory would need to build in strong safeguards against them. Nor is it to say that we should embrace the practice of punishment with fervent wills and easy consciences. We should certainly follow Murphy's injunction that "in punishing, we should act with caution, regret, humility, and with a vivid realization that we are involved in a fallible and finite human institution—one that is necessary but regrettable" (Murphy 1999; 160–61). But it is to say (or to hope) that we could aspire to transform our penal practices into a system of communicative, penitential punishment that, while (like any human practice) far from perfect, would recognizably serve the values of a liberal polity. It is to say, too, that although we must suspect and guard against the potentially oppressive and corrupting power of the state, a system of state punishment is not *inevitably* oppressive and corrupt.

However, even if such worries do not by themselves undermine my account as an account of an in principle practicable ideal of punishment, they point towards certain deeper problems about any attempt to actualize that ideal. As presented so far, the worries concern the content, the internal operations, of the penal system—whether punishments could be so organized and administered that they would constitute genuine attempts to engage in the kind of moral communication that punishment ought to be. But we must also ask about the wider context in which the penal system is set and on which it depends for its legitimacy. Here the problems become even more serious.

2. Preconditions of Criminal Punishment

One task for normative theory is to identify the conditions given which the punishment of a particular offender or the punishments imposed by a particular system are justified. These include, on my account, the requirements that those punished have been duly convicted of what the law defines as a crime, that their punishments are proportionate to their crimes, and that those punishments constitute attempts to engage the offender in the appropriate kind of moral communication. If these conditions are not satisfied, the punishments are not justified. However, a normative theory of punishment must also identify certain further conditions. These are conditions not so much of the legitimacy of particular punishments imposed within a system as of the legitimacy of the system itself: only given such conditions can we justifiably engage in the practice of punishment at all. These are *preconditions* of punishment: they are conditions that must be satisfied before we can engage in this practice and before we can discuss the legitimacy of particular actions taken or policies pursued within the practice.

2.1. Conditions and Preconditions

An analogy and an example should help to clarify the distinction between conditions and preconditions, and the importance of the latter.[5]

For an analogy, consider some of the conditions that bear on the legitimacy of moral criticism and censure. If I criticize another's conduct, censuring her for acting immorally, she might respond by arguing that she did not do what I allege she did, or that it was not wrong, or that it was excusable, or that my censure is excessive (that it was not *that* wrong). Arguments such as these concern the conditions of justified censure. We are engaged in the practice of moral criticism or judgment, and are discussing whether the conditions (conditions internal to that practice) for legitimate criticism of the kind I have made are satisfied. But she might instead respond in different terms, arguing that I lack the right or the moral standing to censure her conduct. What she allegedly did is not my business; it is not for me (although it might be for others) to criticize or to call her to moral account for it. Her argument now is not about the conditions of legitimate censure within that moral practice—about the moral character of what she did or about whether it was justified or excusable. It concerns instead the conditions for engaging in this practice, for raising these questions about the morality or culpability of her conduct, at all. She is claiming that I lack the right or the standing to seek to engage with her in this practice, in relation to this aspect of her conduct. Her argument thus concerns the preconditions of moral criticism.

For an example, consider the case of an alleged offender who has, since the time of the alleged offense, become so mentally disordered that he cannot understand the charges laid against him and could not understand his punishment (were he punished) as a punishment—as a censure-expressing burden imposed on him for his crime. Such a person is not fit to be tried or to be punished. He cannot properly be subjected to the criminal process of trial, conviction, and punishment (see Duff 1986, 14–38, 119–23, 180–84). The point is not that he should be *acquitted,* or that if he is convicted the court should discharge him rather than impose a punishment. Decisions to acquit or to grant a discharge are taken *within* the practice of trying and punishing offenders, whereas his fitness to be tried or to be punished is a condition of subjecting him to that practice at all. His fitness is a *precondition* of criminal liability and punishment. It is a condition that must be satisfied before he can be tried, and thus before the question can even be raised whether he should be convicted (rather than acquitted) or what sentence (if any) the court should impose if he is convicted.

The requirement that an alleged offender be fit to be tried and punished is an aspect of the requirement that he be a responsible citizen. By 'responsible' here I mean 'answerable'.[6] I am responsible for something (in this context, for some alleged past action of mine) if I am answerable for it: if I can properly be called to account for it, to explain or to justify it, or (if blame is at issue) to accept blame for it if I cannot justify or excuse it.[7] The criminal process of trial and punishment presupposes that the defendant is answerable. The trial calls her to answer to the charge against her; a conviction censures her as someone who is answerable for, who should accept censure for, the wrong she has been proved to have committed (see ch. 3.2.2); and her punishment, as an attempt to persuade her to recognize and repent her crime, addresses her as someone who could understand and respond to her punishment as such a communicative enterprise. But to be answerable, to be properly called to answer, I must be *capable* of answering. If an alleged offender cannot understand the charge against him (as a charge of criminal wrongdoing) or cannot understand his trial, he is not capable of answering the charge and is therefore not responsible. His trial, which purports to call him to answer the charge, becomes a travesty. So too, if he cannot understand the meaning of his conviction or punishment, if he could not accept as justified (because he cannot understand) the censure they convey, he is not responsible. His conviction and punishment, which purport to communicate that censure to him and to seek his acceptance of it, become travesties. He might have committed the offense and might have been at that time a responsible agent, but he is not now responsible for that past crime, since he cannot now answer for it.[8]

It is an essential precondition of criminal liability and punishment that the person who is to be tried and (if convicted) punished be a responsible citizen. That precondition is not satisfied if the person is not fit to be tried and punished—if he lacks the capacities necessary to answer the charge that he faces or to understand and respond appropriately to conviction and punishment. But there is more to being a responsible citizen than the possession of such capacities, and it is this 'more' that primarily concerns us in this section. In particular, I discuss three further preconditions of criminal liability and punishment that the idea of being a responsible citizen includes. One concerns the person's obligations to or under the law. Another concerns the question who has the standing to call her to answer for her alleged crimes. A third concerns the language in which she is called to answer.

(In each instance, as for fitness to be tried or punished, the law itself will usually specify *legal* preconditions of liability and punishment: that the person be fit, that the laws under which she is charged are binding on her, that the court has the authority to try her, that her trial be in a language she can understand—if necessary, through an interpreter. But my concern is with the preconditions that the law *should* specify rather than with those that it in fact specifies—the preconditions that must be satisfied if a person is to be *justly* convicted and punished.)

All three of these preconditions reflect the conception of political community on which my account of criminal punishment depends—though any plausible normative account of punishment will need to include versions of them (see p. 198, below). All three concern ways in which people can be included in, or excluded from, a political community (see ch. 3.1). That is why I speak of responsible *citizenship* rather than of responsible *agency* as a precondition of criminal liability and punishment. What matters is not whether the person is in some general or abstract sense a responsible agent (though only responsible agents can be responsible citizens) but whether she is responsible *as a citizen* of the polity under whose laws she is to be tried and punished, and that depends on the extent to which she is included as a member of that political community.[9]

2.2. Political Obligation

If someone is to be justly tried and punished for a crime, she must be bound by the laws that define her conduct as criminal and by the laws that provide for her trial, conviction, and punishment. If she is not bound by those laws, then however wrong her conduct might have been, she cannot justly be held liable for it under those laws. The question whether she is bound by those laws is here the question whether she is *morally* bound by them, not whether she is *legally* bound by them—whether their claim to bind her is morally legitimate (cf. Bottoms 1998, 91–94, on "legitimacy").

The question whether she is bound by those laws is often taken to be equivalent to the question whether she has an obligation to obey them—not just a legal obligation, but a political or moral obligation as a citizen. But the matter is not quite that simple: the aspects of the criminal law that define the central *mala in se* should not be understood as *prohibitions* that citizens are obligated to *obey* (see ch. 2.4.1). Someone who is convicted of wounding is not convicted for *disobeying* the law that defines such conduct as criminal, but for committing a (prelegal) wrong in which the community takes a legitimate interest through the criminal law. The initial question is not whether she is obligated to obey the law, but whether she is bound by the values that the law embodies and expresses. However, the question of a defendant's obligation to obey the law soon arises, in two ways.

First, even with central and uncontroversial *mala in se*, to justify holding the agent criminally liable it must be shown not only that she is bound (as a member of this political community or simply as a human being) by the values that her conduct infringed, but also that she is bound or obligated to answer for that conduct in the criminal courts: that the law has the legitimate authority to define her conduct as a public wrong and to bring her to trial for it. Even if she does not have an obligation to obey the laws that define her conduct as criminal, we can thus properly talk of her obligation to obey the laws that provide for her trial and punishment; and such an obligation to answer for her conduct through the criminal process is a precondition of her criminal liability. This is an aspect of the requirement (see sec. 2.3, below) that those who call her to answer for her criminal conduct must have the authority or standing to do so.

Second, we can talk of an obligation to obey the substantive criminal law insofar as it deals with controversial *mala in se*, or with controversial *determinationes* of *mala in se*, or with *mala prohibita* (see ch. 2.4.4). In such instances the law does demand the citizen's obedience, and she can be called to answer for her alleged disobedience only if she has an obligation to obey the law.

This is not the place for a full discussion of the conditions under which people have, or lack, an obligation to obey the law. I want simply to note some factors that might undermine that supposed obligation and so threaten the legitimacy of holding those whose obligation is thus undermined criminally liable for the crimes they commit. I focus on questions concerning, not the content of the law (although these are certainly important), but the larger context in which it is set.

Consider some crimes of the disadvantaged. An impoverished single parent steals clothes from a supermarket for her children or defrauds the social security system by concealing her earnings. A group of unemployed youths living in a run-down and ill-provided housing estate vandalize a local council building or escalate a protest against heavy-handed policing into a riot. A homeless couple looking for somewhere to sleep break into an empty office building, where they cause some damage to property. Such cases as these rightly worry those who are concerned about the problem of doing penal justice in an unjust society. Can we honestly say that these people are justly punished if they are brought to court for their actions—which do, under our existing laws, constitute criminal offenses? But why should we be uneasy about their punishment?

We might think in some such cases that the person's action is morally justified and that the law should recognize such a justification; or that these actions are, if not justified, at least excusable in a way that the law should recognize.[10] These issues are important, but I do not discuss them here. For they presuppose that the agent is bound by the law—that she is bound by the values it declares as the values of the political community and by its *determinationes* of those values, that she is obligated to obey it even if she does not agree with its content. But perhaps that is just what we should question (see Hudson 1995, 68–69).

Suppose we come to believe, in any of the examples given above, that the offenders had suffered not only 'social disadvantage' but serious, persisting, and systematic injustice. They had been excluded from participation in the political life of the community, having no real chance to make their voices heard in those fora in which the laws and policies under which they must live are decided. They had been excluded from a fair share in, or a fair opportunity to acquire, the economic and material benefits that others enjoy. They had been normatively excluded—they had not been treated, by the state or by their fellow citizens collectively, with the respect and concern due to them as citizens (see ch. 3.1.1). Can we still say that they are bound by the laws of the polity that treats them thus? Can we say that they are still normatively included, as being bound by its laws, although in these other ways they are severely excluded? Can we say that this is still their law (see ch. 2.4.2) although, if they are punished for what they have done, it now reinforces the injustices they have suffered?

There is of course no simple answer to this question. We need to ask how stringent the conditions are that must be satisfied if people are to have a obligation to obey the law. What undermines that obligation, I have suggested, is the extent to which people are excluded—politically, materially, normatively—from the community whose law it is, since they can be bound by the law only insofar as they are, and are treated as, members of that community. But how serious must that exclusion be for it to undermine that obligation? How minimal or modest can inclusion be if it is to sustain that obligation? We also need to ask whether really serious exclusion negates, or only weakens, the obligation to obey the law; and whether it negates, or weakens, the excluded people's obligation with respect to every law or only with respect to those laws that are implicated in the injustices they have suffered. But I do not pursue these issues here. My aim is simply to point out that one condition of being responsible as a citizen, and so one precondition of criminal liability and punishment, is that the agent be bound by the laws under which she is to be tried and punished, and that there is reason to doubt whether this precondition is adequately satisfied for many of those who appear before our criminal courts.

To suggest that those who have been systematically excluded or unjustly disadvantaged may not be bound by the law (or not be bound as stringently as others) is not to suggest that their criminal actions are justified, permissible, or excusable. That is a quite separate question, which this argument does not address. It is, rather, to suggest that their actions are not wrong *qua criminal*: that they are not to be judged (justified, excused, or condemned) by the law, in terms of its demands and requirements. An employer who treats his employees unjustly and oppressively might thereby lose whatever claim he had to their obedience to the rules he lays down for their working lives. Employees who then break those rules might still act wrongly, since the rules might forbid conduct that they anyway have good moral reason to avoid. Indeed, the very existence of the rules might give the employees reason to act in conformity with them, if the rules assist the coordination of their shared activities. But what makes their actions right or wrong is not now the fact that they conform, or fail to conform, to rules that they have an obligation to obey as being laid down by an employer with legitimate authority over them. So too with the law. Someone who is not bound by the law, because she has been unjustly disadvantaged and excluded by the polity whose law it is, is not bound to regard the law as a source of authoritative requirements. But her conduct can still be judged and criticized by other values and standards than those concerning its conformity to the law.

This is also to say that her conduct is not to be judged by the law or its institutions. This first precondition of criminal liability, that the person be bound by the law, thus connects with the second, that the law and its courts have the standing to call her to answer for her alleged crimes. Indeed, this second precondition is hardly separable from the first, since the question whether I am bound by the law is in part the question whether I am bound to answer to the law for my alleged failures to conform to its requirements. It also poses a more serious challenge to the legitimacy of punishing those who have been unjustly excluded (to the possibility of doing penal justice in an unjust society). The examples that I have used to raise the question whether the unjustly excluded can be said still to be bound by the law involve crimes that are not amongst the most serious, and that have a direct connection to the exclusions suffered by those who committed them. But if the law lacks the standing to call the unjustly excluded to account, it lacks that standing in relation to *all* crimes, including the most serious *mala in se*.

2.3. To Whom Must I Answer?

To be responsible is to be answerable. To be answerable is to be *capable* of answering: hence the requirement that the defendant be fit to be tried (see sec. 2.1, above). It is also to be answerable *for* something. In the context of criminal liability it is to be answerable for alleged offenses under laws by which the defendant is bound: hence the requirement, discussed in section 2.2, that the defendant be bound by the laws under which she is tried. If she is not bound, she has nothing for which to answer before a criminal court. But to be answerable is also to be answerable *to* someone or something: to my conscience, to God, to my spouse or family, to my friends or colleagues, to my employer. I am answerable to some person or body only if he or it has the standing to call me to account. If I fail in my duties as a teacher, there are various people or bodies to whom I am answerable—who can properly call me to account (to explain, to excuse, or to accept criticism for my failure): my students, my colleagues, my university. But if some stranger heard about my failings and criticized me for them, I could properly reply that it was none of his business—that he lacked the standing to call me to account for them. In responding thus I would not be trying to explain, justify, or excuse my performance as a teacher: I would simply be refusing to answer for it to *him*.

A further precondition of criminal liability and punishment is thus that the person who is to be tried, convicted, and punished must be answerable to those who thus call him to answer for his alleged criminal wrongdoing: that they have the standing to call him to answer. If they lack that standing, they cannot properly try him or judge him. They lack the right either to convict or to acquit him, to decide either that he deserves punishment or that he does not. We must therefore ask who, or what, calls the defendant to answer when he is put on trial. To whom, or to what, is he supposedly answerable? He is called to answer *by* a particular court, but it is not that court *to* which he is answerable. He is answerable to those, or that, in whose name this court speaks and acts. But who, or what, is that?

English legal forms list criminal cases as *"Regina v. D"*—which might suggest that it is the monarch. But this answer is hardly suitable for a liberal polity of citizens (as distinct from mere subjects). A better answer is implicit in such U.S. case titles as *"People v. D"* (see text at ch. 2, n.34, above): defendants are answerable as citizens to their fellow citizens—which is why responsible *citizenship* is a precondition of criminal liability. The court speaks, in the voice of the law, on behalf of the political community whose law it is. It calls citizens to answer to their fellow citizens for their alleged commissions of public wrongs under the community's law—a law that is also meant to be their law, as being the common law of the community of which they are members (see ch. 2.4.2).

Another precondition of criminal liability and punishment is thus that the law, and the political community in whose name it speaks, have the authority and the standing to call this person to answer for his alleged crime. But what gives it, and what could deprive it of, that authority and standing? It can have that authority and standing only if the defendant is bound by the law (the topic of sec. 2.2, above). But that is not, I think, sufficient.

Suppose that an academic institution lays down strict rules for its students concerning their academic behavior, and that the rules are justified in terms of the values that define the institution as an academic institution. They require the students to treat other members of the institution with honesty and respect, to attend classes, to produce essays on time, and so on. These rules are applied and enforced by the academic staff, who are given the authority to call students to account and to penalize them for breaches of the rules. But suppose that the staff themselves treat their students with persistent dishonesty and disrespect. They regularly fail to appear for classes they are due to give, or they appear late. They mark essays carelessly, or they mark them months after they were written. Such behavior might not breach any formal rules of the institution; or if it does breach the formal rules, those rules are never enforced against members of staff. If a student is then called to account by members of staff or by an official committee for an alleged breach of the rules, she might with justice reply that they lack the moral standing thus to call her to account or to judge her: not because she is not bound by the institution's rules (she would be prepared to answer for breaches of them to her fellow students or to members of staff who behaved appropriately towards her) or because she thinks her conduct was justified or excusable (that is not the question she is addressing); but because those who would call her to account have themselves, in their behavior towards her, shown no respect for the values they accuse her of flouting. Similarly, if I criticize another for acting immorally towards me, she might respond by arguing, not that her action was right or that she is not bound by the values to which I appeal or that it is none of my business, but that I have lost the right thus to call her to account by my persistent misconduct towards her. I am not well placed to criticize her for lying to me if I have persistently and unrepentantly lied to her.

Something analogous can also undermine the standing of the law and its courts to call a citizen to answer a charge of criminal wrongdoing. The law and the courts speak and act in the name of the political community. They call a defendant to answer to the community for an offense against its public values as expressed, interpreted, and applied by its law. Suppose, however, that the defendant's treatment by that community (if not directly by the law and its officials, then by the community's political institutions, by its governmental policies, by its social practices and habits) has been persistently and seriously at odds with those values. Suppose that he has been excluded—politically, materially, and normatively—from an adequate share in the community's goods; and that his exclusion has not been recognized as a wrong done to him. Could he not with justice say to the court that, whether or not he is bound by the criminal law, the court lacks the standing to call him to answer for his alleged crime: that since the community in whose name it speaks has so notably failed to treat him in accordance with its declared values, it can hardly claim the right to call him to account for his alleged failure to respect those values as embodied in the criminal law?[11]

It might be said that whatever injustice or exclusion a defendant has suffered is not the concern of the criminal court that is now to try his case. Its concern is with whether he has committed a crime, and its right and authority to call him to answer for that alleged crime is not undermined by the injustices he has suffered at the hands of other aspects or organs of the community's political institutions. The truth in this argument is that *once the defendant is brought to trial*, such injustices will probably not be relevant, unless they generate what the law should recognize as a justification or excuse for what he did. The court will rightly focus on whether the particular charge, that the defendant committed a specified crime, is proved against him. But the defendant's claim here is not that the injustices he has suffered give the court reason to acquit him—that they negate the *conditions* of criminal liability. It is, rather, that the court lacks the standing to try his case, to call him to account in this way, at all: that those injustices negate an essential *precondition* of criminal liability by negating the claim that he is answerable to the political community through its courts. Once a defendant comes to trial, the court should properly attend only to those factors that bear on the conditions of liability, which do not usually include the kinds of injustice to which this defendant appeals. In this way the court's decisions are properly isolated from the broader social and political context in which the law and the criminal process, as particular practices, are set. What this defendant claims, however, is that he should not be subjected to this practice at all—that the conditions for the legitimacy of the practice as it is applied to him (which are preconditions for the legitimacy of particular verdicts reached within it) are not satisfied. But the question whether the practice is legitimate cannot be answered without attending to the context in which it is set.[12]

It might also be argued that, even if the injustice or exclusion a defendant has suffered undermines the court's standing to call him to account for *some* crimes, it cannot undermine its standing in relation to *all* crimes. Perhaps academics lack the standing to call students to account for infringements of values that they themselves persistently and unrepentantly flout in their dealings with the students; and my persistent lying to you might deprive me of the right to call you to account if you lie to me. But the academics can still claim the standing to call students to account for infringing values that they do not themselves flout; and I can still call you to account for other wrongs you commit against me (my lying to you does not undermine my right to condemn you for trying to kill me). So too, even if the court lacks the right to call the defendant to account for some crimes, those involving values that the political community has failed to respect in its treatment of him, it surely still has the right to call him to account for other crimes: for murder or for rape, for instance, since his life and sexual integrity have not been attacked by the community. But, first, we must ask how far the political community and its institutions have respected these values in their dealings with this person or the group or community to which he belongs. If, for instance, the police or the courts have not taken criminal attacks on members of this disadvantaged group seriously, this failure undermines their standing to call members of this group to answer for attacks that they commit, since it shows that the community does not treat the members of the group as fully sharing in those values. Second, the question is whether this person is answerable as a citizen to his fellow citizens: but if their collective treatment of him has effectively excluded him from many of the rights and goods of citizenship, if they have collectively failed to treat him as a citizen, how can they now call him to account as a fellow citizen?

This is not to say that there is *no one* who has the right to call him to account—no one to whom he is answerable. He will normally be answerable to his victim for the moral wrong he has done. He may be answerable to the members of other communities to which he belongs, if he commits a wrong that properly concerns them. But it is to say that he is not answerable, as a citizen, to the political community that has unjustly excluded him, and thus that he is not answerable before the criminal courts, which act in the name of that community and its law.

We must of course ask, as we must ask in relation to political obligation, how serious the unjust exclusion or disadvantage must be if it is to undermine the person's answerability as a citizen—how stringent this precondition of criminal liability ought to be. But I do not pursue this question here. My aim again has simply been to point out another condition of being responsible as a citizen, another precondition of criminal liability and punishment—that the agent be answerable to the political community for his alleged criminal wrongdoing. And I suggest that there is reason to doubt whether this precondition is adequately satisfied for many of those who appear before our criminal courts.

2.4. The Language of the Law

It is a general precondition of criminal liability and punishment that the person who is to be tried and punished be responsible, answerable, as a citizen. She is thus answerable only if she is *capable* of answering—capable of understanding and responding to the charge brought against her. She is thus answerable only if she is answerable *for* her alleged crime, as a citizen who is bound by the law, and only if she is answerable *to* the political community through its courts. But there is a further condition of responsibility as answerability, concerning language.

The criminal process of trial, conviction, and punishment is a communicative process. A trial calls the defendant to answer a charge of criminal wrongdoing. If she is convicted, her conviction communicates to her the censure she has been proved to deserve. Her punishment, I have argued, should aim both to further that communicative enterprise by persuading her to recognize and repent her wrongdoing, and to provide a way in which she can communicate that repentant recognition to others. But communication requires a language in which the charge can be expressed, the case argued, and the censure communicated. So what is that language?

The obvious answer is that it is the language of the law: the (to some degree inevitably specialized) language in which are expressed the substantive rules and requirements of the criminal law, the conditions of criminal liability, and the procedural rules for the trial and for sentencing and the administration of punishment. But a further, crucial question then arises: *whose* language is this—and whose language *should* it be if it is to be the language in which citizens are addressed by the law and in which they are called to answer for their alleged crimes?

There is an equally obvious answer to the question of whose language it *is*. It is the language of legal professionals—most obviously of judges and lawyers. It is a language in which they are at home. They can understand it, and they can use it to express the judgments and arguments that belong to the law. However, it *should* also be a language that is accessible both to the lay participants in the criminal process—defendants, jurors, and lay magistrates—and to the wider community in whose name the criminal process is conducted. If the defendant is to be answerable, she must be called to answer in a language that she can understand. It would be a travesty to try (or pretend to try) a person who cannot understand the language in which she is charged and in which she is supposed to answer. If juries and lay magistrates are to play their roles, deciding on the defendant's legal guilt or innocence, they too must be able to understand the language in which the charge is expressed and in which the trial is conducted. They must be able to understand the meaning of what is said in the trial, and of what they are saying when they bring in their verdict. And if justice is to be seen to be done by those in whose name the courts act, lay members of the polity must also be able to understand the language of the law. That language might not be one with which they are entirely at home or that they can at once understand without assistance. It will inevitably be a specialized language with its own peculiarly legal concepts (or legal versions of extralegal concepts) and its own modes of reasoning. But it must be a language that they *could* understand, with help, if necessary, from those who are fluent in it. An important part of the task of judges, lawyers, and magistrates' clerks is to provide such assistance—to translate, if necessary, the language of the law for lay participants (and one task of defense counsel is to translate the defendant's language into the language of the law).

This might not seem to be a very demanding requirement. But we can see that it is quite demanding if we ask what kind of understanding must be accessible to the lay participants in the criminal process.

First, it must be a *normative*, not merely a factual, understanding. The defendant, and those who must decide her legal guilt or innocence, must be able to understand, not just that she is said to have acted in some factually specifiable way that the law defines as criminal, but that she is charged with criminal *wrongdoing*. She, and they, must therefore be able to understand the values in the light of which her alleged conduct counts as a criminal wrong.

Second, it must be an understanding that would make it possible for the defendant, and for those who must decide her legal guilt or innocence, to *speak* the language of the law in the first person. It must be possible for them to make, not merely the kinds of third-person "detached normative statement" (see Raz 1979, 146, 153–59) that report the requirements of an alien value system that one does not and could not share, but first-person, committed normative statements that express their own acceptance of the law and its values.

These two requirements flow from the role of the criminal law in a liberal polity (see ch. 2.4). If the criminal law is to be a common law rather than an alien imposition, it must express the public values of the political community. It must speak to members of that polity in a language that they can understand as expressing values that are, or could be, theirs. It must speak to them, not merely of demands that they are to be coerced into obeying, but of requirements or obligations that flow from those values, and its language must be one that they can speak for and to themselves. The defendant must be able to understand that she is charged with a public wrong under laws that claim her allegiance to the values they purport to embody. She must be able, if she is duly proved guilty, to express her own repentant recognition of that wrong, since that is what her conviction and punishment call on her to do. The jurors, or lay magistrates, must likewise be able to understand that what they have to determine is whether a charge of wrongdoing has been proved; and since in convicting the defendant they will be censuring her for a wrong that has been proved against her (for that is the meaning of a conviction), they must be able to speak that conviction in the first-person voice of those who accept the law and the values it embodies. They are meant to speak and act on behalf of and in the name of the whole political community. But they must therefore be able to speak the language of the law, as expressing the public values of that community, in the first person. Linguistic inclusion (see ch. 3.1.1) is thus a crucial condition of the law's authority over those whom it claims to bind, and a precondition of criminal liability. The language of the law must be a normative language that the citizens can understand and speak for themselves.

If this is to be possible, the language of the law cannot be entirely detached from the ordinary, extralegal language in which citizens talk to one another (and to themselves)—the language in which they criticize one another's (and their own) conduct, in which they discuss and apply the shared values of the political community. Even if the language of the law is to some degree a specialized, technical language, there must be a bridge by which lay citizens can cross from their ordinary extralegal language into enough of the language of the law for them to be able to speak the relevant aspects of that language in the first person.

That bridge is provided by what we can call, following Bernard Williams, the law's "thick" concepts. "Thick" ethical concepts enable us to describe and judge human actions in terms of substantive ethical values. Obvious examples include such concepts as courage and cowardice, honesty and dishonesty, kindness and cruelty. Such concepts "express a union of fact and value" (B. Williams 1985, 129; see ch. 8, generally). To call an action courageous or cowardly is to describe it as an action of a specific kind. But it is also to describe it, if we are speaking for ourselves in using the terms, as admirable or defective in the light of the values that such concepts express. Such "thick" ethical concepts are central to ethical thought and understanding. "Thick" legal concepts are likewise central to the possibility of the kind of lay understanding of the law that is a precondition of criminal liability. The most obvious examples of such concepts are those that pick out the various kinds of crime (murder, rape, theft, wounding, fraud, dangerous driving, and so on) and the various kinds of fault (intention, recklessness, negligence). While the legal meanings of such terms might not be quite the same as the meanings they carry in extralegal discourse, the legal concepts must be closely enough connected to those extralegal concepts for lay citizens to be able to recognize them as specialized versions of thick ethical concepts with which they are familiar—and thus to recognize as genuine wrongs what the law defines as crimes.

The requirement that the language of the law be accessible to the defendant and to other lay participants in the criminal process might still seem to be easily and typically satisfied—even if it is interpreted, as I have argued it should be, as requiring that lay people be able to speak that language in the first person, as a normative language expressing the shared values of the political community. The law clearly does contain the kinds of thick concept that I argue, are crucial for that purpose. Those concepts are connected sufficiently closely to their extralegal forms to enable lay citizens who grasp the extralegal concepts to grasp and apply the legal concepts. Since the vast majority of lay citizens can grasp and apply those extralegal concepts in their own moral discourse, they therefore have the appropriate access to the language of the law.

There is some truth in the argument that the language of the law is, at least in principle, properly accessible to most citizens. Most people are not psychopaths to whom the normative moral language on which the law draws is alien and inaccessible. The moral languages that most people speak include the kinds of thick concept on which the law draws (concepts concerning, for instance, the significance of various kinds of attack on or endangerment of people and their property, and of various kinds of dishonesty and deception). Lay people might not give those concepts quite the same meaning or scope or significance as the law gives them. But there is still a bridge available from their language to the language of the law, and there is no reason to suppose it to be a bridge that they cannot cross. Surely, then, it is a bridge that they should cross: for the language of the law is the authoritative language of the polity, declaring and defining its public values; as citizens of that polity, they ought to recognize those values as theirs and be ready to be judged (and to judge others) in terms of those values, in the language of the law.

There may still, however, be room to wonder whether it is a bridge that all those whom the law claims to bind can reasonably be expected to cross. The language of the law might be *in principle* accessible to them, but this is not yet to say that it is a language that they can reasonably be expected to hear or to speak as their own—as a language expressing values in which they share as members of the political community.[13]

What someone hears, or can be reasonably expected to hear, when he is addressed depends not just on the content of what is said, but on the context in which it is said, and the accent in which it is spoken.[14] I might speak the language of honest philosophical inquiry to my students, urging them to think for themselves about the issues we discuss and to follow the argument wherever it leads, and offering them what I take to be good arguments for the views I hold and against their views. I might hope (honestly, or self-deceptively) that I will thereby persuade them to make that language their own—to engage for themselves in this practice, to begin to speak in their own philosophical voice. But the context in which I speak to them (which is determined not just by how I behave towards them but by the nature and practices of our academic institution) might be one that makes it subtly or unsubtly clear to them that independent thought is not valued. It might make clear that what matters is to get a good degree by producing work that says what the teachers want to hear, and that their teachers are not really interested in them as potential philosophers but instead see them as necessary but irritating distractions from research. Furthermore, the accents or tones in which I speak to them might reveal all too clearly that I have no real respect for them or their attempts at philosophical thought. My voice might be all too often the voice of irritation or contempt, or of a bullying attempt to force them to accept the views that I take to be right. If that is the context, if those are the accents, in which I speak to my students, I cannot reasonably expect them either to hear what I say as an attempt to speak the language of rational and honest philosophical inquiry to or with them, or to come to speak that language as their own. They will not hear in my voice a commitment to the values of such inquiry or encouragement to engage in it for themselves. They will hear instead a voice that seeks their submissive obedience and that encourages them to parrot what they think I want to hear (see Duff 1998b, 261–64; 1998d, 204–5; 1999, 65–66).

So too with the law. It purports to address all citizens in the language of the political community's values, as a language that they should hear and speak for themselves, and that should be their language as citizens. But suppose that the context in which the law speaks to some of the citizens is one in which they are unjustly excluded or disadvantaged. Suppose that their treatment at the hands of the community and its institutions has not shown respect or concern for them as sharing in those values. Suppose that they are politically, materially, and normatively excluded from many of the community's goods. Suppose too that the accents in which they are addressed (or, given that context, reasonably hear themselves as being addressed) by the law's officials—police officers, judges, and others who administer the law—are the accents not of respect but of contempt, not of authority but of mere power. They cannot then reasonably be expected to hear the language of the law as one that could be theirs, as one that they could and should speak for themselves. They will rather, and reasonably, hear it as an alien voice that they might have to obey but that they could not make their own.

This point has obvious implications for a communicative theory of punishment. If punishment is to communicate with the offender (and enable her to communicate repentance to her fellow citizens) it must speak a language that she can understand and speak for herself as a normative language of censure.[15] But there is ample scope for misunderstandings, both reasonable and unreasonable. Given the context in which punishment is administered (which includes the ways in which the offender has been treated by other political institutions) and the accents in which it is administered by penal officials, some offenders will hear its voice, not as the voice of a community to which they belong and are treated as belonging, but as the voice of an alien and oppressive power; not as a voice that appeals to values that they share and are treated as sharing, but as a voice that seeks to coerce them into submission.

This then is a further condition of being responsible, that is, answerable, as a citizen under the law and a further precondition of criminal liability and punishment: that the language of the law and of punishment be one that the agent can reasonably be expected to understand and speak for herself as a language of public values that are or could be her own. I suspect that this condition too is not adequately satisfied for many of those who appear before our criminal courts.

2.5. Law and Community

The preconditions of criminal liability and punishment discussed in this section concern the existence and scope of an appropriate kind of political community. Citizens are bound by the law as members of the political community whose common law it is. They are answerable to their fellow citizens, through the courts, for their offenses against the community's public values as declared and interpreted by the law. They are answerable in the public language in which those values are expressed and applied. To determine whether criminal punishment can be justified (let alone whether it is justified as it is actually practiced), we must therefore ask not only about the internal workings of a penal system but also about the larger political context in which it is set; not only (the topic of sec. 1) whether the punishments that it imposes could constitute genuine attempts at moral communication, aimed at persuading offenders to repentance, reform, and reconciliation, but also (the topic of this section) whether those who are punished are indeed members of an appropriate kind of political community.

To ask this question is to ask, first, whether such a political community exists at all. Can we discern, in our existing societies, normative political communities of the kind I sketched above (ch. 2.2)? Such communities are constituted by a shared commitment to certain defining values and by their members' mutual regard for one another as fellow citizens. Their members are bound by those values and their laws are structured by them. They must be both normative and linguistic communities, sharing a commitment to certain values and a language in which those values are expressed and discussed, and sharing a form of life—a set of practices and ways of acting—in which that commitment is actualized.

Certain kinds of skepticism might tempt us here. For instance, a MacIntyrean skepticism finds in modern western societies mere "simulacra of morality," "fragments of a conceptual scheme" that no longer makes sense to us. We still use the language of morality, and think that we agree in our use and understanding of moral concepts (or disagree intelligibly about their meaning and application): but those concepts have lost their sense, since we have lost the social and conceptual frameworks within which they once made sense. "We have—very largely, if not entirely—lost our comprehension, both theoretical and practical, of morality" (MacIntyre 1985, 2). We have then also lost the possibility of political community, since we have lost our grasp of the values on which such community depends. A postmodernist skepticism (or, its close relative, the skepticism flowing from the Critical Legal Studies movement) finds in our contemporary societies and legal systems, not a coherent set of intelligible or rational values, but a collection of incoherent, contradictory, and rationally unfounded dogmatisms, that disguise the exercise of brute power beneath the rhetoric of value and of law. We may have the forms and use the rhetoric of 'community', but we lack its reality. A less all-embracing skepticism argues that we can find moral *communities*, but not *political community*, in our contemporary societies. There is no "homogeneous sense or community in society as a whole," but only communities that are "shifting and limited, structurally fractured and conflictual" (Norrie 1998, 116).

These kinds of radical skepticism are, I think, ill-founded. Once we recognize (see ch. 2.2) that normative community is a matter of aspiration as much as of fact, that political community can be partial rather than total, and that it will not be the only community in which its members live or the most important community in their lives, we can find in our own societies imperfect, limited but still genuine political communities. They are not free of conflict and disagreement. But disagreement does not preclude community—it presupposes it, since we can intelligibly disagree only against a background of agreement.[16] They often fail to actualize the values to which they purport to be committed, but we can see that purported commitment as a (to some degree) genuine aspiration, not as mere (self-)deceiving rhetoric. Their members often fail to accord one another the respect and concern due to them as fellow citizens. But they can recognize those failures precisely as *failures* to live as they should live. They may lack any very adequate articulation or theorization of the values by which they are structured, and no doubt lack any rationally compelling *proof* that these are values by which a human polity should be structured. But we should not mistake (as I suspect MacIntyre and others mistake) the lack of adequate theory for the lack of that which is to be theorized, since people might not be able to theorize the values by which their lives are genuinely structured. Nor should we assume (as both rationalists and skeptics mistakenly assume) that values can have a rational claim on our allegiance only if we can provide some a priori demonstration of their validity (see Duff 1998c, 157–67). There may be those who reject some or all of the community's values. But this does not undermine the claim, made by other citizens, that they are members of the community and are bound by its values (see ch. 2.5).

However, we must ask not just about the existence, but also about the scope, of political community: not just whether a political community exists, speaking to its members through its laws, but whether it really does include *all* those who are supposedly bound by those laws as members of the community. On this question, as I have suggested in this section, there is more room for skepticism. A political community can include (can insist on including) some who reject its values or do not want to see themselves as members; it can legitimately insist that they are nonetheless bound by its laws and answerable before its courts. It can often fail to treat some of its members with the respect and concern due to them without undermining the claim that they are bound as citizens by the values in whose light they are also, albeit imperfectly, treated and by the laws that also, albeit imperfectly, protect them. Not every failure *in* community (every failure to act, collectively or individually, as the community's values require) marks a complete failure *of* community—especially if those failures are recognized as such and genuine attempts are made to correct them. But there can come a point where we must talk instead of a failure *of* community. If there are individuals or groups within the society who are (in effect, even if not by design) persistently and systematically excluded from participation in its political life and in its material goods, who are normatively excluded in that their treatment at the hands of the society's governing laws and institutions does not display any genuine regard for them as sharing in the community's values, and who are linguistically excluded in that the voice of the law (through which the community speaks to its members in the language of their shared values) sounds to them as an alien voice that is not and could not be theirs, then the claim that they

are, as citizens, bound by the laws and answerable to the community becomes a hollow one. Sufficiently persistent, systematic, and unrecognized or
uncorrected failures to treat individuals or groups as members of the polity
who share in its goods undermine the claim that they are bound by its laws.
They can be bound only as citizens, but such failures implicitly deny their
citizenship by denying them the respect and concern due to citizens.

I have suggested (although I have not tried to prove) that this skepticism
is warranted in relation to individuals and groups in our own societies, including many of those who appear before our criminal courts and who suffer conviction and punishment for their crimes: many of them, whether individually
or as members of unjustly disadvantaged groups, have suffered such serious
kinds of exclusion that the essential preconditions of criminal liability are not
adequately satisfied. Insofar as that is so, they are not justly tried, or convicted, or punished. The courts cannot properly call them to answer for their
crimes, since they are not answerable for those crimes (as crimes) before
these courts.

One can talk about how 'we' or 'the community' should respond to crimes
and to those who commit them; and the 'we' who talk thus, as theorists or as
policy makers, might see ourselves as members of a political community
whose laws are our laws and whose language is our language. But in talking
thus about what 'we' or 'the community' should do, it is all too easy either to
talk and think as if those policies are needed to deal with a 'them'—with a separate class of actual and potential offenders who are not 'us' (for 'we' do not
often find ourselves facing charges in a criminal court or suffering the coercive
attentions of the penal system); or simply to assume that the 'we' who are to do
something, the community whose penal policies we are discussing, include all
those to whom these policies are to be applied. To think thus of offenders as
constituting a 'them' is to fail to see them as fellow citizens, and to undermine
the legitimacy of punishing them. But to assume without question that they
are bound by and answerable to the law as members of the community is to fail
to attend carefully enough to the implications of the various kinds of exclusion
that so many of those who appear before our courts have suffered.

Those who suffer systematic, persistent exclusion are members of the
community that excludes them. They have a claim on the community and its
other members to be included as fellow citizens who share in its values and
its goods, to be accorded the respect and concern that is their due as members. That is why their exclusion constitutes not a neutral fact but an injustice. But they are not *treated* as members of the community. That is why its
laws and its courts cannot justly hold them answerable, or punish them, for
their crimes. The court cannot claim, as it must be able to claim if it is to justify trying the defendant, that she is answerable through this court to the
community in whose name it acts for a wrong committed against the community, if that community has in other respects utterly failed to treat her as a
member. It cannot claim the right to condemn her if the charge is proved, to

call her to repentance, or to demand a reparative apology from her to those she has wronged. Nor can it claim that her punishment will reconcile her with the community. Such reconciliation presupposes a prior, mutual relationship of recognized fellow citizenship that was damaged and is now to be repaired. But that presupposition is falsified if the defendant has not been treated as a fellow citizen.

3. Can Criminal Punishment Be Justified?

In chapters 3 and 4 I argued that criminal punishment could in principle be justified as a communicative system of secular penances. In this chapter I have raised some doubts about whether that 'in principle' justification can justify punishment in our existing societies. Even if we could aspire so to reform or transform the contents of our existing penal practices that punishment becomes a genuinely communicative, penitential enterprise, we must face the question whether the preconditions of criminal liability and punishment are satisfied. I have suggested that they are not adequately satisfied for many of those who suffer punishment under our existing systems.

If this is right, the conclusion must be that our present practices of criminal punishment are, if not *wholly* unjustified, very largely unjustified. We cannot justly punish the crimes of those who have been seriously and unjustly excluded or disadvantaged—which is to say, of many of those who are tried and sentenced in our courts.

This cannot, however, be the final conclusion of a book that aims not just to engage in idealized intellectual theory, utterly detached from our actual world, but to offer a normative account of punishment that, while still an ideal account, can address our actual practices. If I (and others) believe that our existing penal practices are unjust and unjustified, then I (and they) must face the question what is to be done. Nor can we simply say with Murphy that if we "want to be sure that we have the moral right to punish before we inflict it, then we had better first make sure that we have restructured society in such a way" that punishment could be justified (Murphy 1979c, 110). We should, of course, do what we can to work towards a restructuring of society that would transform it into a genuine, inclusive liberal community (although there are other and better reasons for doing this than a desire to make sure that we are justified in punishing offenders). Perhaps too, if and when that is achieved, "crime itself and the need to punish it would radically decrease if not disappear entirely" (110). But such restructuring takes time—decades, if not lifetimes. If asked what should be done about punishment meanwhile, we cannot just throw up our hands and say, "Nothing"—if only because we are, whether we like it or not, complicit in the penal practices that are still maintained and administered in our names. So what then should we do?

One response would be to go down the abolitionist route: to argue that since punishment cannot, for the time being or in the near future, be adequately justified, it must be abolished. But the ideals to which abolitionists aspire are as distant from our present actualities as is the ideal of punishment that I offer (see ch. 1.5). Their actualization requires, as much as does mine, the (re)creation of genuine communities whose members are united by shared values and mutual respect and concern, are answerable to one another, and can share the task of resolving such "conflicts" or "troubles" as arise. And we must again ask what is to be done until those preconditions are satisfied. Since I have argued that the ideals that abolitionists offer us are themselves misguided, this is not a route we should take.

Another response would be to reject the theory of punishment that I offer, on the grounds that however attractive it might seem as an ideal, a theory that sets such demanding preconditions for criminal liability and punishment is too remote from human life to serve as a guide or goal for our human practices. Alternatively, even if we do not reject it utterly, we might suspend it until such time (if ever) as the preconditions it sets come closer to being satisfied. In its place we might then put a qualified deterrent theory of the kind I discussed in chapter 3 (sec. 3). I have argued in the past that this may be the route we should take (Duff 1986, 291–99; 1991, 441–51): but I now doubt this, for several reasons.

First, though I spelt out the preconditions of punishment in the previous section in terms of a liberal communitarian conception of political society and a communicative theory of punishment, I think that *any* plausible normative theory of punishment will set preconditions similar to these. Any plausible theory will hold that punishment is justified only if it is deserved, and what makes it deserved must be that the person punished committed a crime that he was bound or obligated not to commit. Any plausible theory must hold that we are justified in trying, convicting, and punishing offenders only if they are answerable for their crimes before the courts that are to try them and sentence them. And though other theories do not give moral communication as central or as ambitious a role in punishment as I give it, any plausible theory must surely also hold that we are justified in punishing offenders only if they can be expected to understand their punishment as a justified response to their crimes.[17] Precisely how these requirements are articulated will depend on the details of the theory and of the larger conception of the state on which it depends. Anticommunitarian liberals would not articulate them as I do. But once they are articulated, I think we will also see that on any plausible theory of punishment, its legitimacy is seriously undermined by their nonsatisfaction in our existing societies.

Second, the crimes of the unjustly excluded and disadvantaged are often committed against victims who are similarly situated. Such offenders may still, I suggested (pp. 187–88, above), be answerable for such wrongs to their victims and their local communities. Now to say that since the preconditions of *criminal* liability are not satisfied, the law cannot call offenders to answer for such crimes, would be to say that the victims of those crimes cannot look to the law to help them gain satisfaction for the wrongs they have suffered. It would be to say that if the offenders are to be brought to answer or to apologize for those crimes, this must be done by the victims themselves or by their local communities (if they exist). But this would be to add exclusion to exclusion. Because the offenders have been unjustly excluded from the rights and benefits of community, their victims are also excluded from the law's assistance. The point is not that the law could no longer protect them by preventing crime. They could be thus protected by a system of deterrent or incapacitative punishments—though at the cost of further excluding actual and potential offenders from the normative community. The point is rather that the political community owes it to victims of crime to bring offenders to answer for those crimes (see ch. 3.6.2). To refuse to do this would be to that extent to exclude those victims from the normative community.

This might just seem to make the problem worse. Offenders are treated unjustly if they are called to answer for their crimes by a political community that lacks the standing to call them to account, but victims are treated unjustly if the community refuses to call those who wronged them to account. However, and third, perhaps a way forward lies in recognizing that punishment itself, as an exercise in moral communication, can contribute to that social and political restructuring that is needed if punishment is to be justified; that while its justification would remain radically imperfect and morally tainted until that restructuring is achieved, it might still be justified as the best we can do in our morally problematic situation.

To call someone to answer for her wrongdoing, through the criminal justice system, is to that extent to treat her as a citizen. Now the justification for doing this is, I have argued, undermined to the extent that she has in other respects been persistently excluded from the rights and benefits of citizenship. It is undermined especially if that exclusion is not recognized as such—if the political community displays no awareness of its failure to treat her as a citizen. But suppose that it is recognized. Suppose that there is, through the community's institutions and its government, a collective recognition of the wrongs she (and others similarly placed) have suffered, and a collective commitment to correcting them. That correction will be a large and lengthy task that might take decades to complete; and until it is at least well advanced, the community's right to call those who have suffered such exclusion to answer for their crimes is still undermined. But it is not as radically undermined as it was before: for the very fact of this collective recognition, this collective commitment to correcting the wrongs, displays a recognition of and concern for those who have suffered those wrongs as fellow citizens—as members of the community who share in its goods. Since to call them to answer for their crimes is also, so long as that calling to answer itself constitutes a communicative enterprise of the appropriate kind, to treat them as citizens, perhaps it can be (imperfectly) justified as a part of that very commitment to include them as fully recognized members of the polity.

Of course, the communicative content of this calling to answer must itself reflect a due recognition of the wrongs that those who are called to answer have suffered. In some instances this might require the law and the courts to recognize a 'social disadvantage' defense or to accept such disadvantage as a powerful mitigating factor (see p. 183, above). In other instances, however, unjustly excluded offenders have still committed genuine wrongs, for which they must be called to account and punished. But their punishment must include some recognition of the wrongs they have suffered and of the morally flawed character of their punishment—which is still tainted by those wrongs. This recognition could be expressed in the regretful or apologetic tones of the sentencer, but here there is also perhaps a further, more demanding, role for the probation officers who will be central to a communicative system of punishment (see chs. 3.5.1–2, 4.3.2). Their task would now be not only to try to bring offenders to confront and repent the wrongs they have done and to work out with them an appropriate mode of reparative apology, but also to persuade them to see that their punishment is still justified although its preconditions are far from fully satisfied. As mediators between the offender and the community, their role is to communicate to the offender the community's understanding of the crime. But that understanding must include both a condemnation of the crime as a wrong and a recognition of the wrongs the offender has suffered at the hands of the community.

This is not a comfortable position to take. It does not offer an unqualified justification of criminal punishment as an enterprise in which we can engage or be complicit with clear consciences. At best it offers a highly qualified justification of criminal punishment as a necessary but—for the probably extensive time being—morally tainted enterprise about which our consciences should be far from clear. I suspect, however, that it is the best way forward, and it should not surprise us that there is no way forward that is morally unproblematic or free of moral wrong. Both individuals and collectives can, by their own wrongdoing, get themselves into a position in which there is nothing they can do that will be free of moral wrong, but in which they must do something to try to remedy the situation. This, I suggest, is our collective situation as far as punishment is concerned.

I should end, however, with two cautionary comments. First, what I am offering is not a justification for continuing to punish offenders as we now punish them and in the context in which we now punish them. If criminal punishment is to be justified even in the tentatively doubtful way I am suggesting here, what is minimally required is both a serious collective commitment to reform the content and operations of the penal system (see sec. 1, above), and a serious collective commitment to begin to remedy the kinds of exclusion that undermine the preconditions of criminal liability and punishment. In the absence of such a commitment, we cannot justify the punishments undergone by many offenders at the hands of the criminal justice system (and thus at our hands, insofar as that system acts in our names and we remain complicit in its operations).

Second, that collective commitment requires, most obviously, concerted action by our governments and institutions. But it also makes demands on all citizens, and especially on those who are not unjustly excluded or disadvantaged by the political community. It requires that we argue or campaign for appropriate government action. It also, more significantly, requires that we carefully consider our own attitudes and conduct towards our fellow citizens. Such a consideration will no doubt lead many of us to realize how radically we must change ourselves, since the (re)creation of political community depends on the individual and collective attitudes and conduct of citizens towards one another as well as on the activities of governments and institutions. Furthermore, criminal punishment itself depends for its meaning and its value on the conduct and attitudes of all citizens, as well as on the conduct and attitudes of those directly involved in administering it. If criminal punishment is to communicate to offenders the communal censure that they deserve for their crimes and enable them to apologize and to reconcile themselves with the political community, the other members of that community must themselves be ready to accept such apologies and to reconcile themselves with the offender as a fellow citizen.

The task of justifying criminal punishment is not the task of finding a normative theory that will justify something like our existing penal practices. It is the task of so transforming the content and context of criminal punishment that it can become what it ought to be. That task makes heavy demands on all of us. This conclusion, while it should be disturbing and uncomfortable, should surprise no one who is sensitive to the harsh realities of our existing systems of criminal justice.

Notes

Introduction

1. In 1997, 911,842 people were convicted of felonies in U.S. federal and state courts (U.S. Bureau of Justice Statistics 1998, 421); 32,000 were convicted of indictable offenses in English and Welsh criminal courts (Home Office 1998, 21). These figure omit the many more people who were convicted of misdemeanors in U.S. courts and those convicted of summary offenses in English and Welsh courts.

2. The others avoid (further, formal) punishment by, for instance, being diverted into psychiatric care or receiving an absolute or conditional discharge. See Walker & Padfield 1996, chs. 15, 21.

3. I take the term 'penality' from Garland, who uses it 'to refer to the whole of the penal complex, including its sanctions, institutions, discourses and representations' (Garland 1985, x).

4. For an ambitious sketch of such a theory, see Braithwaite & Pettit 1990; for a salutary corrective, see Ashworth 1994, 1995a, 1995b.

5. See, e.g., Flew 1954; Benn 1958; Hart 1968, 1–27; also Fletcher 1978, 408–14; Scheid 1980.

6. Adler (1992) argues that pain is not a *necessary* feature of punishment. But his account portrays it as necessarily burdensome, as involving some restriction on the offender's "basic rights."

7. I say "(supposed)" and "(supposedly)" to mark the fact that those who claim to 'punish' may lack the requisite authority or may not be punishing actual offenders for actual offenses. See Duff 1986, 151–53.

8. Cf. the use of the 'definitional stop' by some philosophers to ward off objections to certain kinds of penal practice. See Quinton 1953–54; Benn 1958; for criticism, see Hart 1968, 5–6; Honderich 1984a, 62–64.

9. How particular or local should our starting point be? Can we talk of punishment as practiced in 'contemporary western societies' or only of punishment as practiced in a particular society? There are important differences in penal practice and theory between different contemporary western societies. But there is, I believe, enough that is shared both in practice and in theoretical

understandings of practice to make it legitimate to talk in the relatively general terms in which I talk here.

10. Some see this as a symptom of modernity's loss of moral understanding—indeed, of morality (see, e.g., MacIntyre 1985; for a MacIntyrean critique of 'liberal' legal theory, see Norrie 1998). Others take it, more reasonably, to mark a recognition of the genuine conflictual complexity of the moral world (see, e.g., Nagel 1979b; Stocker 1990).

11. Normative theories of punishment have always appealed, explicitly or implicitly, to some political conception of the state, but recent writings have increasingly emphasized this dimension. See, e.g., Philips 1986; Lacey 1988; but cf. M. Davis 1989.

Chapter 1

1. Its actual consequences determine its objective justification. Its reasonably expected consequences determine whether those who operate it act justifiably or reasonably.

2. 'Prevention' should be understood not as complete prevention (which would be absurdly ambitious) but as reduction. See Walker 1980, 24–45.

3. Zimring & Hawkins 1995, 3–17, argue that incapacitation has become, by default, the central rationale for imprisonment.

4. Diana is talking about the aims of probation, as a process from which "any punitive quality has been removed" (see ch. 3.5.1).

5. See, e.g., H. Morris 1968; American Friends Service Committee 1971; Twentieth Century Fund 1976; von Hirsch 1976; Murphy 1979c. For commentaries, see M. Gardner 1976; Tonry & Morris 1978; Bottoms & Preston 1980, chs. 1–3; Allen 1981; Galligan 1981; Radzinowicz & Hood 1981; von Hirsch 1985, ch. 1; Hudson 1987, chs. 1–2.

6. To which some sociological theorists reply that the penal system does 'work', but to serve functions quite other than that of crime-prevention. See Cohen 1985, 21–30; Garland 1990; Abel 1991.

7. See n.4, above; also Rotman 1990; Walker & McCabe 1973, 101–2, on 'occasionalism'.

8. To which it might be added that rehabilitation is a goal that the state should pursue for the sake of offenders as well as of their potential victims. See Cullen & Gilbert 1982; Carlen 1989; Rotman 1990.

9. See Smart 1973, 69–72; Dennett 1987, s.v. "outsmart"—"To embrace the conclusion of one's opponent's reductio ad absurdum argument. 'They thought they had me, but I outsmarted them. I agreed that was sometimes just to hang an innocent man.'"

10. For versions of such an argument see Rawls 1955; Sprigge 1968; Hare 1981, chs. 3, 9.7. In response, see McCloskey 1972; Duff 1986, 162–64; Primoratz 1989a, 45–46, 129–37.

11. Braithwaite & Pettit 1990 (see 71–76 on the right of the innocent not to be punished). For critical discussion and responses, see von Hirsch & Ashworth 1992; Pettit & Braithwaite 1993; von Hirsch & Ashworth 1993; Duff 1996a, 20–25; Pettit 1997; and ch. 3.7.2, below. See also Lacey 1988 on autonomy

and welfare (understood in communitarian terms) as the goods that punishment should serve; on which see Duff 1996a, 18–20.

12. On the idea of 'side-constraints', see Nozick 1974, 28–29; Braithwaite & Pettit 1990, 26–36; Scheid 1997, 448–51.

13. On Hart, see Ten 1987, 81–85; Lacey 1988, 46–56; Morison 1988; Primoratz 1989a, 137–43; Cragg 1992, 59–67. Scheid 1997 offers a sophisticated development of a Hartian account.

14. It might seem that the requirement of proportionality also demands that we punish the guilty no *less* severely than they deserve. I discuss this aspect of proportionality in chapter 4, sec. 1.

15. See, generally, Winch 1972b; B. Williams 1973a; Nagel 1979a; Gaita 1991, ch. 5.

16. For another suggestion, appealing to a Rawlsian notion of fairness, see Walker 1991, ch. 11.

17. For a third argument—that by breaking the law the offender *consents* to becoming liable to punishment as a normative consequence of her action, so that punishment does not then infringe her rights—see Nino 1983; on which see Alexander 1986; Nino 1986; Duff 1996a, 13–14.

18. See Alexander 1980; Quinn 1985 (on which see Brook 1988; Quinn 1988; Alexander 1991; Otsuka 1996); Farrell 1985 (on which see Holmgren 1989; Alexander 1991), 1995; Montague 1995.

19. Some critics argue that retributivism involves either a refusal to *justify* punishment at all (as distinct from appealing to unjustified intuition), or a justification that turns out to be covertly consequentialist (see, e.g., Benn 1958, 326–35; Hart 1968, 9). But this reflects either a failure to attend to the justifications that retributivists actually offer, or an unargued (and untenable) assumption that the justification of such a practice *must* be consequentialist (see Murphy 1979a, 78–79).

20. By contrast, the goals that consequentialists set for punishment, such as the prevention of crime, seem obviously to be goals that the state should pursue (but see ch. 2.4.1 on 'prevention'). The question then is whether the state has the right to pursue such goals *by these means* (see Murphy 1979c, 94–95; 1985, 3).

21. See H. Morris 1968; Finnis 1972; von Hirsch 1976; Murphy 1979c; Sadurski 1985, 1989; Sher 1987, ch. 5; Adler 1992, chs. 5–8; Dagger 1993. See also M. Davis 1992, 1996, arguing that we can found a theory of sentencing, as distinct from a theory of punishment, on this conception of crime. For criticism see Scheid 1990, 1995; Duff 1990a; von Hirsch 1990.

22. See Christie 1981, chs. 6–7; Burgh 1982; Murphy 1985; Duff 1986, ch. 8; Falls 1987; Hudson 1987; Braithwaite & Pettit 1990, 157–59; von Hirsch 1990, 264–69; Dolinko 1991; Hampton 1992a, 4–5; Anderson 1997.

23. See also Hampton's account of crime as conduct that 'demeans' its victim and therefore calls for punishment as a way of 'defeating' the wrongdoer and nullifying the demeaning message of the crime. See Murphy & Hampton 1988, ch. 4; Hampton 1991, 1992a, 1992b. For criticism see Duff 1990b; Dolinko 1991; Dare 1992; S. E. Marshall 1992; Slattery 1992; Golash 1994; Duff 1996a, 36–41.

24. See also Mackie 1985. While the 'retributive emotions' provide no rational justification of punishment, we can give an evolutionary account of why humans have developed this emotional disposition; for criticism, see Hampton in Murphy & Hampton 1988, 117–19.

25. See Murphy & Hampton 1988, chs.1, 3. The quoted phrases occur on 89 and 108. For criticisms, see Hampton's comments in Murphy & Hampton 1988, ch. 2; Duff 1990b; and Murphy's own comments in Murphy 1999. See also Baldwin 1999.

26. Murphy seems to connect this account to the 'unfair advantage' theory (see Murphy & Hampton 1988, 94–95; and sec. 4.2, above). But our anger at the rapist is surely not anger at the unfair advantage he took over the law-abiding.

27. Moore 1987 (the quoted phrase above is from 213), 1993. For criticism (to some of which Moore responds in the revised version of Moore 1993 published in Moore 1997, ch. 4), see Dolinko 1991, 555–59; Knowles 1993; Duff 1996a, 28–29; Murphy 1999.

28. Only 'typically' because *mala prohibita* (tax evasion, for instance) can also provoke our indignation.

29. See, generally, Feinberg 1970; Primoratz 1989b. For critical discussion, see Benn 1958; Hart 1963, 60–69; Walker 1978, 1981; Skillen 1980; M. Davis 1996, 169–81. Lacey (1988) and Braithwaite & Pettit (1990) also offer consequentialist accounts of punishment as (at least in part) expressive.

30. Following von Hirsch (1993), I hereafter use the notion of 'censure' to capture the communicative content of punishment.

31. Feinberg adds that this content might be expressed, for different reasons, to offenders, to their victims, and to the public at large (1970, 101–5). But retributivists will focus on communication with the offender.

32. See Brandt 1961; Nowell-Smith 1961, 301–4; Smart 1973, 49–56; Braithwaite 1989; Braithwaite & Pettit 1990, 87–91, on "reprobative shaming" as an instrumental technique for inducing productive shame in offenders.

33. This is oversimplified in two ways. First, it presupposes that I have the moral standing to comment in this way—that it is my business; I discuss this issue in the context of the criminal law in ch. 5 (sec 2.3). Second, there could be occasions on which I should not speak out—perhaps because it would do more harm than good. But this shows only that my commitment to speaking out is defeasible.

34. See also von Hirsch 1993, 12–14. I discuss his more recent account in ch. 3.3.2.

35. See also Hampton's account of punishment as 'defeating' the wrongdoer; n.23, above.

36. My account has something in common with those who portray punishment as a process of moral (re-)education. See ch. 3.4.1.

37. See, generally Mathiesen 1974, 1986, 1990; Christie 1977, 1981; Hulsman 1981, 1982, 1986, 1991; Abel 1982; Cohen 1985, 1991; Bianchi & van Swaaningen 1986; Scheerer 1986; Steinert 1986; Hudson 1987; de Haan 1990; Bianchi 1994; Sim 1994; Duff 1996a, 67–87.

38. But see Mathiesen 1974, 11–36; 1986, for a principled refusal to offer much in answer to the third question.

39. There are also other theorists who argue for the abolition of punishment but who would not normally be classed as belonging to, or be welcomed as allies by, the 'abolitionist' movement, such as those who would replace punishment by systems of compulsory treatment (e.g., Wootton 1963; Menninger 1968) or by a system of legally organized restitution (see Barnett 1977; Hajdin 1987; for criticisms, see Pilon 1978; Kleinberg 1980; Dagger 1991. Cf. Holmgren 1983, 1989, who aims to justify *punishment* in terms of restitution).

Chapter 2

1. See, generally, Mulhall & Swift 1992; also Avineri & de-Shalit 1992; Kymlicka 1989; Rosenblum 1989.
2. Hence the importance for many liberals of the 'Harm Principle' (that the criminal law should be concerned only with conduct that causes or threatens harm to others; see Feinberg 1984–88) and the idea that the criminal law should be concerned only with (intentional, chosen) conduct, not with the 'private' attitudes or motives that lie behind conduct (see, e.g., Fletcher 1978, 139–59, 170–74; 1986, 107–10). On both these matters, see further ch. 3.8, below.
3. See Sher 1997, ch. 2; Mulhall & Swift 1992, 31–33, 216–19. Here as elsewhere the views I ascribe to 'liberals' are not held by all those who count themselves as 'liberals'. I am simply picking out certain themes that are common in liberal writings; see n.21, below.
4. But see Nino 1983; ch. 1, n.17, above.
5. Even liberals who do not appeal to a social contract can insist on choice as a prerequisite of punishment: hence the attractions of Hart's account (see text at ch.1, n.16, above; also Ashworth 1984, 1987; Duff 1993, 346–61). Justifications of punishment that model it on self-defense could also appeal to choice (see ch.1.3.2, above). It is because offenders choose to break the law, to attack the protected interests of others, that we can properly allocate to them, rather than to their victims, the harm that must ensue.
6. I leave aside here the possibility that it might include *no* penal provisions: for instance, that it might provide only for restitution on a civil law model rather than for punishment under a criminal law. See ch. 1, n.39.
7. The name of the equivalent Scottish body, the "Social Inclusion Network," seems more appropriate to its inclusionary ambitions.
8. Indeed, 'safe communities' are liable to exclude not only offenders but also suspected potential offenders. 'Undesirables' may be excluded from the neighborhoods and facilities of the 'respectable'.
9. This idea of community is thus 'normative' both in that the community is defined by a shared commitment to certain values, and in that those values are portrayed as being worthy of such commitment by its members—and of respect by outsiders. These two aspects are separable: communities can be structured by repugnant as well as by admirable or respectworthy ends and values; no communitarian need believe that every community that is normative in the first sense is valuable or worthy of respect simply in virtue of existing. But I assume here that both academic communities and political communities can be worthy of respect.

10. A number of contemporary 'communitarian' critics of 'liberalism' should indeed be classed as 'liberal communitarians' in this sense. See, e.g., Taylor 1989; Walzer 1983; also R. Dworkin 1986, 195–216, 1989; Lacey 1988, ch. 8; Selznick 1992.

11. To talk thus of its self-definition as a community is not to suggest that its members articulate their self-understanding in these terms. They define themselves as a community not by what they say about community but by what they do—by how they respond to and behave towards one another. To describe them as constituting a community of this (or any other) kind is to interpret their conduct and practices as displaying a commitment to these values (see R. Dworkin 1986, 201).

12. Cf. the normative conception of 'neighbor' in the parable of the Good Samaritan (Luke 10.29–37): to recognize others as my 'neighbors' is to be disposed to respond to their needs if I come into contact with them.

13. See Sandel 1982, criticizing Rawls 1972; Mulhall & Swift 1992, 10–18, 45–54; Carse 1994.

14. See Rawls 1985, 1993; Mulhall & Swift 1992, chs. 5–6; and Taylor 1989, distinguishing "ontological" from "advocacy" issues.

15. For different versions of it, see Sandel 1982; MacIntyre 1985; Taylor 1990. See Mulhall & Swift 1992, chs. 1–3; Carse 1994; Sher 1997, ch. 7.

16. This is not to say that I could, while still being recognizably a rational human agent, be a *pure* egoist, attaching *no* importance to the interests of anyone else and recognizing no values independent of what I take to be my interests. Although the image of pure egoism has loomed large in moral philosophy, as the threatening figure against whom morality must be justified, it is at best dubiously intelligible and even more dubiously tempting. But individuals can have a paramount concern for their own interests (some of which can be other-directed, as involving concern for the well-being of others about whom they care) without being pure egoists (see B. Williams 1973b, 1981b).

17. The possibility of such radical detachment is a feature of any theory that tries to justify morality by arguing from nonmoral premises—to show that someone who had detached herself from all moral values or commitments could still have reason to accept (some) morality (see, e.g., Gauthier 1986). Its impossibility is argued by those who claim that morality neither needs nor can be given any such nonmoral foundation (e.g., Beardsmore 1969; Gaita 1991).

18. Although some people do believe that their family or their friends have an unconditional claim on them, come what may (for a fictional example, see Stephen Blackpool in Charles Dickens's *Hard Times*). I might admire such people and wish that I were capable of such commitment, or think them misguided, but I would not call them irrational.

19. Or even simply as fellow creatures, in a way that includes nonhuman animals as our fellows. See Diamond 1978.

20. We must distinguish temptation from rational questioning. I might be tempted to (try to) deny or ignore the demands that fellowship makes on me when they conflict with some of my own interests. But this is not to subject them to rational questioning; and what is required, to resist that temptation, is not a rational argument to show me that I should accept those demands but a reminder of what I already know—that those bonds are real.

21. There are also 'perfectionist' liberals who reject the 'neutrality' thesis, arguing that the state should not remain wholly neutral between competing substantive conceptions of the good. See Raz 1986 (on which see Mulhall & Swift 1992, ch. 8; George 1993, ch. 6); Sher 1997.
22. See, generally, G. Dworkin 1988, pt. 1; Raz 1986, 369–429; Sher 1997, chs. 2–3.
23. They are, we can say, the capacities necessary if we are to be genuinely the "co-authors of our own narratives" (MacIntyre 1985, 213; see, more generally, ch. 15). But authorship is a social activity, possible only within a social context that determines the shapes and forms it can take and the value it can have.
24. Cf. Berlin 1969 on "positive" and "negative" freedom; cf. the "republican" account of negative freedom as "franchise" or "dominion" in Pettit 1989; Braithwate & Pettit 1990, 61–69.
25. Cf. R. Dworkin 1978, 262–63, on "liberty as license" and "liberty as independence"; and Braithwaite & Pettit 1990, 62–65, on "dominion".
26. I leave aside here issues about criminal liability for omissions (when the law prescribes conduct rather than prohibiting it), and for statuses that seem not to involve 'conduct' at all. See Glazebrook 1978; Husak 1998.
27. But perhaps only partly independent. My reason for obeying the law could be, for instance, partly that it is the law but also that what it requires of me is not morally wrong.
28. See Cotterrell 1995, ch. 11, on the "imperium" model of law; Duff 1998b.
29. Cf. Raz 1994, 343–44. But Raz talks of the law as "prohibiting" such conduct.
30. It might be said that 'prevention' is the aim not of the law's specifications of crimes but of the sanctions attached to the commission of those crimes—though the *Model Penal Code* makes prevention the first purpose of "the provisions governing the definition of offenses" (sec.1.02(a)). See further ch. 3.2–4, below.
31. See, generally, Postema 1986, chs. 1–2; Farmer 1997; also Cotterrell 1995, ch. 11, on the "community" as against the "imperium" model of law; Waldron 1999, 56–60.
32. On *determinationes*, see Finnis 1987, 146–47; MacCormick 1990, 548–49.
33. I am not suggesting that the 'common law' defended by such proponents as Coke, Hale, and Blackstone actually had this character. We might more plausibly see its supposed commonality as one of the dangerous fictions that Bentham so ferociously attacked. But I am talking throughout this chapter of ideals of law and community. On the relation between the ideal and the actual, see ch. 5.
34. These two U.S. ways of entitling cases fit best with the idea of the common law of a liberal polity (as does "*State v. D*"—so long as we can see the state as an official aspect of the political community). By contrast, the standard English description—"*Regina v. D*"—is ill-suited to a community of citizens as distinct from subjects.
35. I leave aside here the possibility of private criminal prosecutions (which in England are still subject to state control in that the Attorney General can take them over and then drop them). The provisions for them can perhaps best be seen as giving citizens a way to pursue cases that, they think, the state wrongly failed to pursue.

36. See Christie 1977, 8, on the need to discuss "How wrong was the thief, how right was the victim?"; Hulsman 1986, 72–73; Bianchi 1994, 71–97.

37. On compensation and reparation see further, ch. 3.4.2, p. 161, below; see also Goodin 1991, on whether all harms or wrongs can be compensated.

38. Cf. Hart 1994, ch. 9, on the "minimum content of Natural Law"; also Winch 1972a.

39. This is not the place for a general discussion of the authority of law (and discussions of that topic tend not to focus on what I think is the rather special case of the criminal law). Raz (1979; 1986, pt. 1; 1994, pt. 2) provides the best discussions of that general topic. I am grateful to Paul Markwick for helpful discussions of authority in the context of the criminal law.

40. This presupposes, of course, that they have access to a political process in which their voices can be heard and through which they can try to persuade others of their view (see further, p. 76, ch. 5.2.2, below). Some theorists will argue that disagreement about the values that even these central aspects of the criminal law purport to reflect is far wider and deeper than I imply here—that disagreement and conflict are normal rather than exceptional (see, e.g., [arguing to very different conclusions], Norrie 1993; Bianchi 1994; Waldron 1999). All I would say here is that insofar as the criminal law should claim to be a 'common' law, it must claim to embody values that are widely, if not universally, shared in the community whose law it is. I comment below on the problem posed by those who do not share those values (sec. 5; ch. 3.7.4) and on the implications of a lack of such consensus on central values (ch. 5.2).

41. See LaFave & Scott 1986, 32–35; G. Williams 1961, 189, 234; 1983, 936–37; Gordon 1978, 17–20.

42. See Duff 1996b, 129, 134–35. Parking offenses are also typically of this kind. The 'mischief' at which parking regulations are aimed may be inconvenience rather than danger, but unreasonably inconveniencing others is morally wrong (albeit a relatively trivial wrong) and so counts as a (relatively trivial) *malum in se.*

43. In these kinds of context the criminal law thus comes closest to claiming the kind of authority that Raz thinks is legitimate. See Raz 1986, ch. 3.

44. I leave aside the issue whether we should distinguish a class of minor 'violations' from 'crimes' properly speaking (see *Model Penal Code* s.1.04(5); Ashworth 1995b, 50–51). I think, however, that they should be kept within the realm of the criminal law. They still constitute kinds of (minor) wrongdoing that properly concern the community, and those accused of committing them should receive the protections built into the criminal process.

45. See Husak 1995; Duff 1996b, ch. 5; Ashworth 1995b, ch. 11.

46. For a useful liberal discussion of the issues here, see Ashworth 1995b, 22–57 (esp. 31–35 on 'minimalism'); see also Feinberg 1984–88.

47. What I can say here will barely touch on this large and complex issue. See Horton 1992 for a useful survey of recent trends in the discussion, and a communitarian account of political obligation in terms of what it is to recognize oneself as a member of a polity (ch. 6). However, I think he underestimates the problem posed by those who do not thus recognize themselves (159–62; see Simmons 1996, 261–65).

48. On versions of these first two arguments, see Horton 1992, ch. 2.

49. For references and criticism, see Simmons 1996, 261–65.

50. I am speaking here of those born into a political community. The appeals to those who move into a community, or to temporary visitors, would need to be rather different.

51. On 'informal justice' see, generally, Christie 1977, 1981; Abel 1982; Cain 1985; Cohen 1985; Matthews 1988; de Haan 1990; Hulsman 1991; T. F. Marshall 1994.

52. I cannot discuss here the various kinds of coercion involved in the pretrial process of investigation (see Sanders & Young 1994, chs. 3–4), or in detention pending trial (see Sanders & Young 1994, 282–94; Ashworth 1994, ch. 7; Duff 1986, 139–40).

Chapter 3

1. See Bianchi 1986, 113–14; Hulsman 1991, 681–84. The points made here do not, however, apply to *all* criminals. There are crimes committed by 'us', notably driving offenses and white-collar crimes, which do not have such exclusionary implications.

2. For insightful and critical discussions of the exclusionary character of much modern punishment (and penal theory), see Dubber 1994, 1995, 1996, 1998. Dubber emphasizes, as I want to emphasize, the importance of seeing offenders as our fellows. But he appeals to a Kantian notion of our common rationality (which seems to me inadequate to the task; see Gaita 1991, ch. 3), whereas I appeal to our fellowship in contingent communities.

3. This is not yet to say that purely incapacitative or preventive sentences could never be justified. But they could be justified only by arguing that those who are to be subjected to them have excluded themselves from the normative community. See further ch. 4.4.2.

4. See ch. 2.4.2. This is a communitarian version of a familiar Kantian objection to a purely deterrent system of punishment (see Duff 1986, 178–86).

5. See also Dubber 1998 on the exclusionary character of 'rehabilitation' (in at least some of its forms) as a penal aim.

6. See further sec. 6.1, below. If the defendant pleads guilty as a genuine admission of wrongdoing (not just as a result of tactical plea-bargaining), the conviction serves as a formal and public confirmation of that confession.

7. See von Hirsch 1993, ch. 2; 1999; Narayan 1993. On von Hirsch, see Bottoms 1998.

8. To which we could add (see von Hirsch, Bottoms, Burney & Wikström 1999, 39–40) that the deterrent efficacy of hard treatment punishment can also depend on the underlying normative element of justified censure. See also Bottoms 1998, 90–95.

9. Cf. Goldman 1979 on the tension involved in positing both a deterrent justifying aim for punishment and retributivist side-constraints on our pursuit of that aim.

10. See Plato, *Gorgias*; H. Morris 1981; Hampton 1984. For criticism, see Deigh 1984; Murphy 1985; Shafer-Landau 1991. Garvey 1998 also advocates an "educating model" of punishment. But his account is actually closer to that which I offer than to these views of punishment as a matter of moral education.

11. See H. Morris 1981, 265; Duff 1986, 254–57; Lacey 1988, 171–73; Oldenquist 1988; Reitan 1996. Cf. also Plato's *Gorgias* for the view that wrongdoing separates one from the Good, on which one's own good depends; and Nozick on crime as disconnecting the offender from "correct values" (1981, 374–79).

12. See H. Morris 1981; Hampton 1984; Duff 1986, 254–66. Cf. Oldenquist 1988, 471.

13. Some critics might object that I take too narrow a view of 'moral education': that it involves not merely teaching people what is right or wrong but teaching or training them to care as they should about, and to attend as they should to, the moral aspects of their actions—educating their emotions and attitudes (as Aristotle emphasized). It might also be objected that those who do not attend to or care enough about the wrongs that they do *are* in need of moral (re-)education. There is some truth in this. But we should resist the temptation to make it a definitional truth that all wrongdoing shows the wrongdoer to be in need of moral (re-)education.

14. For useful routes into the voluminous literature on mediation and restorative justice, see Matthews 1988; Marshall & Merry 1990; Cragg 1992; Brown 1994; Dignan 1994; Daly & Immarigeon 1998; von Hirsch & Ashworth 1998, ch. 7; Braithwaite 1999; Dignan 1999.

15. It also follows that it is not open to the victim to charge the offender with conduct that the law does not define as criminal.

16. As distinct from regret at harm which another suffered but not through my agency. See B. Williams on "agent regret" (1981a, 27–31).

17. Analogously, though the ritual of a funeral is important in providing a structure for the expression of grief at another's death, it cannot be expected to provide closure when that other is a close friend or relative. The loss and the grief go deeper than that.

18. This raises the question whether there are any wrongs so terrible that apology and reconciliation are impossible. See ch. 4.4.

19. See, e.g., Dignan 1999, 48. For further references, and criticism, see Daly & Immarigeon 1998, 32–34. For a useful critical discussion, see Zedner 1994.

20. And see Adler 1992, ch. 2, on the "conscientious paradigm" of punishment.

21. It might be said that, while they 'knew' that their actions were wrong in the way that Tolstoy's Ivan Ilych 'knew' that he would die, they had not fully grasped or understood their wrongfulness (see Tolstoy [1886] 1960, sec. 6, 131–34). But this need not be true, and even if it is true, what is required is not so much 'education' as a proper attention (see n.13, above).

22. And our own civil procedures provide both for apologies and for reparative or compensatory damages.

23. On probation see, generally, Raynor 1985; Harding 1987; Morris & Tonry 1990, ch. 7; Ashworth 1995a, 269–75; Brownlee 1998, chs. 3–4.

24. Diana 1970, 48. On this development, see, generally, McWilliams 1985, 1986.

25. Apart from items already cited, see Weston 1978; McWilliams 1987; McWilliams & Pease 1990; Faulkner & Gibbs 1998.

26. Beaumont 1989 (the quotations are drawn from 99–101), responding to Home Office 1988.

27. The distinction drawn in this paragraph between responsible, culpable offenders and nonresponsible, nonculpable offenders is oversimplified. The

very distinction between the responsible and the nonresponsible is fraught with difficulty, and no doubt many of those sentenced in our courts are not (fully) responsible or not (unqualifiedly) culpable. Though my concern here is with what probation should mean for those who *are* responsible and culpable, one could also see a less punitive role for probation officers in helping those whom the law has wrongly portrayed and condemned as fully responsible and culpable. See p. 200, below.

28. Diana 1970, 48; see text at n.24, above. On 'occasionalism', see Walker & McCabe 1973, 101–2.

29. Such punishments must be 'proportionate' to the crimes for which they are imposed. See ch. 4.1.

30. I skate over two difficult issues here. One concerns the victims' role. One one hand, mediation can be painful and demanding for the victims, and we might think that it should, as far as they are concerned, be optional. On the other hand, if we take the bonds of citizenship seriously, perhaps victims *should* be ready to take part in mediation (see further p. 115, below). The other concerns the offender's consent or willingness to take part in mediation, or in any other program that depends on his cooperation. It might seem that such programs should be *offered* to offenders but not be *imposed* on them, since they would then be ineffectual. This is an oversimplified contrast, however. Depending on the alternatives, an offender's acceptance of an 'offer' might be far from free or willing, and a person can cooperate with a program that he would not have entered voluntarily but is required (told that he ought) to enter.

31. Cf. the provisions for compensation orders under English criminal law (see Walker & Padfield 1996, 245–50) and for reparation orders for young offenders under sec. 67 of the Crime and Disorder Act 1998.

32. See, generally, Pease & McWilliams 1980; Pease 1985; Morris & Tonry 1990, ch. 6; McIvor 1994; Ashworth 1995a, 277–81; Brownlee 1998, 10–11, 114–17.

33. Though such a reconciliation depends not just on her but on how her fellow citizens respond to her. See further p. 201, below.

34. If the offender refuses to take part in such a discussion, a sentence must then simply be imposed by the court, in the light of the probation officer's advice.

35. Community Service Orders can of course involve work that citizens might undertake voluntarily rather than as punishment. Kahan (1996, 1998) argues that they are therefore, as currently organized, labeled, and understood, expressively inadequate as punishments, since they do not express the requisite kind or degree of condemnation. To turn them into suitable punishments, we should change the name to "shameful service" (cf. the English Home Secretary's proposal to call them "Criminal Work Orders") and make sure that their content is humiliating and degrading (Kahan 1996, 651–62). While Kahan rightly emphasizes the importance of what different modes of punishment mean (see ch. 4.2, below), he is wrong to look for punishments that will humiliate and degrade. That is not how we should treat fellow citizens (see von Hirsch 1993, 82–86). He also ignores the way in which context helps to determine meaning. A piece of work—for instance, cleaning up a vandalized public park—has one kind of meaning if it is undertaken voluntarily by a concerned local person and quite a different meaning if it is undertaken as a

punishment by an offender. The requirement to undertake such work as a punishment, while it (rightly) does not degrade or humiliate the offender, can communicate appropriate censure of the offense for which it is imposed. Undertaking that work as a punishment can also communicate (in a way that undertaking it as a voluntary act of civic help would not) the agent's apology for the offense.

36. I am here developing and refining the account offered in Duff 1986. For criticisms of that account, to some of which I respond below, see Bickenbach 1988, 1992; Harrison 1988; Lipkin 1988; Ten 1990; Baker 1992a, 1992b; Cragg 1992, 67–77; Narayan 1993; von Hirsch 1993, ch. 8; 1999; Murphy 1997; Norrie 1998, 110–17; Baldwin 1999.

37. On the multiplicity of 'R's in this area, see Daly & Immarigeon 1998, n. 17. See also Dignan 1999, 48, on "Responsibility, Restoration and Reintegration." I could add recognition and reparation to my three 'R's of repentance, reform, and reconciliation: but recognition is subsumed by repentance, and reparation by reconciliation.

38. Reform as an aim of punishment on this account is thus quite different from reform as a penal aim understood in simple consequentialist terms. See sec. 4.1, above.

39. This way of putting this objection is due to Andrew von Hirsch. For a defense of punitive "apology rituals," see Garvey 1998, 791–94.

40. Thus Kahan (1996, 631–37) commends various "shaming penalties," (some of which involve a kind of public apology) precisely as "degradation penalties" (636) that may involve "self-debasement" (634). Some of them are, given their content, necessarily humiliating (for instance, requiring juvenile offenders to apologize on their hands and knees; 634); and on his account all are intended to be and should be seen as being degrading (see n.35, above). On the relation between the ideal account of what punishment ought to be, which I offer here, and the actualities of existing penal practice, see ch. 5.1, below.

41. Those who take a paternalistic view of punishment might also say that the state owes it to its citizens as potential *criminals* to protect them from the harm they would suffer in committing crimes. But I have argued (sec. 4.1, above) that, while we may believe that crime is injurious to the criminal and that penitential punishment is thus a benefit to the criminal, this benefit cannot provide a justifying aim of punishment.

42. This raises again the question whether there are any wrongs so serious that such reconciliation is morally impossible (see n.18 above). On the further question of how the victim or the wider community should respond to offenders who remain unrepentant and unapologetic, see sec. 7.4, below.

43. For useful recent discussions of shame, see Gibbard 1990, ch. 7; B. Williams 1993, ch. 4. See also Garvey 1998, 765–66.

44. For a good illustration of these points, see Trollope 1864, ch. 25.

45. My account therefore has no room for the kinds of *degrading* "shaming penalties" advocated by Kahan (1996; see nn.35, 40, above). See Garvey 1998, 743–62.

46. We must distinguish this case from one in which the offender has suffered serious harm unrelated to his crime, which he does not see as a punishment for that crime. We might then, especially if the harm is serious and the crime is

relatively minor, see reason to exempt the offender from punishment. But this would be a matter of mercy, not of penal justice. We would say, not that he had already been *punished* enough, but that his suffering made it inappropriate to punish him. I cannot discuss mercy here (but see Murphy & Hampton 1988, 157–86). I think, however, that in the context of punishment, mercy—as something distinct from justice—involves the thought that it would be cruel to focus our attention and to try to focus the offender's attention on his crime, when we should rather be attending sympathetically to the other disasters or harms that are quite reasonably occupying his attention.

47. My account might also seem to imply either a system of indeterminate sentencing (since we cannot tell in advance how quickly an offender will come to repentance) or one that imposes harsher punishments on those who seem likely to be stubborn—which would conflict with the requirements of proportionality (see von Hirsch 1993, 75–76). I meet this objection below (sec. 7.4, ch. 4.1).

48. Those who think that criminal liability should depend on 'character' might want to go further than this, arguing that genuine repentance at any point should be a mitigating factor, since one who repents displays a less vicious or dangerous character than one who does not. But I have argued elsewhere (Duff 1993) that criminal liability should be grounded in action, not in 'character', and only an immediate repentance can alter the moral character of the criminal action.

49. Should there then be no penal discount for pleading guilty? I think there should not. If the criminal justice system aims to do justice, it should not bribe defendants to plead guilty (especially since this can also put pressure on the innocent to plead guilty). If it is objected that the system would then be unworkable, since it can function only if many defendants do plead guilty, the answer is that if we are serious about doing justice we must provide the resources it requires.

50. See Bickenbach 1988, 780–83; Ten 1990, 204–5; Baker 1992b, 157–59; Cragg 1992, 74–77; von Hirsch 1993, 10.

51. It might be objected that, once I admit that a liberal polity's central values cannot be rationally demonstrated to be binding even on those who reject them (see ch. 2.5), I must also admit that any punitive attempt to bring them to accept those values will deny their "value sovereignty" as autonomous moral agents—that it will constitute an attempt to *impose* on them values that they are not rationally bound to accept (see Bickenbach 1988, 780–85; Cragg 1992, 74–77). This objection would be sound if the admission that those values cannot be rationally demonstrated undermined any claim that those who do not accept them *ought* to do so. But it does not (see p. 71, above; Duff 1988). So long as the dissidents are not politically excluded, so long as there exists an appropriate political forum in which they can argue their case and have it heard, we can properly insist that they *ought* to accept the values of the political community. So long as they retain the freedom to remain unpersuaded, we can properly punish them in a forceful attempt to get them to listen to this message.

52. Similarly, the wrongfulness of reckless conduct that endangers but does not attack the interests of others consists not just in the fact that the agent know-

ingly creates a risk but in the practical indifference that his conduct manifests. See Duff 1990c, ch. 7.

Chapter 4

1. See, generally, Robinson 1987a, 1987b; Morris & Tonry 1990; von Hirsch
   1992, 1993; Tonry 1996; von Hirsch & Ashworth 1998.
2. See von Hirsch (1985, ch. 4; 1993, 18–19) on the distinction between 'ordinal'
   and 'cardinal' proportionality.
3. A requirement of relative proportionality also includes a requirement of
   'spacing' (see von Hirsch 1993, 18): that the extent to which one offender's
   punishment is more, or less, severe than another's should depend on the extent to which his crime was more, or less, serious.
4. Consequentialists might argue that we could in principle work out which
   modes and levels of punishment would most efficiently serve the aims of the
   penal system. But it is at best far from clear that we could even in principle
   carry through the requisite calculus of costs and benefits. Some retributivists
   might appeal to *Lex Talionis*, saying that we should try (perhaps subject to certain constraints of humanity) to inflict on offenders punishments that match
   their crimes in both content and severity. But the notion of penal desert for
   which I argue, as making sense of the retributivist slogan that the guilty deserve to suffer, does not justify such a claim (see sec. 2, below).
5. And see sec. 4.1, below, on the relevance (if any) of prior criminal record in
   judging the seriousness of the current offense.
6. Cf. J. Gardner 1994; Horder 1994 on the English law of offenses against the
   person. See also J. Gardner 1998a.
7. See, generally, Wasik & von Hirsch 1988, 1990; von Hirsch, Wasik & Greene
   1989; von Hirsch 1990, 1993, chs. 7–8.
8. See von Hirsch, Wasik & Greene 1989; von Hirsch 1992, 1993, ch. 7; 1999,
   76–78. On von Hirsch, see Bottoms 1998, 55–77; see also Rex 1998.
9. On this point see, e.g., Frase 1997, 367–68; Tonry 1998, 292.
10. See, e.g., Slote 1989. Note that what dissuades the satisficer from trying to op-
    timize is not just the costs (time, effort, the possibility of error) of doing so.
    She would then simply be a sophisticated optimizer who built those costs
    into her calculus. Her view is, rather, that attempting to optimize is incoher-
    ent (if we are dealing with incommensurable goods that could not even in
    principle be ranked on a single scale) or distorting (if we try to translate in-
    commensurable goods into commensurable goods) or pointless, since we
    should be content with what is 'good enough'.
11. For versions of such a justification, see Schoeman 1979; Wood 1988. For criti-
    cism, see Duff 1998a, 147–51.
12. In this respect my account of the proper demands of proportionality differs
    most obviously from the 'limiting retributivism' espoused by Morris and
    Tonry (see sec. 1.2, above). On their account, within the limits set by the
    constraints of negative proportionality, sentences should be determined
    by the sentencer's "purposes at sentencing"—purposes that might in differ-
    ent cases include incapacitation, deterrence, rehabilitation, or retribution
    (see Morris & Tonry 1990, 77–78, 90–91; Tonry 1998, 292–93). On my

account, however, the "purpose at sentencing" is still that of appropriate moral communication.

13. But see Garland 1990, chs. 9–10, on the relation between culture and penality; and von Hirsch 1993, ch. 9, on the notion of "acceptable penal content."

14. Another kind of punishment, which I cannot discuss here, is disqualification, which forbids the offender to engage in an activity in which citizens can normally engage (perhaps without any special qualification, as with keeping pets; or by obtaining a license, as with driving; or by obtaining some specialist qualification, as with medical practice). Some such disqualifications are seen as civil rather than punitive, even when they follow on a criminal conviction (see von Hirsch & Wasik 1997 for a very useful discussion), but I think that they should often be seen as partly or wholly punitive, communicating the message that the offender has shown herself to be unfit to engage in that activity (see Duff 1998a, 157–59).

15. To talk of the meanings of different modes of punishment is not, of course, to talk of meanings that they have a priori or ahistorically. Their meanings depend upon the historical cultures in which they are set, on the "mentalities" and "sensibilities" (see Garland 1990, chs. 9–10) that exist in those cultures. My concern is with what punishments mean or could mean in cultures like ours, and within a liberal political community.

16. See Bottoms 1983; Young 1994; Ashworth 1995a, 261–68; Walker & Padfield 1996, 230–45; also Morris & Tonry 1990, ch. 5, arguing that much more use should be made of fines in the United States (an argument that this subsection aims to counter). My comments on the meaning of fines also apply to compensation orders (see Ashworth 1995a, 256–61; Walker & Padfield 1996, 245–50), under which offenders make payments directly to victims. Fines stand to compensation orders somewhat as Community Service Orders stand to reparative work undertaken through a mediation process. But both fines and compensation orders must be distinguished from restitution orders and confiscations of the proceeds of crime (Walker & Padfield 1996, 250–53). Simply to deprive offenders of the material proceeds of their crimes is not to punish them.

17. See Hillsman 1990; Morris & Tonry 1990, 143–46; Ashworth 1995a, 262–64; Brownlee 1998, 143–47; Greene 1998.

18. Cf. Kahan 1996, 617–24. But see ch. 3, n.35, above, on his argument.

19. Amongst such requirements we should distinguish those that are imposed simply to ensure offenders' participation in some specified program from those that are themselves imposed as part of their punishment. In both instances the requirement must be justified. But only in the latter instance, which is the one that concerns me here, will the justification refer to the meaning of custody as a punishment.

20. Must this always be true, or might there be crimes (or persistent patterns of crime) so serious that no such return is possible? See sec. 4.2, below.

21. Which implies that they should retain the right to vote (see p. 77, above). The loss of that right is a symbol of the loss of citizenship.

22. This slogan informed many recent initiatives in penal policy aimed at reducing the use of imprisonment. See, e.g., Home Office 1988; Petersilia 1998.

23. Another implication of my account is that we should where possible prefer a

system of requiring offenders who are sentenced to imprisonment to present themselves to serve their sentences on a specified date: not primarily because this makes it easier to manage prison numbers, but because it gives offenders a more active role in their own punishment.

24. For useful ways into the larger debates, see Bedau 1987; Nathanson 1987; Primoratz 1989a, ch. 8; Bigel 1994; Davis 1996, chs. 1–6; Hood 1998.

25. We should note that reducing individual sentencers' discretion by subjecting them to strict rules or guidelines that specify a fixed penalty or a small range of penalties for each offense also *increases* the discretionary role of prosecutors in indirectly determining sentences, since more then hangs on what charges they decide to press and on what pleas they decide to accept (see Zimring 1976).

26. Arguments in favor of strong statutory or quasi-statutory sentencing guidelines also have much in common with arguments for a codified criminal law: a mistrust of judges, and a concern that the law should be visibly clear, certain, and consistent. We might add the assumption that the law can be rational and consistent only insofar as it is structured by determinate general rules, an assumption given which common law modes of case-by-case reasoning (whether in the substantive criminal law or in sentencing) will be seen as radically imperfect. I think that this assumption is seriously misguided, but cannot pursue that issue here. See J. Gardner 1998a; Duff 1996b, 65–66.

27. See Morris & Tonry 1990, 82–83, on the conflict between "the requirement of fairness—that there be general standards that apply to all—and the requirement of justice—that all legitimate grounds for distinguishing between individuals be taken into account when decisions about individuals are made." The criminal law's abstraction has been a target for 'critical' theorists (see, e.g., Hudson 1987, 1993; Norrie 1993; for a partial response, see Duff 1998c). But see, e.g., Norrie 1993, 31–32, 223–25, on the way that such abstraction can also protect individual citizens against the state.

28. See, generally, Hudson 1987, espec. ch. 3; Ashworth 1995a, ch. 13; Tonry 1996; von Hirsch & Ashworth 1998, ch. 5 (which includes a comprehensive bibliography).

29. See Tonry 1994, 1996, chs. 2–3; von Hirsch 1998b. For a useful brief introduction to these issues, see Ashworth's introduction to von Hirsch & Ashworth 1998, ch. 5.

30. But the considerations that should guide them in exercising that discretion are quite different on my account from those that Tonry thinks should guide them. See n.12, above.

31. I leave aside here the role of "victim impact statements" (see Ashworth 1993a). They are formally evidence on which sentencers can draw rather than direct contributions to the sentencing decision. Some U.S. states also allow for "victim statements of opinion" about the appropriate sentence (see Erez 1994; Zedner 1997, 601). I comment on the role of the victim later in this subsection.

32. For a suggestion that in many ways resembles mine, see Cavadino & Dignan 1998. See also Zedner 1994.

33. The discussion is also limited to the nature and implications of the crime for which the offender has been convicted. It is not an occasion for a wider dis-

cussion that forces the offender to attend to matters not involved in the crime. See p. 126, above.

34. There could also be provision for the negotiation to produce a suggested sentence not included in the specified range, which the court would then approve or reject.

35. I leave aside here the question whether the state should provide compensation for victims who cannot obtain it from the offender. See Ashworth 1986.

36. Cf. the provisions for Compensation Orders under English criminal law. See Ashworth 1995a, 256–61; Walker & Padfield 1996, 245–50.

37. I must leave aside here the question whether other interested individuals (the family or friends of the victim or the offender, other members of the local community) should have a role, as they do in some kinds of mediation process.

38. But see further p. 200, below.

39. I discuss the role of "the court" in approving proposed sentences as if that is obviously a task for the judge or magistrate. But why should it not be a task for the jury, as representing the wider community? I cannot pursue this issue here (but see Dubber 1997, 551–53, 591–95), but two reasons for at least leaving the final decision to judges or magistrates are, first, that they should be better placed to ensure that the demands of relative (negative) proportionality are satisfied, and, second, that they should be better placed to understand what is involved in, and to judge the practicability of, different possible sentences. This is not to say that our judges and magistrates are always in fact well equipped in either of these ways—only that they ought to be.

40. Even this is arguable, given the difficulty of establishing any significant correlation between increased severity (as distinct from certainty) of punishment and lower crime rates. See von Hirsch, Bottoms, Burney & Wikström 1999.

41. For an illuminating critical discussion of the U.S. laws, see Dubber 1995. For the English provisions, see Crime (Sentences) Act 1997, sec. 2 (mandatory life sentence for a second "serious" offense; "serious" offenses include some offenses related to homicide, but also wounding with intent, rape and attempted rape, sexual intercourse with a girl under thirteen years old, robbery while possessing a firearm or imitation firearm, and some other firearm offenses), sec. 3 (minimum seven-year sentence for third class-A drug trafficking offense), and sec. 4 (minimum three-year sentence for third domestic burglary).

42. See, e.g., Greenwood & Abrahamse 1982; Wilson 1983, ch. 8. For further references and discussion, see Duff 1998a, 143–51.

43. See Duff 1998a, 141–42, 151–56. I leave aside those whose offenses are connected to drug dealing, since it is at least controversial whether a liberal polity should criminalize the kinds of drug use that generate such crimes (see Husak 1992a). I also leave aside offenders (persistently drunken drivers, for instance, or firms that operate with unsafe procedures) whose offenses might cause more material harm than those of offenders more typically classified as 'dangerous' (see Bottoms 1977, 83–87; Floud & Young 1981, 6–7, 10–15) but who do not directly attack other people. We should certainly take their crimes more seriously than we often do (on corporations, see Wells 1993), but we can also hope that they could be dissuaded from crime without extraordinary measures.

44. See Wasik 1987; Roberts 1997, 322–26, 331–33, 335–41. The notion of "the same kind" of offense is admittedly vague. But see J. Gardner 1998a, 247–49.

45. Only previous convictions should count—not, for instance, previous arrests (see Roberts 1997, 325). If we take the presumption of innocence seriously, we cannot allow alleged offenses for which the offender was not convicted and which he has not admitted to affect his sentence.

46. See Roberts 1997 for a useful survey of prior-record provisions in the United States and of the theoretical issues; also Ashworth 1995a, ch. 6, and Wasik & von Hirsch 1994 on the role of prior record in England; von Hirsch 1985, ch. 7; 1991, 1998a.

47. Cf. the English Criminal Justice Act 1993 sec. 66(6): "In considering the seriousness of any offense, the court may take into account any previous convictions of the offender or any failure of his to respond to previous sentences." But see Ashworth 1995a, 160–62, arguing for a narrow interpretation of this provision.

48. Put to me forcefully by Andrew von Hirsch.

49. If exile (after some appropriate punishment) were a possibility, would it be justified? If another political community was willing to receive the offender, perhaps he should have that option (unless, for instance, the offer came from a regime that planned to employ his criminal capacities in oppressing its subjects). But if, as is more likely, there was no such possibility of emigration, exile would be exile from any human community—which is not something we should do to a human being.

Chapter 5

1. See Murdoch 1970, 61–63, on Matt. 5.48.

2. There is of course ample scope for self-deception in such cases—to persuade myself that I should not intervene, thus sparing myself the burden of trying to help while gaining some self-satisfaction from my (supposedly) humble awareness of my own inadequacies. But there are genuine as well as self-deceptive instances. For a useful discussion of this and related phenomena, see Phillips 1982, esp. 42–45.

3. See Murphy 1999 for an insightful discussion of this and related worries about the moral character and standing of retributivist motivations to punish.

4. Cf. Duff 1986, 293–99, and 1991, 441–51.

5. See Duff 1998d. I do not suggest that this distinction is always clear, or determinable independently of the context in which and the purposes for which it is drawn. But it can help us to understand the different ways in which the satisfaction or nonsatisfaction of different kinds of condition bear on the legitimacy of punishment.

6. See Lucas 1993, ch. 1; Hart 1968, 264–65. The notion of answerability overlaps with all four of the varieties of responsibility distinguished by Hart (1968, 211–30). I am answerable for the performance or nonperformance of my role-responsibilities (to say that something is my role-responsibility is to say, in part, that I am thus answerable). I am answerable for at least much of that for which I am causally responsible (to hold me causally responsible is often to hold me answerable). I am answerable for that for which I am liable,

legally or morally (to hold me liable for X is to call me to answer for X). But I am answerable only for that as to which I have "capacity-responsibility."

7. Responsibility in this sense neither constitutes nor entails blameworthiness. Even if we are, typically, called to answer for our actions only when what we are called to answer is a charge of some kind, the charge need not be one of wrongdoing of a kind that would attract blame. I can be called to answer for alleged deficiencies in this book and be criticized if I cannot answer those charges, but philosophical criticism is not blame. Furthermore, even if blameworthiness is at issue, I can avert blame by justifying my action. But in justifying it I do not deny, indeed I presuppose, that I am responsible for it.

8. By contrast, a defendant who is a responsible agent at the time of his trial might not have been a responsible agent at the time when he committed the offense, if he was then suffering a temporary mental disorder that entitles him to an acquittal. The *precondition* of criminal liability, that he now be a responsible agent who can be called to answer for his conduct, is satisfied. But an essential *condition* of criminal liability for that conduct is not satisfied.

9. The claim that citizenship is a precondition of criminal liability and punishment needs qualifying in two ways. First, temporary visitors to a country, as well as its citizens, can be held liable and punished for crimes under its laws. Although versions of these preconditions apply to visitors, they will not be quite the same as those that apply to citizens. Second, as Augusto Pinochet has found, a person might find himself being tried and punished under the laws of a state of which he is not a citizen for crimes committed outside that state's territory against victims who were not its citizens. I do not discuss here the complex issues raised by such cases, in which elements of international law are incorporated into national law and applied by municipal courts. It is worth noting, however, that the moral arguments about Pinochet's case revolve around the question to whom he should be answerable or by whom he can properly be called to account for his alleged crimes. And the moral arguments justifying his extradition can be read as appealing to the idea that (until we have a properly functioning international criminal court) national courts should sometimes act on behalf of a wider international community, as well as of their own municipal community.

10. See Delgado 1985 (criticized by Dressler 1989, 1377–85); Bazelon 1976 (criticized by Morse 1976); von Hirsch 1993, 97–99, 106–8; Hudson 1995, 70–72, on a possible defense of "economic duress"; Duff 1998c, 184–98.

11. But see von Hirsch 1999, 80–82 for critical comments on this line of thought. For similar suggestions, see Bazelon 1976, 388–89 (but he fails to distinguish the question of standing from that of excuse; see Dressler 1988, 685–86); Delgado 1985, 68–75 (on which see Dressler 1989, 1379, n.246).

12. See further Duff 1998c. I argue there that we can find the truth in critical theorists' claims that liberal criminal law is riven by "contradictions" (e.g., Kelman 1981; Norrie 1993) by focusing not, as they focus, on the law's *internal* coherence but on the *preconditions* of criminal liability—the conditions that must be satisfied if the very enterprise of criminal law is to be legitimate.

13. In talking of what it is "reasonable" to expect of someone I am talking of normative, not of predictive expectations: of what we can reasonably claim

or demand that she ought to do, not of what we can reasonably predict that she will in fact do.

14. Indeed, the content or sense of what is said cannot be divorced from the context in which it is said. See Travis 1989.

15. The language of punishment is more than a purely verbal language. Punishment speaks to the offender, not just through the words that are said to her, but through the material forms that it takes. Imprisonment, fines, Community Service Orders, and other kinds of sentence have their own meanings (see ch. 4.2). But this is a general point about the language of the law: it is a language rich in nonverbal symbols and meanings.

16. If we are to disagree rather than simply talk uncomprehendingly past one another, we must share a language in which we can disagree. But "if language is to be a means of communication, there must be agreement not only in definitions but also (queer as this may sound) in judgments"—which itself depends on "agreement . . . in form of life" (Wittgenstein 1963, paras. 242, 241).

17. These claims about what "any plausible theory" must hold will of course be rejected by some theorists—notably by pure consequentialists who argue that punishment is justified so long as it achieves more good than any currently available alternative. I do not rehearse the objections to consequentialism here (see ch. 1.1–3), Any nonconsequentialist theory that takes seriously the demand that punishment treat offenders as responsible agents must, I think, set some such preconditions.

References

Abel, R. 1991. "The Failure of Punishment as Social Control." *Israel Law Review* 25:740–52.

———, ed. 1982. *The Politics of Informal Justice*. (2 vols.). New York: Academic Press.

Adler, J. 1992. *The Urgings of Conscience*. Philadelphia: Temple University Press.

Alexander, L. 1980. "The Doomsday Machine: Proportionality, Punishment and Prevention." *The Monist* 63:199–227.

———. 1983. "Retributivism and the Inadvertent Punishment of the Innocent." *Law and Philosophy* 2: 233–46.

———. 1986. "Consent, Punishment, and Proportionality." *Philosophy and Public Affairs* 15:178–82.

———. 1991. "Self-Defense, Punishment, and Proportionality." *Law and Philosophy* 10: 323–38.

Alldridge, P. 1990. "Rules for Courts and Rules for Citizens." *Oxford Journal of Legal Studies* 10:487–504.

Allen, F. A. 1981. *The Decline of the Rehabilitative Ideal*. New Haven: Yale University Press.

American Friends Service Committee. 1971. *Struggle for Justice*. New York: Hill and Wang.

Anderson, J. L. 1997. "Reciprocity as a Justification for Retributivism." *Criminal Justice Ethics* 16:13–25.

Ardal, P. 1984. "Does Anyone Ever Deserve to Suffer?" *Queen's Quarterly* 91–92:241–57.

Ashworth, A. J. 1984. "Sharpening the Subjective Element in Criminal Liability." In *Philosophy and the Criminal Law*, edited by R. A. Duff and N. E. Simmonds. Stuttgart: Franz Steiner, 79–89.

———. 1986. "Punishment and Compensation: Victims, Offenders and the State." *Oxford Journal of Legal Studies* 6:86–122.

———. 1987. "Belief, Intent and Criminal Liability." In *Oxford Essays in Jurisprudence*, 3rd series, edited by J. Eekelaar & J. Bell. Oxford: Oxford University Press, 1–31.

————. 1993a. "Victim Impact Statements and Sentencing." *Criminal Law Review*, 498–509

————. 1993b. "Some Doubts about Restorative Justice." *Criminal Law Forum* 4:277–99.

————. 1994. *The Criminal Process: An Evaluative Study*. Oxford: Oxford University Press.

————. 1995a. *Sentencing and Criminal Justice*. 2nd ed. London: Butterworths.

————. 1995b. *Principles of Criminal Law*. 2nd ed. Oxford: Oxford University Press.

Ashworth, A. J., & Player, E. 1998. "Sentencing, Equal Treatment, and the Impact of Sanctions." In *Fundamentals of Sentencing Theory*, edited by A. J. Ashworth & M. Wasik. Oxford: Oxford University Press, 251–72.

Avineri, S., & de-Shalit, A., eds. 1992. *Communitarianism and Individualism*. Oxford: Oxford University Press.

Baker, B. M. 1992a. "Penance as a Model for Punishment." *Social Theory and Practice* 18:311–31.

————. 1992b. "Consequentialism, Punishment and Autonomy." In *Retributivism and Its Critics*, edited by W. Cragg. Stuttgart: Franz Steiner, 149–61.

Baldwin, J., & McConville, M. 1977. *Negotiated Justice*. London: Martin Robertson.

Baldwin, T. 1999. "Punishment, Communication, and Resentment." In *Punishment and Political Theory*, edited by M. Matravers. Oxford: Hart Publishing, 124–32.

Barnett, R. E. 1977. "Restitution: A New Paradigm of Criminal Justice." *Ethics* 87:279–301.

Bazelon, D. L. 1976. "The Morality of the Criminal Law." *Southern California Law Review* 49:385–405.

Beardsmore, R. W. 1969. *Moral Reasoning*. London: Routledge.

Beaumont, B. 1989. "Professional Reactions and Comments." In *Punishment, Custody and the Community*, edited by H. Rees & E. Hall Williams. London: London School of Economics, 87–111.

Becker, L. 1974. "Criminal Attempts and the Theory of the Law of Crimes." *Philosophy and Public Affairs* 3:262–94.

Bedau, H. A. 1987. *Death Is Different*. Boston: Northeastern University Press.

Benn, S. I. 1958. "An Approach to the Problems of Punishment." *Philosophy* 33:325–41.

Bentham, J. [1789] 1970. *An Introduction to the Principles of Morals and Legislation*, edited by J. H. Burns and H. L. A. Hart. London: Athlone Press.

Berlin, I. 1969. "Two Concepts of Liberty." In *Four Essays on Liberty*. Oxford: Oxford University Press, 118–72.

Beyleveld, D. 1979. "Identifying, Explaining and Predicting Deterrence." *British Journal of Criminology* 19:205–24.

Bianchi, H. 1986. "Abolition: Assensus and Sanctuary." In Bianchi & van Swaaningen 1986, 113–26. Reprinted in *A Reader on Punishment*, edited by R. A. Duff & D. Garland. Oxford: Oxford University Press, 1994.

————. 1994. *Justice as Sanctuary: Toward a New System of Crime Control*. Bloomington: Indiana University Press.

Bianchi, H., & van Swaaningen, R., eds. 1986. *Abolitionism: Towards a Non-Repressive Approach to Crime*. Amsterdam: Free University Press.

Bickenbach, J. E. 1988. "Critical Notice of R. A. Duff, *Trials and Punishments.*" *Canadian Journal of Philosophy* 18:765–86.

———. 1992. "Duff on Non-Custodial Punishment." In *Retributivism and Its Critics*, edited by W. Cragg. Stuttgart: Franz Steiner, 69–74.

Bigel, A. I. 1994. "Justices Brennan and Marshall on Capital Punishment." *Notre Dame Journal of Law, Ethics, and Public Policy* 8:11–163.

Blum, L. A. 1994. *Moral Perception and Particularity*. Cambridge: Cambridge University Press.

Bottoms, A. E. 1977. "Reflections on the Renaissance of Dangerousness." *Howard Journal* 16:70–96.

———. 1983. "Neglected Features of Contemporary Penal Systems." In *The Power to Punish*, edited by D. Garland & P. Young. London: Heinemann, 166–202.

———. 1998. "Five Puzzles in von Hirsch's Theory of Punishment." In *Fundamentals of Sentencing Theory*, edited by A. J. Ashworth & M. Wasik. Oxford: Oxford University Press, 53–100.

Bottoms, A. E., & McWilliams, W. 1979. "A Non-Treatment Paradigm for Probation Practice." *British Journal of Social Work* 9:159–202.

Bottoms, A. E., & Preston, R. H., eds. 1980. *The Coming Penal Crisis*. Edinburgh: Scottish Academic Press.

Braithwaite, J. 1989. *Crime, Shame and Reintegration*. Cambridge: Cambridge University Press.

———. 1999. "Restorative Justice: Assessing Optimistic and Pessimistic Accounts." In *Crime and Justice: A Review of Research*, vol. 23, edited by M. Tonry. Chicago: University of Chicago Press, 241–367.

Braithwaite, J., & Pettit, P. 1990. *Not Just Deserts*. Oxford: Oxford University Press.

Brandt, R. B. 1961. "Determinism and the Justifiability of Moral Blame." In *Determinism and Freedom in the Age of Modern Science*, edited by S. Hook. New York: Collier-Macmillan, 149–54.

Brook, R. 1988. "Threats and Punishment." *Philosophy and Public Affairs* 17:235–39.

Brown, J. G. 1994. "The Use of Mediation to Resolve Criminal Cases: A Procedural Critique." *Emory Law Journal* 43:1247–309.

Brownlee, I. 1994. "Hanging Judges and Wayward Mechanics: Reply to Michael Tonry." In *Penal Theory and Practice*, edited by R. A. Duff, S. E. Marshall, R. E. Dobash & R. P. Dobash. Manchester: Manchester University Press, 84–92.

———. 1998. *Community Punishment: A Critical Introduction*. London: Longman.

Brudner, A. 1993. "Agency and Welfare in the Penal Law." In *Action and Value in Criminal Law*, edited by S. Shute, J. Gardner & J. Horder. Oxford: Oxford University Press, 21–53.

Burgh, R. W. 1982. "Do the Guilty Deserve Punishment?" *Journal of Philosophy* 79:193–210.

Cain, M. 1985. "Beyond Informal Justice." *Contemporary Crises* 9:335–73.

Carlen, P. 1989. "Crime, Inequality, and Sentencing." In *Paying for Crime*, edited by P. Carlen & D. Cook. Milton Keynes: Open University Press, 8–28. Reprinted in *A Reader on Punishment*, edited by R. A. Duff & D. Garland. Oxford: Oxford University Press, 1994.

Carse, A. 1994. "The Liberal Individual: A Metaphysical or Moral Embarrassment?" *Nous* 28:184–209.

Cavadino, M., & Dignan, J. 1997. *The Penal System: An Introduction*. 2nd ed. London: Sage.

———. 1998. "Reparation, Retribution and Rights." In *Principled Sentencing*. 2nd ed., edited by A. von Hirsch & A. J. Ashworth. Oxford: Hart Publishing, 348–58.

Charvet, J. 1966. "Criticism and Punishment." *Mind* 75:573–79.

Christie, N. 1977. "Conflicts as Property." *British Journal of Criminology* 17:1–15.

———. 1981. *Limits to Pain*. London: Martin Robertson.

Coates, A. J. 1997. *The Ethics of War*. Manchester: Manchester University Press.

Cockburn, D. 1991. "Capital Punishment and Realism." *Philosophy* 66:177–90.

Cohen, S. 1985. *Visions of Social Control*. Cambridge: Polity Press; Oxford: Blackwell.

———. 1991. "Alternatives to Punishment: The Abolitionist Case." *Israel Law Review* 25:729–39.

Cotterrell, R. 1995. *Law's Community*. Oxford: Oxford University Press.

Cottingham, J. 1979. "Varieties of Retribution." *Philosophical Quarterly* 29:238–46.

Cragg, W. 1992. *The Practice of Punishment: Towards a Theory of Restorative Justice*. London: Routledge.

Cullen, F. T., & Gilbert, K. E. 1982. *Reaffirming Rehabilitation*. Cincinnati: Anderson.

Dagger, R. 1991. "Restitution: Pure or Punitive?" *Criminal Justice Ethics* 10:29–39.

———. 1993. "Playing Fair with Punishment." *Ethics* 103:473–88.

Daly, K., & Immarigeon, R. 1998. "The Past, Present, and Future of Restorative Justice." *Contemporary Justice Review* 1:21–45.

Dare, T. 1992. "Retributivism, Punishment, and Public Values." In *Retributivism and Its Critics*, edited by W. Cragg. Stuttgart: Franz Steiner, 35–41.

Davis, L. H. 1972. "They Deserve to Suffer." *Analysis* 32:136–40.

Davis, M. 1989. "The Relative Independence of Punishment Theory." *Law and Philosophy* 7:321–50.

———. 1992. *To Make the Punishment Fit the Crime*. Boulder, Colo.: Westview Press.

———. 1996. *Justice in the Shadow of Death: Rethinking Capital and Lesser Punishments*. Lanham: Rowman & Littlefield.

Dean-Myrda, M. C., & Cullen, F. T. 1998. "The Panacea Pendulum: An Account of Community as a Response to Crime." In *Community Corrections*, edited by J. Petersilia. New York: Oxford University Press, 3–18.

de Haan, W. 1990. *The Politics of Redress: Crime, Punishment and Penal Abolition*. London: Unwin Hyman.

Deigh, J. 1984. "On the Right to Be Punished: Some Doubts." *Ethics* 94:191–211.

Delgado, R. 1985. "'Rotten Social Background': Should the Criminal Law Recognize a Defense of Severe Environmental Deprivation?" *Law and Inequality* 3:9–90.

Dennett, D. C., ed. 1987. *The Philosophical Lexicon*. 8th ed. Oxford: Blackwell.

Diamond, C. 1978. "Eating Meat and Eating People." *Philosophy* 53:465–79.

Diana, L. 1970. "What Is Probation?" In *Probation and Parole*, edited by R. M. Carter & L. T. Wilkins. New York: John Wiley, 39–55.

Dignan, J. 1994. "Reintegration through Reparation: A Way Forward for Restorative Justice?" In *Penal Theory and Practice*, edited by R. A. Duff, S. E. Marshall, R. E. Dobash & R. P. Dobash. Manchester: Manchester University Press, 231–44.

———. 1999. "The Crime and Disorder Act and the Prospects for Restorative Justice." *Criminal Law Review*, 48–60.

Dimock, S. 1997. "Retributivism and Trust." *Law and Philosophy* 16:37–62.

Dobash, R. E., & Dobash, R. P. 1992. *Women, Violence and Social Change*. London: Routledge.

Dolinko, D. 1991. "Some Thoughts about Retributivism." *Ethics* 101:537–59.

Dressler, J. 1988. "Reflections on Excusing Wrongdoers: Moral Theory, New Excuses, and the Model Penal Code." *Rutgers Law Journal* 19:671–716.

———. 1989. "Exegesis of the Law of Duress: Justifying the Excuse and Searching for Its Proper Limits." *Southern California Law Review* 62:1331–86.

Dubber, M. 1994. "Rediscovering Hegel's Theory of Crime and Punishment." *Michigan Law Review* 92:1577–621.

———. 1995. "Recidivist Statutes as Arational Punishment." *Buffalo Law Review* 43:689–724.

———. 1996. "The Pain of Punishment." *Buffalo Law Review* 44:545–611.

———. 1997. "American Plea Bargains, German Lay Judges, and the Crisis of Criminal Procedure." *Stanford Law Review* 49:547–605.

———. 1998. "The Right to Be Punished: Autonomy and Its Demise in Modern Penal Thought." *Law and History Review* 16:113–62.

Duff, R. A. 1986. *Trials and Punishments*. Cambridge: Cambridge University Press.

———. 1988. "A Reply to Bickenbach." *Canadian Journal of Philosophy* 18:787–93.

———. 1990a. "Auctions, Lotteries, and the Punishment of Attempts." *Law and Philosophy* 9:1–37.

———. 1990b. "Justice, Mercy, and Forgiveness." *Criminal Justice Ethics* 9:51–63.

———. 1990c. *Intention, Agency and Criminal Liability*. Oxford: Blackwell.

———. 1991. "Retributive Punishment: Ideals and Actualities." *Israel Law Review* 25:422–51.

———. 1993. "Choice, Character, and Criminal Liability." *Law and Philosophy* 12:345–83.

———. 1996a. "Penal Communications: Recent Work in the Philosophy of Punishment." In *Crime and Justice: A Review of Research*, vol. 20, edited by M. Tonry. Chicago: University of Chicago Press, 1–97.

———. 1996b. *Criminal Attempts*. Oxford: Oxford University Press.

———. 1998a. "Dangerousness and Citizenship." In *Fundamentals of Sentencing Theory*, edited by A. J. Ashworth & M. Wasik. Oxford: Oxford University Press, 141–63.

———. 1998b. "Inclusion and Exclusion: Citizens, Subjects, and Outlaws." *Current Legal Problems* 51:241–66.

———. 1998c. "Principle and Contradiction in the Criminal Law: Motives and Criminal Liability." In *Philosophy and the Criminal Law: Principle and Critique*, edited by R. A. Duff. Cambridge: Cambridge University Press, 156–204.

———. 1998d. "Law, Language and Community: Some Preconditions of Criminal Liability." *Oxford Journal of Legal Studies* 18:189–206.

————. 1999. "Punishment, Communication, and Community." In *Punishment and Political Theory*, edited by M. Matravers. Oxford: Hart Publishing, 48–68.

Dworkin, G. 1988. *The Theory and Practice of Autonomy*. Cambridge: Cambridge University Press.

Dworkin, R. 1978. *Taking Rights Seriously*. 2nd imp. London: Duckworth.

————. 1986. *Law's Empire*. London: Fontana.

————. 1989. "Liberal Community." *California Law Review* 77:479–504.

Erez, E. 1994. "Victim Participation in Sentencing: And the Debate Goes On . . ." *International Review of Victimology* 3:17–32.

Falls, M. M. 1987. "Retribution, Reciprocity, and Respect for Persons." *Law and Philosophy* 6:25–51.

Farmer, L. 1997. *Criminal Law, Tradition and Legal Order*. Cambridge: Cambridge University Press.

Farrell, D. M. 1985. "The Justification of General Deterrence." *Philosophical Review* 94:367–94.

————. 1995. "Deterrence and the Just Distribution of Harm." *Social Philosophy and Policy* 12:220–240.

Faulkner, D., & Gibbs, A, eds. 1998. *New Politics, New Probation?* Oxford: University of Oxford Centre for Criminological Research.

Feeley, M. 1979. *The Process Is the Punishment*. New York: Russell Sage Foundation.

Feinberg, J. 1970. "The Expressive Function of Punishment." In *Doing and Deserving*, Princeton, N.J.: Princeton University Press, 95–118. Reprinted in *A Reader on Punishment*, edited by R. A. Duff & D. Garland. Oxford: Oxford University Press, 1994.

————. 1984–88. *The Moral Limits of the Criminal Law*. 4 vols. New York: Oxford University Press.

————. 1988. *Harmless Wrongdoing*. vol. 4 of *The Moral Limits of the Criminal Law*. New York: Oxford University Press.

Fingarette, H. 1977. "Punishment and Suffering." *Proceedings of the American Philosophical Association* 51:499–525.

Finnis, J. M. 1972. "The Restoration of Retribution." *Analysis* 32:131–35.

————. 1987. "On 'The Critical Legal Studies Movement.'" In *Oxford Essays in Jurisprudence*, 3rd series, edited by J. Eekelaar & J. Bell. Oxford: Oxford University Press, 145–65.

Fletcher, G. 1978. *Rethinking Criminal Law*. Boston: Little, Brown.

————. 1982. "The Recidivist Premium." *Criminal Justice Ethics* 1:54–59.

————. 1986. "Constructing a Theory of Impossible Attempts." In *Crime, Justice, and Codification*, edited by P. Fitzgerald. Toronto: Carswell, 87–113.

Flew, A. G. N. 1954. "The Justification of Punishment." *Philosophy* 29:291–307.

Floud, J. E., & Young, W. 1981. *Dangerousness and Criminal Justice*. London: Heinemann.

Frase, R. S. 1997. "Sentencing Principles in Theory and Practice." In *Crime and Justice: A Review of Research*, vol. 22, edited by M. Tonry. Chicago: University of Chicago Press, 363–433.

Gaita, R. 1991. *Good and Evil: An Absolute Conception*. London: Macmillan.

Galligan, D. J. 1981. "The Return to Retribution in Penal Theory." In *Crime, Proof and Punishment*, edited by C. F. H. Tapper. London: Butterworths, 144–71.

————. 1987. "Regulating Pre-Trial Decisions." In *Criminal Law and Justice*, edited by I. H. Dennis. London: Sweet & Maxwell, 177–202.

Gardner, J. 1994. "Rationality and the Rule of Law in Offences against the Person." *Cambridge Law Journal* 53:502–23.

————. 1998a. "On the General Part of the Criminal Law." In *Philosophy and the Criminal Law: Principle and Critique*, edited by R. A. Duff. Cambridge: Cambridge University Press, 205–55.

————. 1998b. "Crime: In Proportion and in Perspective." In *Fundamentals of Sentencing Theory*, edited by A. J. Ashworth & M. Wasik. Oxford: Oxford University Press, 31–52.

Gardner, M. 1976. "The Renaissance of Retribution: An Examination of 'Doing Justice'." *Wisconsin Law Review*: 781–815.

Garland, D. 1985. *Punishment and Welfare*. Aldershot: Gower.

————. 1990. *Punishment and Modern Society*. Oxford: Oxford University Press.

Garvey, S. P. 1998. "Can Shaming Punishments Educate?" *University of Chicago Law Review* 65:733–94.

Gauthier, D. 1986. *Morals by Agreement*. Oxford: Oxford University Press.

George, R. P. 1993. *Making Men Moral: Civil Liberties and Public Morality*. Oxford: Oxford University Press.

Gibbard, A. 1990. *Wise Choices, Apt Feelings*. Oxford: Oxford University Press.

Glazebrook, P. R. 1978. "Situational Liability." In *Reshaping the Criminal Law*, edited by P. R. Glazebrook. London: Stevens, 108–19.

Golash, D. 1994. "The Retributive Paradox." *Analysis* 54:72–78.

Goldman, A. H. 1979. "The Paradox of Punishment." *Philosophy and Public Affairs* 9:42–58.

————. 1982. "Toward a New Theory of Punishment." *Law and Philosophy* 1:57–76.

Goodin, R. E. 1991. "Theories of Compensation." In *Liability and Responsibility*, edited by R. Frey & C. Morris. Cambridge: Cambridge University Press, 257–89.

Gordon, G. H. 1978. *The Criminal Law of Scotland*. 2nd ed. Edinburgh: W. Green.

Greene, J. 1998. "The Unit Fine: Monetary Sanctions Apportioned to Income." In *Principled Sentencing*, 2nd ed., edited by A. von Hirsch & A. J. Ashworth. Oxford: Hart Publishing, 268–72.

Greenwood, P. W., & Abrahamse, A. 1982. *Selective Incapacitation*. Santa Monica, Calif.: Rand Corporation.

Gur-Arye, M. 1991. "The Justification of Punishment: A Comment on Retribution and Deterrence." *Israel Law Review* 25:452–59.

Hajdin, M. 1987. "Criminals as Gamblers: A Modified Theory of Pure Restitution." *Dialogue* 26:77–86.

Hampton, J. 1984. "The Moral Education Theory of Punishment." *Philosophy and Public Affairs* 13:208–38.

————. 1991. "A New Theory of Retribution." In *Liability and Responsibility*, edited by R. G. Frey and C. W. Morris. Cambridge: Cambridge University Press, 377–414.

————. 1992a. "An Expressive Theory of Retribution." In *Retributivism and Its Critics*, edited by W. Cragg. Stuttgart: Franz Steiner, 1–25.

———. 1992b. "Correcting Harms versus Righting Wrongs: The Goal of Retribution." *UCLA Law Review* 39:201–44.

Harding, J., ed. 1987. *Probation and the Community*. London: Tavistock.

Hare, R. M. 1981. *Moral Thinking: Its Levels, Methods and Point*. Oxford: Oxford University Press.

Harrison, R. 1988. "Punishment No Crime." *Proceedings of the Aristotelian Society* 62(suppl.): 139–51.

Hart, H. L. A. 1963. *Law, Liberty and Morality*. New York: Random House.

———. 1968. *Punishment and Responsibility*. Oxford: Oxford University Press.

———. 1994. *The Concept of Law*, 2nd ed. Oxford: Oxford University Press.

Hegel, G. W. F. [1821] 1942. *The Philosophy of Right*, translated by T. Knox. Oxford: Oxford University Press.

Hillsman, S. T. 1990. "Fines and Day Fines." In *Crime and Justice: A Review of Research*, vol. 12, edited by M. Tonry. Chicago: University of Chicago Press, 49–98.

Holmgren, M. H. 1983. "Punishment as Restitution: The Rights of the Community." *Criminal Justice Ethics* 2:36–49.

———. 1989. "The Backward Looking Component of Weak Retributivism." *Journal of Value Inquiry* 23:135–46.

Home Office. 1988. *Punishment, Custody and the Community* (Cm. 424). London: HMSO.

———. 1998. *Criminal Statistics, England and Wales, 1997*. London: HMSO.

Honderich, T. 1984a. *Punishment: The Supposed Justifications*. Rev. ed. Harmondsworth: Penguin Books.

———. 1984b. "Culpability and Mystery." In *Philosophy and the Criminal Law*, edited by R. A. Duff and N. E. Simmonds. Stuttgart: Franz Steiner, 71–77.

Hood, R. 1998. *The Death Penalty: A World-Wide Perspective*. 2nd rev. ed. Oxford: Oxford University Press.

Horder, J. 1992. *Provocation and Responsibility*. Oxford: Oxford University Press.

———. 1994. "Rethinking Non-Fatal Offences against the Person." *Oxford Journal of Legal Studies* 14:335–51.

Horton, J. 1992. *Political Obligation*. London: Macmillan.

Hudson, B. 1987. *Justice through Punishment: A Critique of the "Justice" Model of Corrections*. London: Macmillan.

———. 1993. *Penal Policy and Social Justice*. London: Macmillan.

———. 1994. "Punishing the Poor: A Critique of the Dominance of Legal Reasoning in Penal Policy and Practice." In *Penal Theory and Practice*, edited by R. A. Duff, S. E. Marshall, R. E. Dobash & R. P. Dobash. Manchester: Manchester University Press, 292–305.

———. 1995. "Beyond Proportionate Punishment: Difficult Cases and the 1991 Criminal Justice Act." *Crime, Law & Social Change* 22:59–78.

Hulsman, L. 1981. "Penal Reform in the Netherlands I." *Howard Journal* 20:150–59.

———. 1982. "Penal Reform in the Netherlands II." *Howard Journal* 21:35–47.

———. 1986. "Critical Criminology and the Concept of Crime." *Contemporary Crises* 10:63–80.

———. 1991. "The Abolitionist Case: Alternative Crime Policies." *Israel Law Review* 25:681–709.

Husak, D. 1990. "'Already Punished Enough.'" *Philosophical Topics* 18:79–99.

———. 1992a. *Drugs and Rights*. New York: Cambridge University Press.

———. 1992b. "Why Punish the Deserving?" *Nous* 26:447–64.

———. 1995. "The Nature and Justifiability of Nonconsummate Offenses." *Arizona Law Review* 37:151–83.

———. 1998. "Does Criminal Liability Require an Act?" In *Philosophy and the Criminal Law: Principle and Critique*, edited by R. A. Duff. Cambridge: Cambridge University Press, 60–100.

Ignatieff, M. 1978. *A Just Measure of Pain*. New York: Random House.

Kahan, D. M. 1996. "What Do Alternative Sanctions Mean?" *University of Chicago Law Review* 63:591–653.

———. 1998. "Punishment Incommensurability." *Buffalo Criminal Law Review* 1:691–708.

Kant, I. [1785] 1948. *Groundwork of the Metaphysic of Morals*, translated by H. Paton as *The Moral Law*. London: Hutchinson.

———. [1797] 1965. *The Metaphysical Elements of Justice*. Part I of *The Metaphysic of Morals*, translated by J. Ladd. Indianapolis: Bobbs-Merrill.

Kelman, M. 1981. "Interpretive Construction in the Substantive Criminal Law." *Stanford Law Review* 33:591–673.

King, J. F. S., ed. 1969. *The Probation and After-Care Service*. 3rd ed. London: Butterworths.

Kleinberg, S. S. 1980. "Criminal Justice and Private Enterprise." *Ethics* 90:270–82.

Kleinig, J. 1991. "Punishment and Moral Seriousness." *Israel Law Review* 25:401–21.

Knowles, D. 1993. "Unjustified Retribution." *Israel Law Review* 27:50–58.

Kymlicka, W. 1989. *Liberalism, Community, and Culture*. Oxford: Oxford University Press.

Lacey, N. 1988. *State Punishment: Political Principles and Community Values*. London: Routledge.

Lacey, N., & Zedner, L. 1995. "Discourses of Community in Criminal Justice." *Journal of Law and Society* 22:301–25.

LaFave, W. R., & Scott, A. W. 1986. *Criminal Law*. 2nd ed. St Paul: West.

Lewis, C. S. 1940. *The Problem of Pain*. Glasgow: Collins.

———. 1953. "The Humanitarian Theory of Punishment." *Res Judicatae* 6. Reprinted in *Readings in Ethical Theory*, 2nd ed., edited by W. Sellars and J. Hospers. New York: Appleton-Century-Crofts, 1970.

Lipkin, R. J. 1988. "Punishment, Penance and Respect for Autonomy." *Social Theory and Practice* 14:87–104.

Lucas, J. R. 1968–69. "Or Else." *Proceedings of the Aristotelian Society* 69:207–22.

———. 1980. *On Justice*. Oxford: Oxford University Press.

———. 1993. *Responsibility*. Oxford: Oxford University Press.

MacCormick, D. N. 1982. "Against Moral Disestablishment." In *Legal Right and Social Democracy*. Oxford: Oxford University Press, 18–38.

———. 1990. "Reconstruction after Deconstruction: A Response to CLS." *Oxford Journal of Legal Studies* 10:539–58.

MacIntyre, A. 1985. *After Virtue*. 2nd ed. London: Duckworth.

Mackenzie, M. M. 1981. *Plato on Punishment*. Berkeley: University of California Press.

Mackie, J. L. 1985 "Morality and the Retributive Emotions." In *Persons and Values*. Oxford: Oxford University Press, 206–19.

Marshall, S. E. 1992. "Harm and Punishment in the Community." In *Retributivism and Its Critics*, edited by W. Cragg. Stuttgart: Franz Steiner, 75–82.

―――. 1998. "The Community of Friends." In *Communitarianism and Citizenship*, edited by E. Christodoulidis. Aldershot: Ashgate, 208–19.

Marshall, S. E., & Duff, R. A. 1982. "Camus and Rebellion, from Solipsism to Morality." *Philosophical Investigations* 5:116–134.

―――. 1998. "Criminalization and Sharing Wrongs." *Canadian Journal of Law & Jurisprudence* 11:7–22.

Marshall, T. F. 1994. "Grassroots Initiatives Towards Restorative Justice: The New Paradigm?" In *Penal Theory and Practice*, edited by R. A. Duff, S. E. Marshall, R. E. Dobash & R. P. Dobash. Manchester: Manchester University Press, 245–60.

Marshall, T. F., & Merry, S. 1990. *Crime and Accountability: Victim/Offender Mediation in Practice*. London: HMSO.

Mason, A. 1993. "Liberalism and the Value of Community." *Canadian Journal of Philosophy* 23:215–39.

Mathiesen, T. 1974. *The Politics of Abolition*. London: Martin Robertson.

―――. 1986. "The Politics of Abolition." *Contemporary Crises* 10:81–94.

―――. 1990. *Prison on Trial*. London: Sage.

Matravers, M. 2000. *Justice and Punishment*. Oxford: Oxford University Press.

Matthews, R., ed. 1988. *Informal Justice*. London: Sage.

McCloskey, H. J. 1972. "'Two Concepts of Rules': A Note." *Philosophical Quarterly* 22:344–48.

McIvor, G. 1994. "Community Service: Progress and Prospects." In *Penal Theory and Practice*, edited by R. A. Duff, S. E. Marshall, R. E. Dobash & R. P. Dobash. Manchester: Manchester University Press, 171–84.

McWilliams, W. 1983. "The Mission to the English Police Courts 1876–1936." *Howard Journal* 22:129–47.

―――. 1985. "The Mission Transformed: Professionalisation of Probation between the Wars." *Howard Journal* 24:257–74.

―――. 1986. "The English Probation System and the Diagnostic Ideal." *Howard Journal* 25:241–60.

―――. 1987. "Probation, Pragmatism and Policy." *Howard Journal* 26:97–121.

McWilliams, W., & Pease, K. 1990. "Probation Practice and an End to Punishment." *Howard Journal* 29:14–24.

Melden, A. I. 1959. *Rights and Right Conduct*. Oxford: Blackwell.

―――. 1977. *Rights and Persons*. Oxford: Blackwell.

Menninger, K. 1968. *The Crime of Punishment*. New York: Viking Press.

Michael, M. A. 1992. "Utilitarianism and Retributivism: What's the Difference?" *American Philosophical Quarterly* 29:173–82.

Mill, J. S. 1859. *On Liberty*. London: Parker.

Montague, P. 1995. *Punishment as Societal Defense*. Lanham: Rowman & Littlefield.

Moore, M. S. 1987. "The Moral Worth of Retribution." In *Responsibility, Character and the Emotions*, edited by F. Schoeman. Cambridge: Cambridge University Press, 179–219.

———. 1993. "Justifying Retribution." *Israel Law Review* 27:15–49.

———. 1997. *Placing Blame: A Theory of Criminal Law*. Oxford: Oxford University Press.

Morison, J. 1988. "Hart's Excuses: Problems with a Compromise Theory of Punishment." In *The Jurisprudence of Orthodoxy*, edited by P. Leith and P. Ingram. London: Routledge, 117–46.

Morran, D. & Wilson, M. 1994. "Confronting Domestic Violence: An Innovative Criminal Justice Response in Scotland." In *Penal Theory and Practice*, edited by R. A. Duff, S. E. Marshall, R. E. Dobash & R. P. Dobash. Manchester: Manchester University Press, 216–27.

Morris, C. W. 1991. "Punishment and Loss of Moral Standing." *Canadian Journal of Philosophy* 21:53–79.

Morris, H. 1968. "Persons and Punishment." *The Monist* 52:475–501.

———. 1981. "A Paternalistic Theory of Punishment." *American Philosophical Quarterly* 18:263–71. Reprinted in *A Reader on Punishment*, edited by R. A. Duff & D. Garland. Oxford: Oxford University Press, 1994.

Morris, N. 1974. *The Future of Imprisonment*. Chicago: University of Chicago Press.

Morris, N., & Tonry, M. 1990. *Between Prison and Probation: Intermediate Punishments in a Rational Sentencing System*. New York: Oxford University Press.

Morse, S. J. 1976. "The Twilight of Welfare Criminology: A Reply to Judge Bazelon." *Southern California Law Review* 49:1247–68.

Mulhall, S., & Swift, A. 1992. *Liberals and Communitarians*. Oxford: Blackwell.

Murdoch, I. 1970. *The Sovereignty of Good*. London: Routledge.

Murphy, J. G. 1979a. "Three Mistakes about Retributivism." In *Retribution, Justice, and Therapy*. Dordrecht: Reidel, 77–81.

———. 1979b. "Kant's Theory of Criminal Punishment." In *Retribution, Justice, and Therapy*. Dordrecht: Reidel, 82–92.

———. 1979c. "Marxism and Retribution." In *Retribution, Justice, and Therapy*. Dordrecht: Reidel, 93–115. Reprinted in *A Reader on Punishment*, edited by R. A. Duff & D. Garland. Oxford: Oxford University Press, 1994.

———. 1979d. "Cruel and Unusual Punishments." In *Retribution, Justice, and Therapy*. Dordrecht: Reidel, 223–49.

———. 1985. "Retributivism, Moral Education and the Liberal State." *Criminal Justice Ethics* 4:3–11.

———. 1997. "Repentance, Punishment, and Mercy." In *Repentance: A Comparative Perspective*, edited by A. Etzioni & D. E. Carney. Totowa, N.J.: Rowman & Littlefield, 143–70.

———. 1999. "Moral Epistemology, the Retributive Emotions, and the 'Clumsy Moral Philosophy' of Jesus Christ." In *The Passions of Law*, edited by S. A. Bandes. New York: NYU Press, 149–67.

Murphy, J. G., & Hampton, J. 1988. *Forgiveness and Mercy*. Cambridge: Cambridge University Press.

Nagel, T. 1979a. "War and Massacre." In *Mortal Questions*. Cambridge: Cambridge University Press, 53–76.

———. 1979b. "The Fragmentation of Value." In *Mortal Questions*. Cambridge: Cambridge University Press, 128–41.

Narayan, U. 1993. "Appropriate Responses and Preventive Benefits: Justifying Censure and Hard Treatment in Legal Punishment." *Oxford Journal of Legal Studies* 13:166–82.

Nathanson, S. 1987. *An Eye for an Eye? The Morality of Punishing by Death*. Totowa, N.J.: Rowman & Littlefield.

Nelken, D. 1985. "Community Involvement in Crime Control." *Current Legal Problems* 38:239–67.

Nino, C. S. 1983. "A Consensual Theory of Punishment." *Philosophy and Public Affairs* 12:289–306.

———. 1986. "Does Consent Override Proportionality?" *Philosophy and Public Affairs* 15:183–87.

Norrie, A. W. 1991. *Law, Ideology and Punishment*. Dordrecht: Kluwer.

———. 1993. *Crime, Reason and History*. London: Weidenfeld & Nicolson.

———. 1998. "'Simulacra of Morality'? Beyond the Ideal/Actual Antinomies of Criminal Justice." In *Philosophy and the Criminal Law: Principle and Critique*, edited by R. A. Duff. Cambridge: Cambridge University Press, 101–55.

Nowell-Smith, P. H. 1961. *Ethics*. Harmondsworth: Penguin.

Nozick, R. 1974. *Anarchy, State, and Utopia*. Oxford: Blackwell.

———. 1981. *Philosophical Explanations*. Oxford: Oxford University Press.

Oldenquist, A. 1988. "An Explanation of Retribution." *Journal of Philosophy* 85: 464–78.

Orwell, G. 1965. "A Hanging." In *Decline of the English Murder and Other Essays*. Harmondsworth: Penguin Books, 14–19.

Otsuka, M. 1996. "Quinn on Punishment and Using Persons as Means." *Law and Philosophy* 15:201–8.

Palmer, T. 1994. *A Profile of Correctional Effectiveness and New Directions for Research*. Albany: SUNY Press.

Parfit, D. 1984. *Reasons and Persons*. Oxford: Oxford University Press.

Pease, K. 1985. "Community Service Orders." *Crime and Justice* 6:51–94.

Pease, K., & McWilliams, W., eds. 1980. *Community Service by Order*. Aberdeen: Scottish Academic Press.

Petersilia, J., ed. 1998. *Community Corrections*. New York: Oxford University Press.

Pettit, P. 1989. "The Freedom of the City: A Republican Ideal." In *The Good Polity*, edited by A. Hamlin & P. Pettit. Oxford: Blackwell, 141–68.

———. 1997. "Republican Theory and Criminal Punishment." *Utilitas* 9:59–79.

Pettit, P., & Braithwaite, J. 1993. "Not Just Deserts, Even in Sentencing." *Current Issues in Criminal Justice* 4:225–39.

Philips, M. 1986. "The Justification of Punishment and the Justification of Political Authority." *Law and Philosophy* 5:393–416.

Phillips, D. Z. 1982. "Some Limits to Moral Endeavour." In *Through a Darkening Glass*. Oxford: Blackwell, 30–50.

Pilon, R. 1978. "Criminal Remedies: Restitution, Punishment, or Both?" *Ethics* 88:348–57.

Postema, G. J. 1986. *Bentham and the Common Law Tradition*. Oxford: Oxford University Press.

Primoratz, I. 1989a. *Justifying Legal Punishment.* Atlantic Highlands, N.J.: Humanities Press.

———. 1989b. "Punishment as Language." *Philosophy* 64:187–205.

Quinn, W. 1985. "The Right to Threaten and the Right to Punish." *Philosophy and Public Affairs* 14:327–73.

———. 1988. "Reply to Brook." *Philosophy and Public Affairs* 17:240–47.

Quinton, A. 1953–54. "Punishment." *Analysis* 14:133–42.

Radzinowicz, L., & Hood, R. 1981. "The American Volte-Face in Sentencing Thought and Practice." In *Crime, Proof and Punishment*, edited by C. F. H. Tapper. London: Butterworths, 127–43.

Rawls, J. 1955. "Two Concepts of Rules." *The Philosophical Review* 64:3–32.

———. 1972. *A Theory of Justice.* Oxford: Oxford University Press.

———. 1985. "Justice as Fairness: Political Not Metaphysical." *Philosophy and Public Affairs* 14:223–51.

———. 1993. *Political Liberalism.* New York: Columbia University Press.

Raynor, P. 1985. *Social Work, Justice and Control.* Oxford: Blackwell.

Raz, J. 1979. *The Authority of Law.* Oxford: Oxford University Press.

———. 1986. *The Morality of Freedom.* Oxford: Oxford University Press.

———. 1994. *Ethics in the Public Domain.* Oxford: Oxford University Press.

Reitan, E. 1996. "Punishment and Community: The Reintegrative Theory of Punishment." *Canadian Journal of Philosophy* 26:57–81.

Rex, S. 1998. "A New Form of Rehabilitation." In *Principled Sentencing*, 2nd ed., edited by A. von Hirsch & A. J. Ashworth. Oxford: Hart Publishing, 34–41.

Roberts, J. 1989. *The Guardian*, October 13, 4.

Roberts, J. V. 1997. "The Role of Criminal Record in the Sentencing Process." In *Crime and Justice: A Review of Research*, vol. 22, edited by M. Tonry. Chicago: University of Chicago Press, 303–62.

Robinson, P. 1987a. "Hybrid Principles for the Distribution of Criminal Sanctions." *Northwestern University Law Review* 82:19–42.

———. 1987b. "A Sentencing System for the Twenty-first Century?" *Texas Law Review* 66:1–61.

———. 1990. "Rules of Conduct and Principles of Adjudication." *University of Chicago Law Review* 57:729–71.

Rosenblum, N. L., ed. 1989. *Liberalism and the Moral Life.* Cambridge, Mass.: Harvard University Press.

Rotman, E. 1990. *Beyond Punishment: A New View of the Rehabilitation of Offenders.* New York: Greenwood Press.

Sadurski, W. 1985. "Distributive Justice and the Theory of Punishment." *Oxford Journal of Legal Studies* 5:47–59.

———. 1989. "Theory of Punishment, Social Justice, and Liberal Neutrality." *Law and Philosophy* 7:351–73.

Sandel, M. 1982. *Liberalism and the Limits of Justice.* Cambridge: Cambridge University Press.

Sanders, A., and Young, R. 1994. *Criminal Justice.* London: Butterworths.

Schedler, G. 1980. "Can Retributivists Support Legal Punishment?" *The Monist* 63:185–98.

Scheerer, S. 1986. "Towards Abolitionism." *Contemporary Crises* 10:5–20.

Scheid, D. E. 1980. "Note on Defining 'Punishment'." *Canadian Journal of Philosophy* 10:453–62.
———. 1990, "Davis and the Unfair-Advantage Theory of Punishment: A Critique." *Philosophical Topics* 18:143–70.
———. 1995. "Davis, Unfair Advantage Theory, and Criminal Desert." *Law and Philosophy* 14:375–409.
———. 1997. "Constructing a Theory of Punishment, Desert, and the Distribution of Punishments." *Canadian Journal of Law and Jurisprudence* 10:441–506.
Schoeman, F. D. 1979. "On Incapacitating the Dangerous." *American Philosophical Quarterly* 16:27–35.
Schünemann, B., von Hirsch, A., and Jareborg, N., eds. 1998. *Positive Generalprävention*. Heidelberg: C. F. Müller.
Scourfield, J., & Dobash, R. P. 1999. "Programmes for Violent Men: Recent Developments in the UK." *Howard Journal of Criminal Justice* 38:128–43.
Scull, A. 1984. *Decarceration*. 2nd ed. Cambridge: Polity Press.
Selznick, P. 1992. *The Moral Commonwealth: Social Theory and the Promise of Community*. Berkeley: University of California Press.
Shafer-Landau, R. 1991. "Can Punishment Morally Educate?" *Law and Philosophy* 10:189–219.
———. 1996. "The Failure of Retributivism." *Philosophical Studies* 82:289–316.
Sher, G. 1987. *Desert*. Princeton: Princeton University Press.
———. 1997. *Beyond Neutrality*. Cambridge: Cambridge University Press.
Sim, J. 1994. "The Abolitionist Approach: A British Perspective." In *Penal Theory and Practice*, edited by R. A. Duff, S. E. Marshall, R. E. Dobash & R. P. Dobash. Manchester: Manchester University Press, 263–84.
Simmons, A. J. 1996. "Associative Political Obligations." *Ethics* 106:247–73.
Skillen, A. J. 1980. "How to Say Things with Walls." *Philosophy* 55:509–23.
Slattery, B. 1992. "The Myth of Retributive Justice." In *Retributivism and Its Critics*, edited by W. Cragg. Stuttgart: Franz Steiner, 27–34.
Slote, M. 1989. *Beyond Optimizing: A Study of Rational Choice*. Cambridge, Mass.: Harvard University Press.
Smart, J. J. C. 1973. "An Outline of a System of Utilitarian Ethics." In *Utilitarianism: For and Against*, by J. J. C. Smart & B. Williams. Cambridge: Cambridge University Press, 1–74.
Smith, J. C., & Hogan, B. 1996. *Criminal Law*. 8th ed. London: Butterworths.
Sowle, S. D. 1994–95. "A Regime of Social Death: Criminal Punishment in the Age of Prisons." *New York University Review of Law and Social Change* 21:497–565.
Sprigge, T. L. S. 1968. "A Utilitarian Reply to Dr McCloskey." In *Contemporary Utilitarianism*, edited by M. D. Bayles. Garden City, N.Y.: Doubleday, 261–99.
Steinert, H. 1986. "Beyond Crime and Punishment." *Contemporary Crises* 10:21–38.
Stephen, J. F. [1873] 1967. *Liberty, Equality, Fraternity*, edited by J White. Cambridge: Cambridge University Press.
Stocker, M. 1990. *Plural and Conflicting Values*. Oxford: Oxford University Press.
Sypnowich, C. Forthcoming. "The Civility of Law: Between Public and Private." In *Public and Private: Legal, Political, and Philosophical Perspectives*, edited by M. d'Entrèves & U. Vogel. London: Routledge.

Taylor, C. 1989. "Cross-Purposes: The Liberal-Communitarian Debate." In *Liberalism and the Moral Life*, edited by N. Rosenblum. Cambridge, Mass.: Harvard University Press, 159–82.

———. 1990. *Sources of the Self*. Cambridge: Cambridge University Press.

Teichman, J. 1973. "Punishment and Remorse." *Philosophy* 48:335–46.

Ten, C. L. 1987. *Crime, Guilt, and Punishment*. Oxford: Oxford University Press.

———. 1990. "Positive Retributivism." *Social Philosophy and Policy* 7:194–208.

Tolstoy, L. [1886] 1960. "The Death of Ivan Ilych." Translated by A. Maude. In Tolstoy, *The Death of Ivan Ilych and Other Stories*, edited by D. Magarshack. New York: New American Library, 95–156.

Tonry, M. 1994. "Proportionality, Parsimony, and Interchangeability of Punishments." In *Penal Theory and Practice*, edited by R. A. Duff, S. E. Marshall, R. E. Dobash & R. P. Dobash. Manchester: Manchester University Press, 59–83. Reprinted in *A Reader on Punishment*, edited by R. A. Duff & D. Garland. Oxford: Oxford University Press, 1994.

———. 1996. *Sentencing Matters*. New York: Oxford University Press.

———. 1997. *Intermediate Sanctions in Sentencing Guidelines*. U.S. National Institute of Justice.

———. 1998. "Interchangeability, Desert Limits and Equivalence of Function." In *Principled Sentencing*, edited by A. von Hirsch & A. J. Ashworth. Oxford: Hart Publishing, 291–96.

Tonry, M., & Morris, N. 1978. "Sentencing Reform in America." In *Reshaping the Criminal Law*, edited by P. R. Glazebrook. London: Stevens, 434–48.

Travis, C. 1989. *The Uses of Sense*. Oxford: Oxford University Press.

Trollope, A. 1864. *The Small House at Allington*. London: Smith, Elder.

Twentieth Century Fund (Task Force on Criminal Sentencing). 1976. *Fair and Certain Punishment*. New York: McGraw-Hill.

U.S. Bureau of Justice Statistics. 1998. *Sourcebook of Criminal Justice Statistics 1997*. Washington, D.C.: U.S. Government Printing Office.

von Hirsch, A. 1976. *Doing Justice: The Choice of Punishments*. New York: Hill and Wang.

———. 1985. *Past or Future Crimes*. Manchester: Manchester University Press.

———. 1990. "Proportionality in the Philosophy of Punishment: From 'Why Punish?' to 'How Much?'" *Criminal Law Forum* 1:259–90.

———. 1991. "Criminal Record Rides Again." *Criminal Justice Ethics* 10:55–57.

———. 1992. "Proportionality in the Philosophy of Punishment." In *Crime and Justice: A Review of Research*, vol. 16, edited by M. Tonry. Chicago: University of Chicago Press, 55–98.

———. 1993. *Censure and Sanctions*. Oxford: Oxford University Press.

———. 1998a. "Desert and Previous Convictions." In von Hirsch & Ashworth 1998, 190–97.

———. 1998b. "The Swedish Sentencing Law." In von Hirsch & Ashworth 1998, 240–52.

———. 1999. "Punishment, Penance and the State." In *Punishment and Political Theory*, edited by M. Matravers. Oxford: Hart Publishing, 69–82.

von Hirsch, A., & Ashworth, A. J. 1992. "Not Not Just Deserts: A Response to Braithwaite and Pettit." *Oxford Journal of Legal Studies* 12:83–98.

————. 1993. "Desert and the Three Rs." *Current Issues in Criminal Justice* 5:9–12.

————. eds. 1998. *Principled Sentencing*. 2nd ed. Oxford: Hart Publishing.

von Hirsch, A., Bottoms, A. E., Burney, E., & Wikström, P-O. 1999. *Criminal Deterrence and Sentence Severity*. Oxford: Hart Publishing.

von Hirsch, A., & Jareborg, N. 1991. "Gauging Criminal Harm: A Living-Standard Analysis." *Oxford Journal of Legal Studies* 11:1–38.

von Hirsch, A., & Wasik, M. 1997. "Civil Disqualifications Attending Conviction." *Cambridge Law Journal* 56:599–626.

von Hirsch, A., Wasik, M., & Greene, J. 1989. "Punishment in the Community and the Principles of Desert." *Rutgers Law Journal* 20:595–618.

Waldron, J. 1988. "When Justice Replaces Affection: The Need for Rights." *Harvard Journal of Law and Public Policy* 11:625–47.

————. 1992. "Lex Talionis." *Arizona Law Review* 34:25–51.

————. 1999. *Law and Disagreement*. Oxford: Oxford University Press.

Walker, N. 1978. "Punishing, Denouncing or Reducing Crime." In *Reshaping the Criminal Law*, edited by P. R. Glazebrook. London: Stevens, 391–403.

————. 1980. *Punishment, Danger and Stigma*. Oxford: Blackwell.

————. 1981. "The Ultimate Justification." In *Crime, Proof and Punishment*, edited by C. F. H. Tapper. London: Butterworths, 109–26.

————. 1991. *Why Punish?* Oxford: Oxford University Press.

Walker, N., & McCabe, S. 1973. *Crime and Insanity in England*. Vol. 2. Edinburgh: Edinburgh University Press.

Walker, N., & Padfield, N. 1996. *Sentencing: Theory, Law and Practice*. 2nd ed. London: Butterworths.

Walzer, M. 1983. *Spheres of Justice*. New York: Basic Books.

Wasik, M. 1987. "Guidance, Guidelines and Criminal Record." In *Sentencing Reform: Guidance or Guidelines?* edited by M. Wasik & K. Pease. Manchester: Manchester University Press, 105–25.

Wasik, M., & von Hirsch, A. 1988. "Non-Custodial Penalties and the Principles of Desert." *Criminal Law Review*: 555–72.

————. 1990. "Statutory Sentencing Principles: The 1990 White Paper." *Modern Law Review* 53:508–17.

————. 1994. "Section 29 Revisited: Previous Convictions in Sentencing." *Criminal Law Review*, 409–18.

Wells, C. 1993. *Corporations and Criminal Responsibility*. Oxford: Oxford University Press.

Weston, W. R. 1978. "Probation in Penal Philosophy: Evolutionary Perspectives." *Howard Journal* 17:7–22.

Williams, B. 1973a. "Ethical Consistency." In *Problems of the Self*. Cambridge: Cambridge University Press, 166–86.

————. 1973b. "Egoism and Altruism." In *Problems of the Self*. Cambridge: Cambridge University Press, 250–65.

————. 1981a. "Moral Luck." In *Moral Luck*. Cambridge: Cambridge University Press, 20–39.

————. 1981b. "Internal and External Reasons." In *Moral Luck*. Cambridge: Cambridge University Press, 101–13.

————. 1985. *Ethics and the Limits of Philosophy*. London: Fontana.

————. 1993. *Shame and Necessity*. Berkeley: University of California Press.

Williams, G. 1961. *Criminal Law: The General Part*. 2nd ed. London: Stevens.

————. 1983. *Textbook of Criminal Law*. 2nd ed. London: Stevens.

Wilson, J. Q. 1983. *Thinking about Crime*. Rev. ed. New York: Basic Books.

Winch, P. 1972a. "Nature and Convention." In *Ethics and Action*. London: Routledge, 50–72.

————. 1972b. "The Universalizability of Moral Judgments." In *Ethics and Action*. London: Routledge, 151–70.

————. 1972c. "Can a Good Man be Harmed?" In *Ethics and Action*. London: Routledge, 193–209.

————. 1972d. "Ethical Reward and Punishment." In *Ethics and Action*. London: Routledge, 210–28.

Wittgenstein, L. 1963. *Philosophical Investigations*, translated by G. E. M. Anscombe. Oxford: Blackwell.

Wood, D. 1988. "Dangerous Offenders, and the Morality of Protective Sentencing." *Criminal Law Review*: 424–33.

Wootton, B. 1963. *Crime and the Criminal Law*. London: Stevens.

Young, P. 1994. "Putting a Price on Harm: The Fine as a Punishment." In *Penal Theory and Practice*, edited by R. A. Duff, S. E. Marshall, R. E. Dobash & R. P. Dobash. Manchester: Manchester University Press, 185–96.

Zedner, L. 1994. "Reparation and Retribution: Are They Reconcilable?" *Modern Law Review* 57:228–50.

————. 1997. "Victims." In *The Oxford Handbook of Criminology*, edited by M. Maguire, R. Morgan & R. Reiner. Oxford: Oxford University Press, 577–612.

Zimring, F. E. 1976. "Making the Punishment Fit the Crime: A Consumer's Guide to Sentencing Reform." *Hastings Center Report* 6:13–21. Reprinted in *A Reader on Punishment*, edited by R. A. Duff & D. Garland. Oxford: Oxford University Press, 1994.

Zimring, F. E. & Hawkins, G. 1995. *Incapacitation: Penal Confinement and the Restraint of Crime*. New York: Oxford University Press.

Index

N.B. Bare bibliographical references are not indexed.